D1478000

The Economics of Liberty

Edited by
Llewellyn H. Rockwell

The Ludwig von Mises Institute

Auburn, Alabama 36849

The Ludwig von Mises Institute gratefully acknowledges
the Patrons whose generosity made the publication of
this book possible:

O.P. Alford, III

Morgan Adams, Jr.
The Adams Fund

Anonymous (4)

Dr. J.C. Arthur

Joe Baidinger

V.S. Boddicker
*The Boddicker
Investment Co.*

Brenda Bretan

Franklin M. Buchta

E.O. Buck

Mrs. Harold B. Chait

J.E. Coberly, Jr.

William B. Coberly, Jr.
Coberly-West Co.

Dr. Everett S. Coleman

Christopher P. Condon

Morgan Cowperthwaite

Charles G. Dannelly

Carl A. Davis
Davis-Lynch, Inc.

Robert E. Derges

John Dewees

William A. Diehl

Robert T. Dofflemyer

Dr. William A. Dunn
*Dunn Capital
Management*

Mrs. Card G. Elliott, Jr.

Mr. & Mrs. C.R. Estes
Estes Enterprises

Jason H. Fane

Alice B. Fawcett

Willard Fischer

Mr. & Mrs. James R.
Focht

John G. Ford

James W. Frevert

John B. Gardner

Martin Garfinkel

Thomas E. Gee

Bernard G. Geuting

W.B. Grant
AANGS Co.

W. Grover
Freeway Fasteners

Dr. Robert M. Hansen

Harry H. Hoiles

Charles Hollinger

T.D. James

G.E. Johnson

Michael L. Keiser

John F. Kieser

H.E. King
*The M.H. King
Foundation*

W.H. Kleiner
*Julius and Emma
Kleiner Foundation*

Dr. Richard J.
Kossmann

John L. Kreischer

Robert H. Krieble
Krieble Associates

Norma R. Lineberger

Robert D. Love
Love Box Co.

William Lowndes, III
The Lowndes Corp.

Walter Marcyan

Forrest E. Mars, Sr.

William W. Massey, Jr.

Richard A. Maussner

Ellice McDonald, Jr.

Dr. J.L. McLean

Robert E. Miller

A. Minis, Jr.

Dr. K. Lyle Moore

Dr. Francis Powers

Donald Mosby Rembert

James M. Rodney

Catherine Dixon Roland

Sheldon Rose

Dwight Rounds

Gary G. Schlarbaum

Stanley Schmidt

Charles K. Seven

Vincent J. Severini

E.D. Shaw, Jr.
Shaw Oxygen Co.

Russell Shoemaker
Shoemaker's Candles

Abe Siemens

Clyde A. Sluhan

Donald R. Stewart

David F. Swain, Jr.

Walter F. Taylor

Dr. Benjamin H.
Thurman

C.S. Trosper

Edgar J. Uihlein

Lawrence Van
Someren, Sr.

Charles H. Wacker, III

Frederick G. Wacker, Jr.

W.F. & Sue T. Whitfield
Trammell-Whitfield Co.

Tom Zignego
The Zignego Co.

Library of Congress Catalog Card Number: 90-062-46
ISBN: 0-945466-08-0

DEDICATION

To O. P. ALFORD, III,
entrepreneur and activist
for liberty

Contents

Introduction
Llewellyn H. Rockwell 13

1. ECONOMIC TRUTH VS. POLITICAL POWER

Outlawing Jobs: The Minimum Wage,
Once More
Murray N. Rothbard 17

The Scourge of Unionism
Llewellyn H. Rockwell 21

Keynesianism Redux
Murray N. Rothbard 27

The Keynesian Dream
Murray N. Rothbard 32

The Free-Rider Confusion
Tom Bethell 35

Property Rights, Taxation, and
the Supply-Siders
Tom Bethell 41

The Regulatory Attack on the Market
Llewellyn H. Rockwell 47

Are Savings Too Low?
Murray N. Rothbard 51

The "We" Fallacy
Sheldon L. Richman 55

U.S. Trade Law: Losing Its Bearings
Alex Tabarrok 59

Statistics: Destroyed from Within?
Murray N. Rothbard 63

The Truth About Economic Forecasting
Graeme B. Littler 66

Michael R. Milken: Political Prisoner?
Llewellyn H. Rockwell 70

The Economic Wisdom of the Late Scholastics
Jeffrey A. Tucker 73

2. DEBUNKING THE BANKERS

Bring Back the Bank Run!
James Grant 79

Nick and Jim Dandy to the Rescue
Bradley Miller 84

Q&A on the S&L Mess
Murray N. Rothbard 88

Inflation Redux
Murray N. Rothbard 95

Faustian Economics
John V. Denson 98

A Gold Standard for Russia?
Murray N. Rothbard 101

The Source of the Business Cycle
Jeffrey A. Tucker 104

The Key to Sound Money
Edwin Vieira, Jr. 108

Foreclose on the World Bank
E. Cort Kirkwood 112

3. UNMASKING THE BUREAUCRATS

Why Bureaucracy Must Fail
Llewellyn H. Rockwell 119

Your Visit to Our Nation's Capital
Llewellyn H. Rockwell 124

The Case Against NASA
Sheldon L. Richman 127

Kemp at HUD: Should Free-Marketeers
Be Optimistic?
Greg Kaza 132

Government and Hurricane Hugo:
A Deadly Combination
Murray N. Rothbard 136

Big Government: An *Un*natural Disaster
Llewellyn H. Rockwell 140

In Defense of Congress
Llewellyn H. Rockwell 144

Exxon: Biggest Victim of the Alaskan Oil Spill
Llewellyn H. Rockwell 148

"Afraid to Trust the People With Arms"
Stephen P. Halbrook 153

4. THE GOVERNMENT MESS

Back to First Principles
Joseph Sobran 159

Why Government Grows
Llewellyn H. Rockwell 169

Our Tentative Economic Freedoms
Llewellyn H. Rockwell 174

The Great Society and 25 Years of Decline
William Murchison 178

Civil Rights and the Politics of Theft
Joseph Sobran 182

Triumph of Liberty? Not in the U.S.
Robert Higgs 187

The Federal Agricultural Swamp
    James Bovard 191

Government Garbage
    Llewellyn H. Rockwell 197

Artistic "Entitlement"
    Doug Bandow 201

What To Do About Traffic Congestion
    Walter Block 207

Time for An American *Perestroika*
    Robert Higgs 211

Immigration and Private Property
    Llewellyn H. Rockwell 216

5. THREATS AND OUTRAGES

End the War on Drugs
    Joseph Sobran 221

Drugs and Adultery
    Llewellyn H. Rockwell 226

Would Legalization Increase Drug Use?
    Lawrence W. Reed 231

Mickey Leland: Humanitarian?
    Llewellyn H. Rockwell 235

Choice in Schooling
    Sheldon L. Richman 238

The High Court Stems the
Tupperware Threat
    Sheldon L. Richman 244

Welcoming the Vietnamese
    Murray N. Rothbard 247

The Double Danger of AIDS
    Richard Hite 249

The Megaeconomic Threat
Llewellyn H. Rockwell 253

Controlling the World Economy
Graeme B. Littler and *Jeffrey A. Tucker* 257

The Dangers of "National Service"
Sheldon L. Richman 263

The Mandated-Benefits Scheme
Sheldon L. Richman 267

Animal Crackers
Llewellyn H. Rockwell 272

Christian Economics
Carl C. Curtis, III 276

Breaking Up the Opinion Cartel
Llewellyn H. Rockwell 280

Lyndon Baines Bush?
Llewellyn H. Rockwell 285

The Environmentalist Threat
Llewellyn H. Rockwell 289

6. THE COMMUNIST CRACKUP

Mises Vindicated
Llewellyn H. Rockwell 313

The Freedom Revolution
Murray N. Rothbard 318

The Old Right Was Right
Sheldon L. Richman 322

The Vanishing Spectre of Communism
Doug Bandow 332

The Socialist Holocaust in Armenia
Llewellyn H. Rockwell 334

How to Desocialize?
Murray N. Rothbard 338

A Radical Prescription for the
Socialist Bloc
Murray N. Rothbard 342

Mises in Moscow! An Interview
with an Austrian Economist
From the U.S.S.R.
Jeffrey A. Tucker 346

Cambodian Catharsis
Lawrence W. Reed 354

Mises's Blueprint for the Free Society
Sheldon L. Richman 359

APPENDIX

A FOREIGN POLICY FOR A FREE-MARKET
AMERICA: TWO VIEWS

A New Nationalism
Patrick J. Buchanan 363

America First, Once More
Bill Kauffman 368

INDEX 375

ABOUT THE CONTRIBUTORS 391

INTRODUCTION

T oday, the whole world knows about the socialist fiasco. But in 1920, when Ludwig von Mises's journal article on "Economic Calculation in the Socialist Commonwealth" was published, he was a lone voice of truth.

"Socialism," he wrote in the book that followed two years later, "is the watchword and the catchword of our day." It "dominates the modern spirit" and "has set its seal upon our time. When history comes to tell our story it will write above the chapter 'The Epoch of Socialism.'"

Until the glorious year of 1989, almost everyone seemed to agree that history was indeed on the side of socialism. The only question was the pace of the transition. The Marxists and Nazis wanted immediate revolution; the Fabians and New Dealers wanted gradualism. But for all of them, laissez-faire capitalism was the enemy.

Yet no socialist had ever written a scientific defense of socialism, nor a blueprint for exactly how the economy would function when the means of production were collectively owned.

According to Karl Marx's doctrine, anyone questioning the socialist scheme lacked class consciousness. Bourgeois values prevented an understanding of the logic of history.

Because "people were not allowed to talk or to think about the nature of the socialist community," Mises notes, socialism became "the dominant political movement of the late nineteenth and early twentieth centuries."

But Mises refused to play by the socialist rules, and he challenged left-wing intellectuals with questions they were unable to answer.

If there is no private ownership of the factors of production, and thus no market prices for them, how can we calculate profit and loss? Without the ability to make profit and loss calculations, how can we judge the value of resources, determine the correctness of various methods of production, or tell whether time and resources are being wasted or put to good use?

In a market economy, prices tell us the needs of society and the best ways to meet those needs. Without prices, economic decision must be arbitrary.

Mises criticized socialism on other grounds—that it politicizes society, fosters laziness, and relies on violence, for example—but his calculation argument is the most important. With it, he showed that socialism is inherently irrational and uneconomic, as the wreckage of the East Bloc and the Third World demonstrates today.

One socialist response to Mises was to invent pretend market prices, missing the point that private property is necessary for real prices. And that is why the Misesian calculation argument has relevance for the mixed economy. It shows what is wrong with all government interventions in the free market.

In a government agency, there are no private owners. There are no market prices for its goods or services. There is no way to determine profits or losses. So its decisions must be arbitrary.

Mises's case against socialism is also the case for laissez-faire capitalism, "the only conceivable form of social economy which is appropriate to the fulfillment of the demands which society makes of any economic organization."

But despite their economic failure, socialist systems survived until men and women of courage brought about their political downfall. And that is what we need in America, one of the nations still moving towards bigger and more intrusive government.

The answer is not more policy analysis that accepts big government categories and advocates meaningless reforms. It is not the "privatization" of illegitimate government functions. It is not alleged free-marketeers installed in big Washington jobs.

The answer, as in Eastern Europe, is men and women willing to tell the truth about the coercion, plunder, corruption, and lies of Washington, D.C. And this is what the Ludwig von Mises Institute's monthly *Free Market* tries to do, through an uncompromising advocacy of the free market, private property, individual liberty, and sound money.

In this publication and through many other Institute programs, we battle old threats like central banking and bureaucracy, and new threats like civil rights and Green-o-mania.

The first *Free Market Reader* proved popular on campus and among the general public. This second collection is even more timely.

To Perry Alford and the other generous donors who made this book possible, heartfelt thanks. Without men and women like this, whether in 1776 or today, the cause of liberty would be lost.

Thanks also to Murray Rothbard, dean of the Austrian school of economics, for his contributions to this volume and his inspiration; to the indispensable Jeff Tucker, managing editor of *The Free Market*; to Norma Marchman, for keeping everything on track; to Judy Thommesen, for wizardry in publishing; and to Lianne Araki, for proofreading.

Llewellyn H. Rockwell
Auburn, Alabama
November 22, 1990

1

ECONOMIC TRUTH
VS.
POLITICAL POWER

Outlawing Jobs:
The Minimum Wage, Once More

Murray N. Rothbard

There is no clearer demonstration of the essential identity of the two political parties than their position on the minimum wage. The Democrats proposed to raise the legal minimum wage from $3.35 an hour, to which it had been raised by the Reagan administration during its allegedly free-market salad days in 1981. The Republican counter was to allow a "subminimum" wage for teenagers, who, as marginal workers, are the ones who are indeed hardest hit by any legal minimum.

This stand was quickly modified by the Republicans in Congress, who proceeded to argue for a teenage subminimum that would last only a piddling 90 days, after which the rate would rise to the higher Democratic minimum (of $4.55 an hour). It was left, ironically enough, for Senator Edward Kennedy to point out the ludicrous economic effect of this proposal: to induce employers to hire teenagers and then fire them after 89 days, to rehire others the day after.

Finally, and characteristically, George Bush got the Republicans out of this hole by throwing in the towel altogether, and pumping for a Democratic plan, period. We were left with the Democrats forthrightly proposing a big increase in the minimum wage, and the Republicans, after a series of illogical waffles, finally going along with the program.

In truth, there is only one way to regard a minimum wage law: it is compulsory unemployment, period. The law says: it is illegal, and therefore criminal, for anyone to hire anyone else below the level of X dollars an hour. This means, plainly and simply, that a large number of free and voluntary wage contracts are now outlawed and hence that there will be a large amount of unemployment. Remember that the minimum wage law provides no jobs; it only outlaws them; and outlawed jobs are the inevitable result.

All demand curves are falling, and the demand for hiring labor is no exception. Hence, laws that prohibit employment at any wage that is relevant to the market (a minimum wage of 10 cents an hour would have little or no impact) must result in outlawing employment and hence causing unemployment.

If the minimum wage is, in short, raised from $3.35 to $4.55 an hour, the consequence is to disemploy, permanently, those who would have been hired at rates in between these two rates. Since the demand curve for any sort of labor (as for any factor of production) is set by the perceived marginal productivity of that labor, this means that the people who will be disemployed and devastated by this prohibition will be precisely the "marginal" (lowest wage) workers, e.g., blacks and teenagers, the very workers whom the advocates of the minimum wage are claiming to foster and protect.

The advocates of the minimum wage and its periodic boosting reply that all this is scare talk and that minimum wage rates do not and never have caused any unemployment. The proper riposte is to raise them one better; all right, if the minimum wage is such a wonderful anti-poverty measure, and can have no unemployment-raising effects, why are you such pikers? Why are you helping the working poor by such piddling amounts? Why stop at $4.55 an hour? Why not $10 an hour? $100? $1,000?

It is obvious that the minimum wage advocates do not pursue their own logic, because if they push it to such heights, virtually the entire labor force will be disemployed. In short, you can have as much unemployment as you want, simply by pushing the legally minimum wage high enough.

It is conventional among economists to be polite, to assume that economic fallacy is solely the result of intellectual error. But there are times when decorousness is seriously misleading, or, as Oscar Wilde once wrote, "when speaking one's mind becomes more than a duty; it becomes a positive pleasure." For if proponents of the higher minimum wage were simply wrong-headed people of good will, they would not stop at $3 or $4 an hour, but indeed would pursue their dimwit logic into the stratosphere.

The fact is that they have always been shrewd enough to stop their minimum wage demands at the point where only marginal workers are affected, and where there is no danger of disemploying, for example, white adult male workers with union seniority. When we see that the most ardent advocates of the minimum wage law have been the AFL-CIO, and that the concrete effects of the minimum wage laws has been to cripple the low-wage competition of the marginal workers as against higher-wage workers with union seniority, the true motivation of the agitation for the minimum wage becomes apparent.

This is only one of a large number of cases where a seemingly purblind persistence in economic fallacy only serves as a mask for special privilege at the expense of those who are supposedly to be "helped."

In the current agitation, inflation—supposedly brought to a halt by the Reagan administration—has eroded the impact of the last minimum wage hike in 1981, reducing the real impact of the minimum wage by 23%. Partially as a result, the unemployment rate has fallen from 11% in 1982 to under six percent today. Possibly chagrined by this drop, the AFL-CIO and its allies are pushing to rectify this condition, and to boost the minimum wage rate by 34%.

Once in a while, AFL-CIO economists and other knowledgeable liberals will drop their mask of economic fallacy and candidly admit that their actions will cause unemployment; they then proceed to justify themselves by claiming that it is more "dignified" for a worker to be on welfare than to work at a low wage. This of course, is the doctrine of many people on welfare themselves. It is truly a strange concept of "dignity" that has been fostered by the interlocking minimum wage-welfare system.

Unfortunately, this system does not give those numerous workers who still prefer to be producers rather than parasites the privilege of making their own free choice.

The Scourge of Unionism
Llewellyn H. Rockwell

Any business owner whose employees deliberately set out to harass and even endanger customers could do only one thing: fire the offenders, and maybe sue them for damages as well. Nothing else would be compatible with free enterprise and private property. But thanks to a whole host of government interventions, unionized companies, like most airlines, cannot take the actions that morality and economics would dictate.

Long before the now-famous strike, Eastern Airlines was hobbled by a legacy of bureaucratic management. During the bad old days when airlines were fully regulated by the government, managements were cozily in cahoots with the government and the union bosses. The resulting featherbedding and other mandated inefficiencies were foisted off on the hapless flyer through higher prices and inferior service, as were the above-market wages extorted by unionized airline employees.

When partial deregulation came along during the Carter administration, sclerotic Eastern started a long downhill slide, guided by ex-astronaut Frank Borman, whose managerial nirvana was the obese NASA. Only the attempt of entrepreneurial chairman Frank Lorenzo to forcefeed some economic rationality into Eastern had a chance of saving the company from bankruptcy. But his efforts were hamstrung by politically-favored unions. And then they attacked Eastern's customers by striking, as well as encouraging their cohorts in the rest of the industry to engage in a work slowdown designed to cause chaos.

Labor unions, it must be remembered, are not simple associations of workers. They are conspiracies against the public interest. In the past, striking union members have done everything from breaking kneecaps to sending out false air traffic control signals. And when they do so, they are immune from justice.

Through laws and court decisions, the federal government gives these organizations and their bosses a whole range of special-interest privileges. For example, unions are virtually immune from prosecution for assaults and property damage during strikes.

We all have the right to quit our jobs. We also have the right to quit as a group. But we emphatically do not have the right to set up harassing picket lines and criminally assault those who choose to work. Yet that is what a strike consists of: the threat and actuality of violence against workers who want to support their families rather than obey union bosses. Thanks to government-granted favors, unions get away with things that would send anyone else to the crowbar motel—and rightly so.

With the Eastern strike, and the union attempt to spread it to all other forms of transportation, the unions have taken a serious risk. Union power has dwindled in recent years and this could help it along. Tormented consumers must know who to blame for their purgatory: unions.

But that is not easy, since there is so much disinformation about unions—spread by union propagandists, leftists, and the government itself. Even the standard historical account is an accumulation of myths.

One myth says that unions have played a crucial role in representing U.S. workers. In truth, unions have historically represented only a small fraction. Today, only about 15% of the civilian workforce is unionized. Even at their height in 1955, unions comprised only 25%. And labor economist Morgan Reynolds says that union membership could drop in a few years below 10%.

Before 1860, there were virtually no unions in America. After the Civil War, socialists and communists tried to organize workers—from ideological rather than economic motives. But the organizations inevitably declined and disbanded amidst public hostility to widespread bombings and killings by union organizers.

The founding of the American Federation of Labor in 1881 gave a temporary boost to the nationwide craft unions, but 20 years later, with fewer than 500,000 members, unions still had little influence.

That all changed with World War I. As part of its central wartime planning, the U.S. government declared a national emergency and promoted unionism—as a useful adjunct to cartelized big business—through wage and labor boards.

In a precedent-setting move, the government even approved union violence by (1) outlawing "interference" with coercive union activities; (2) forcing companies to rehire violent union members with full back pay; and (3) seizing the assets of companies that refused to go along. At one point, the government even created a union, the Loyal Legion of Loggers and Lumbermen.

After the war—over the opposition of government contractors and their unions—the labor market was deregulated, and union membership plummeted, with the biggest losses in those industries closest to the government.

Contrary to another myth, union membership took a free fall with the Great Depression. It wasn't until the New Deal labor legislation that union membership began to grow again. A flood of legislation authorized federal fixing of minimum wages, maximum hours, and working conditions, and bolstered union cartelization by allowing them to fix terms of employment.

Especially objectionable were the Norris-LaGuardia Act, which prohibited court injunctions against union violence, and the Wagner Act, which forced employers to "bargain in good faith" with unions, i.e., to give in to their demands.

As culpable as Franklin Roosevelt was for all this legislation, however, Herbert Hoover had actually laid the groundwork. As secretary of commerce under Harding and Coolidge—as Murray N. Rothbard has pointed out— he was an ardent union defender, praising their activities, encouraging collective bargaining, and preaching the "humanitarian" goals of union organizing. After the Crash, as president, Hoover used government power to keep wages high for unions—exactly the opposite of what should have happened during a depression.

As a result of all this, union membership increased by 160% from 1933 to 1940.

Unions received yet another boost from World War II, when the federal government again cartelized the economy. Wages were set by government decree and business had to obey dictates from Washington, including the many that favored unions. By the end of the war, union membership had nearly doubled.

After World War I, when the wartime socialism-fascism was dismantled, unions fell apart. But this didn't happen in the much milder dismantling after World War II. Thanks to the New Deal laws and pro-union government agencies, unions were able to avoid market competition and thus sustain their membership. As always, one of their major tools in this was violence and the threat of violence.

Eventually, however, a public outcry against this led Congress to pass another major piece of union legislation, this time over Harry Truman's veto: the Taft-Hartley Act of 1947. It was a blow to union power, but rather than repeal existing pro-union laws, it gave the government even more power, especially to intervene in labor disputes and to force employees back to work.

Nevertheless, Taft-Hartley marked a turning point. Eight years later, union membership peaked, and it has fallen ever since. And in the absence of new federal interventions, it will continue to do so.

Many people are unaware of this decline, in part because of the visibility of public-sector unions like the postal workers and the National Education Association. These unions, observes Constitutional lawyer Edwin Vieira, have "quasi-governmental power" that is "incompatible" with "constitutional liberties." Even here, however, unions represent a minority—34%—of government employees.

Another myth is that unions were founded to assist the poor and oppressed. In fact, they have always concentrated on high-wage, cohesive groups that are easy to organize, like construction tradesmen and railroad workers, and which can wreak broad havoc with strikes and other anti-competitive practices.

Today, the purpose of unions is largely to protect middle-upper class workers from wage competition. Typical are the Air Line Pilots Association, where some senior captains make $150,000 to fly less than 11 hours per week. The average annual salary of ALPA members is $85,000 for less than 19 hours of work a week. And no one thinks of Eastern's $52,000 mechanics and $43,000 baggage handlers as the oppressed proletariat—especially when massive overtime caused by deliberate union makework is added to these high incomes.

This creates what Morgan Reynolds calls a "two-way dependency" between unions and wages: high-wage workers are more likely to unionize, which creates confusion about the sequence of causes. In truth, unions do not and cannot raise wages in general. Wages are determined by the productivity of the individual laborer, which in turn is largely determined by the amount of capital invested per worker.

The best way to raise wages is to increase the productivity of labor, which means creating a freer economy with more capital investment.

Unions can and do raise their own pay, but only at the expense of non-union and marginal workers. This is why unions promote such anti-competitive government interventions as minimum wages, which are designed to throw out of work those whose market worth is less than the minimum. This process enriches unions at the expense of the most vulnerable members of society.

Even with their limited numbers, unions enact a dreadful toll on our economy. They stymie competition, thwart the will of consumers, and promote misallocation of resources. Businesses and consumers have to bear the costs of arcane work rules and other mandated inefficiencies, absenteeism, and delays of new technology. And finally, there are the costs that strikes cause through disruption and violence.

It is impossible to measure precisely how much damage unions do to the U.S. economy. But Morgan Reynolds's "unsubstantiated hunch" is that real income would rise 10% if unions disappeared.

The solution to union violence and inefficiency—as with all our economic problems—is simple: cut off the government's tentacles. In this case, that means repealing the laws which grant the unions privileges and immunities. Justice for private property, working people, and consumers allows nothing less.

Keynesianism Redux

Murray N. Rothbard

One of the ironic but unfortunately enduring legacies of the eight years of Reaganism has been the resurrection of Keynesianism. From the late 1930s until the early 1970s, Keynesianism rode high in the economics profession and in the corridors of power in Washington,

promising that, so long as Keynesian economists continued at the helm, the blessings of modern macroeconomics would surely bring us permanent prosperity without
inflation. Then something happened on the way to Eden:
the mighty inflationary recession of 1973-74.

Keynesian doctrine is, despite its algebraic and geo-
metric jargon, breathtakingly simple at its core: recessions are caused by underspending in the economy,
inflation is caused by overspending. Of the two major
categories of spending, consumption is passive and determined, almost robotically, by income; hopes for the proper
amount of spending, therefore, rest on investment, but
private investors, while active and decidedly non-robotic,
are erratic and volatile, unreliably dependent on fluctua-
tions in what Keynes called their "animal spirits."

Fortunately for all of us, there is another group in the
economy that is just as active and decisive as investors,
but which is also—if guided by Keynesian economists—
scientific and rational, able to act in the interests of all:
Big Daddy government. When investors and consumers
underspend, government can and should step in and
increase social spending via deficits, thereby lifting the
economy out of recession. When private animal spirits
get too wild, government is supposed to step in and
reduce private spending by what the Keynesians
revealingly call "sopping up excess purchasing power"
(that's ours).

In strict theory, by the way, the Keynesians could just
as well have called for lowering government spending
during inflationary booms rather than sopping up our
spending, but the very idea of cutting government budgets (and I mean actual cut-cuts, not cuts in the rate of

increase) is nowadays just as unthinkable, as, for example, adhering to a Jeffersonian strict construction of the
Constitution of the United States, and for similar reasons.

Originally, Keynesians vowed that they, too, were in
favor of a "balanced budget," just as much as the fuddy-
duddy reactionaries who opposed them. It's just that
they were not, like the fuddy-duddies, tied to the year as
an accounting period; they would balance the budget,
too, but over the business cycle. Thus, if there are four
years of recession followed by four years of boom, the
federal deficits during the recession would be compen-
sated for by the surpluses piled up during the boom; over
the eight years of cycle, it would all balance out.

Evidently, the "cyclically balanced budget" was the
first Keynesian concept to be poured down the Orwellian
memory hole, as it became clear that there weren't going
to be any surpluses, just smaller or larger deficits. A
subtle but important corrective came into Keynesianism:
larger deficits during recessions, smaller ones during
booms.

But the real slayer of Keynesianism came with the
double-digit inflationary recession of 1973-74, followed
soon by the even more intense inflationary recessions of
1979-80 and 1981-82. For if the government were supposed to step on the spending accelerator during recessions, and step on the brakes during booms, what in
blazes is it going to do if there is a steep recession (with
unemployment and bankruptcies) and a sharp inflation
at the same time? What can Keynesianism say? Step on
both accelerator and brake at the same time? The stark
fact of inflationary recession violates the fundamental

assumptions of Keynesian theory and the crucial program of Keynesian policy. Since 1973-74, Keynesianism has been intellectually finished, dead from the neck up.

But very often the corpse refuses to lie down, particularly an elite which would have to give up their power positions in the academy and in government. One crucial law of politics or sociology is: no one ever resigns. And so, the Keynesians have clung to their power positions as tightly as possible, never resigning, although a bit less addicted to grandiose promises.

A bit chastened, they now only promise to do the best they can, and to keep the system going. Essentially, then, shorn of its intellectual groundwork, Keynesianism has become the pure economics of power, committed only to keeping the Establishment-system going, making marginal adjustments, babying things along through yet one more election, and hoping that by tinkering with the controls, shifting rapidly back and forth between accelerator and brake, something will work, at least to preserve their cushy positions for a few more years.

Amidst the intellectual confusion, however, a few dominant tendencies, legacies from their glory days, remain among Keynesians: (1) a penchant for continuing deficits, (2) a devotion to fiat paper money and at least moderate inflation, (3) adherence to increased government spending, and (4) an eternal fondness for higher taxes, to lower deficits a wee bit, but more importantly, to inflict some bracing pain on the greedy, selfish, and short-sighted American public.

The Reagan administration managed to institutionalize these goodies, seemingly permanently on the American scene, and the Bush administration has continued the tradition. Deficits are far greater and apparently forever; the difference now is that formerly free-market Reaganomists and Bushonomists are out-Keynesianing their liberal forebears in coming up with ever more ingenious apologetics for huge deficits. The only dispute now is within the Keynesian camp, with the allegedly "conservative" supply-siders enthusiastically having joined Keynesians in devotion to inflation and cheap money, and differing only on their call for moderate tax cuts as against tax increases.

The triumph of Keynesianism within the Reagan and Bush administrations stems from the rapid demise of the monetarists, the main competitors to the Keynesians within respectable academia. Having made a series of disastrously bad predictions, they who kept trumpeting that "science is prediction," the monetarists retreated in confusion, trying desperately to figure out what went wrong and which of the many Ms they should fasten on as being the money supply. The collapse of monetarism was first symbolized by Keynesian James Baker's take-over as Secretary of the Treasury from monetarist-sympathizer Donald Regan. With Keynesians dominant during the second Reagan term, the transition to a Keynesian Bush team—Bush having always had strong Keynesian leanings—was so smooth as to be almost invisible.

Perhaps it is understandable that an administration and a campaign that reduced important issues to sound bites and TV images should also be responsible for the restoration to dominance of an intellectually bankrupt economic creed, the very same creed that brought us the political economics of every administration since the second term of Franklin D. Roosevelt.

It is no accident that the same administration that managed to combine the rhetoric of "getting government off our backs" with the reality of enormously escalating Big Government, should also bring back a failed and statist Keynesianism in the name of prosperity and free enterprise.

The Keynesian Dream

Murray N. Rothbard

For a half-century, the Keynesians have harbored a Dream. They have long dreamed of a world without gold, a world rid of any restrictions upon their desire to spend and spend, inflate and inflate, elect and elect. They have achieved a world where governments and Central Banks are free to inflate without suffering the limits and restrictions of the gold standard. But they still chafe at the fact that, although national governments are free to inflate and print money, they yet find themselves limited by depreciation of their currency. If Italy, for example, issues a great many lira, the lira will depreciate in terms of other currencies, and Italians will find the prices of their imports and of foreign resources skyrocketing.

What the Keynesians have dreamed of, then, is a world with one fiat currency, the issues of that paper currency being generated and controlled by one World Central Bank. What you call the new currency unit doesn't really matter: Keynes called his proposed unit at the Bretton Woods Conference of 1944, the "bancor;" Harry Dexter White, the U.S. Treasury negotiator at that time, called his proposed money the "unita," and recently, the London Economist has dubbed its suggested new world money the "phoenix." Fiat money by any name smells as sour.

Even though the United States and its Keynesian advisers dominated the international monetary scene at the end of World War II, they could not impose the full Keynesian goal; the jealousies and conflicts of national sovereignty were too intense. So the Keynesians reluctantly had to settle for the jerry-built dollar-gold international standard at Bretton Woods, with exchange rates flexibly fixed, and with no World Central Bank at its head.

As determined men with a goal, the Keynesians did not fail from not trying. They launched the Special Drawing Right (SDR) as an attempt to replace gold as an international reserve money, but SDRs proved to be a failure. Prominent Keynesians such as Edward M. Bernstein of the International Monetary Fund and Robert Triffin of Yale launched well-known Plans bearing their names, but these too were not adopted.

Ever since the Bretton Woods system, hailed for nearly three decades as stable and eternal, collapsed in 1971, the Keynesians have had to suffer the indignity of floating exchange rates. Ever since the accession of Keynesian James R. Baker as Secretary of the Treasury in 1985, the United States has abandoned its brief commitment to a monetarist hands-off the foreign exchange market policy, and has tried to engineer a phase transformation of the international monetary system. First, fixed exchange rates would be obtained by coordinated action by the large Central Banks. This has largely been achieved, at first covertly and then openly; the leading Central Banks picked a target point or zone, for, say, the dollar, and then by buying and selling dollars, manipulated exchange rates to stay within that zone. Their main difficulty has been figuring out what target to pick, since, indeed, they have no wisdom in rate-fixing beyond that of the market. Indeed, the concept of a just exchange-rate for the dollar is just as inane as the notion of the "just price" for a particular good.

A tempting opportunity for mischief has been offered the Keynesians by the European Community. The Keynesians, led by now-Secretary of State James Baker, have been pushing for a new currency unit for this United Europe, to be issued by a European-wide Central Bank. This would not only mean an international economic government for Europe, it would also mean that it would become relatively easy for the post-1992 European Central Bank to become coordinated with the Central Banks of the United States and Japan, and to segue without too much trouble to the long-cherished goal of the World Central Bank and world currency unit.

Inflationist European countries, such as Italy and France, are eager for the coordinated European-wide inflation that a regional Central Bank would bring about. Hard-money countries such as West Germany, however, are highly critical of inflationary schemes. You would expect Germany, therefore, to resist these Europeanist demands; so why don't they? The problem is that, ever since World War II, the United States has had enormous political leverage upon West Germany, and the United States and its Keynesian foreign secretary Baker have been pushing hard for European monetary unity. Only Great Britain, happily, has been throwing a monkey-wrench into these Keynesian proceedings. Hard-money oriented, and wary of infringements on its sovereignty—and also influenced by Monetarist adviser Sir Alan Walters—Britain might just succeed in blocking the European Central Bank indefinitely.

At best, the Keynesian Dream is a long shot. It is always possible that, not only British opposition, but also the ordinary and numerous frictions between sovereign nations will insure that the Dream will never be achieved. It would be heartening, however, if principled opposition to the Dream could also be mounted. For what the Keynesians want is no less than an internationally coordinated and controlled world-wide paper money inflation, a fine-tuned inflation that would proceed unchecked upon its merry way until, whoops! it landed the entire world smack into the middle of the untold horrors of global runaway hyperinflation.

The Free-Rider Confusion

Tom Bethell

I f property is not privately owned, then it must be either state owned or communally owned. We know state-owned property results in economic failure. What happens when we consider the case of communal property? Why does this too not seem to work very well?

A main reason is that common ownership encourages "free riding" by the joint owners. There is no satisfactory way to assure the communal owners of a just "ratio" between the effort they individually expend producing goods and their ultimate consumption of goods. What one person sows another can reap. Before long, this results in a general laziness—the bane of communes. He who toils finds that the fruits of his labor are tossed into a common pool, where they may be consumed by his less industrious brethren. Slackers profit from the conscientious. This is a classic illustration of the free-rider problem—a problem that arises when the institutional setting does not permit property rights to be well-defined.

The free-rider problem arises because it is a characteristic of human nature that if we are offered a free good, we are strongly inclined to accept it. By the same token, we are strongly disinclined to labor if the fruits of our labor are promptly made available to others, free of charge.

If you turn to economics textbooks, however, and look up "Free-Rider Problem," you find something quite unexpected. You find that the concept of free riding is always discussed in a context of "market failure," almost never in a context of "collective failure." Indeed, current economics textbooks do not so much as entertain the idea that there is any such thing as a "common-pool problem" or "collective failure." They point out that a problem of "public goods" arises when it is technically difficult to prevent those who do not pay for certain goods from using them. One example frequently given, albeit historically inaccurate, is that of lighthouses.

It is true, of course, that in certain situations it is technically difficult to confine the use of certain economic goods to those who pay for them. In such cases, there is said to be a "positive externality," in which non-payers receive an "external benefit." To the extent that this is true, a theorist may well perceive a "market failure." But it is not a particularly serious problem. It does not prevent commercial (i.e., private) radio stations from operating profitably. And technological changes make private security and roads increasingly practical.

The mere technical difficulty of confining the use of goods to those who pay for them is as nothing compared to the institutional difficulties that arise when property is owned in common. Here the free-rider problem strikes with a vengeance. It becomes (in any commune above family size) impossible to apportion consumption to production, and a great sense of injustice begins to take hold. But try to find an economics book that uses the free-rider problem to illustrate the concept of collective failure.

Some would say that communal ownership is so limited in the modern world that it is not particularly relevant or important. Economists argue that in socialist countries, such as the Soviet Union, the free-rider problem does not exist because the ill-defined ownership of common property has been replaced by the monopoly ownership of the state—or by a "single will," as Ludwig von Mises put it.

In practice, however, the free-rider problem exists on a giant scale in all socialist countries. F.A. Hayek has drawn attention to the difficulties of organizing production in centrally planned economies, pointing out that the central planning authority can never have at its disposal sufficient information to issue intelligent commands.

The problem with Hayek's objection to planning is that it implies that people are willing slaves, eager to toil for socialist construction if only their masters at the central planning bureau would issue the right commands. But people, including Soviet people, are not made that way. In the Soviet Union, as in all institutional settings in which the individual is not primary, people are reluctant to work when they can't capture the fruits of their labors, and when they are paid (minimally, it is true) whether they work or not.

The Associated Press reported the following from Moscow: "'The food problem is far from solved,' Gorbachev said in one of his frankest admissions of the Soviet Union's problems. 'The housing problem is acute. There is a dearth of consumer goods in the shops. The list of shortages is growing. The state's financial position is grave.'" He diagnosed the problem in this way: "Many people have forgotten how to work. They got used to being paid," he said, "just for coming to work."

And there, in spades, you have the free-rider problem posing difficulties for socialism: state socialism, not just communitarian socialism. By comparison, the problem that the free riders pose for markets is minimal. But you wouldn't know it from our economics texts.

In his famous text *Economics* (11th edition), Paul Samuelson notes that "wherever there are externalities, a strong case can be made for supplanting complete individualism by some kind of group action." He does not seem to realize that these externalities above all arise in a setting where individualism has in fact been supplanted by group action, or perhaps never existed in the first place.

"Because of their characteristics," Robert Heilbroner and James K. Galbraith argue in *The Economic Problem* (8th edition, 1987), "all public goods share a common difficulty: their provision cannot be entrusted to the decision-making mechanism of the market." This is true, but tautological. Public goods are so defined in their book. The authors' discussion of the problem of externalities is confined to the negative externalities that arise in a free-market system (e.g., pollution), and overlooks the positive externalities that arise in a communal system (the institutional arrangement that permits me to reap what you sow). Hence the free-rider problem is seen as causing difficulties only for the market, and their discussion arises in a chapter entitled "Where the Market Fails."

"Externalities lie at the heart of some of society's most pressing problems," William J. Baumol and Alan S. Blinder write in *Economics: Principles and Policy* (2nd edition, 1982). They cite "the problems of the cities, the environment, research policy and a variety of other critical issues. For this reason, the concept of externalities is one of our 12 Ideas for Beyond the Final Exam. It is a subject that will recur again and again...." Even so, their discussion is limited to the kind of "externality" that is alleged to cause a problem for the market. All this is in a chapter headed "Shortcomings of the Market Mechanism and Government Attempts to Remedy Them." They do not bring up the severe externality problem that arises when the "market mechanism" is supplanted by collectivism.

Stanley Fischer and Rudiger Dornbusch (*Economics*, 1983) likewise confine their discussion of the free-rider problem to the realm of market problems.

Roy J. Ruffin and Paul R. Gregory (*Principles of Economics*, 2nd edition, 1986) note that "externalities are a classic example of market failure," adding: "Many externalities are the result of poorly defined property rights." They proceed to give examples of the failure of communal ownership—overfishing of communally owned fishing grounds, and so on. But their whole argument is set in a chapter entitled "Market Failure, Environment, Energy."

Oddly, in light of this chapter title, their diagnosis of the problem of externalities is the same as that of Harold Demsetz in his famous article "Toward A Theory of Property Rights," (*American Economic Review*, May 1967). Demsetz really did establish the key point that free-riding undermines communalism. The Labrador Indians overhunted beavers on communal hunting grounds because the benefits of such hunting were enjoyed by individual hunters (i.e., were privatized), while the costs were borne by other members of the tribe (i.e., socialized, or "externalized"). The solution, Demsetz said, was to establish private hunting grounds, which would save the beaver.

Communal ownership, Demsetz wrote, "fails to concentrate the costs associated with any person's exercise of his activities on that person.... The effect of a person's activities on his neighbors and on subsequent generations will not be taken into account fully. Communal property results in great externalities." Privatizing the land would "internalize the externalities," Demsetz wrote.

Ruffin and Gregory write, "the solution is to internalize, or put a private price tag on, externalities. This price must be paid by the one imposing the cost or received by the one imposing the benefit." In the 20 years that separate Demsetz and Ruffin & Gregory, what has changed? The problem under discussion, formerly perceived as a problem of communalism, has been construed as a problem of the market.

James Gwartney and Richard Stroup discuss the free-rider problem in Chapter 28 of their *Economics: Public and Private Choice* (4th edition, 1987). They point out that where there are external benefits, people can become free riders (true). They add that "the problems caused by externalities stem from a failure (or an inability) to clearly define and enforce property rights" (also true). They do discuss the externality problems that arise with communal property—the overgrazing of English commons in the 16th century, the overhunting of beavers by the Montagnais Indians in the 17th century—and here they are indeed making the case that massive free riding, hence over-use, tends to destroy communal property. What is misleading is that all this information is conveyed in a chapter entitled "Problem Areas for the Market."

Unexpectedly joining the crowd is Paul Heyne, whose lucid text *The Economic Way of Thinking* (5th edition, 1987) is unusually free of professional group-think. But like everyone else, he uses the free-rider problem to illustrate public goods and market failure—e.g., the difficulty of forming a volunteer police force.

Property Rights, Taxation, and the Supply-Siders
Tom Bethell

I t was a decade ago that most of us began to hear about the supply-side movement, although its origins go further back than that. The movement was given great impetus by the inflation of the 1970s, which combined with the progressive income-tax code to shift everybody into higher tax brackets. Since purchasing power was not increasing, this was widely understood to be unjust. Notice that it was the unlegislated nature of the tax increase that was deemed unfair; not the progressive tax code itself.

In retrospect the claims then made by supply-siders were extremely modest. They argued that tax rates above a certain point are counter-productive from the point of view of the revenue collector. In effect, supply-siders proposed the following deal with the socialists (now called liberals in the U.S.): "You want more revenue, and we want to be able to keep a greater percentage of what we earn at the margin. Both objectives can be attained by reducing the top income tax rates." But what extraordinary rage and scorn poured forth from the liberals in response to this mild observation, offered in a spirit of compromise.

Perhaps the liberals were angry because they suspected supply-siders were insincere in their pose as the pragmatic allies of the revenue collector. Perhaps, indeed, the supply-siders ought to have opposed the progressive income tax as immoral in itself rather than unproductive at the margin.

Nonetheless, the supply-siders' suggested compromise with the advocates of big government contained at its core an analysis that was highly unwelcome to the statists and the mainstream economists. The supply-siders were saying that incentives do matter after all, that if the government takes away too much of what people have worked for, they will not in the future be so productive.

At that time, economists had reason to believe that the whole subject of incentives had been eliminated from economic analysis; as outmoded as the cavalry charge, and as little likely to return. The pretense was that "the economy" was a machine, activated (like a water mill) by an "income stream." Human psychology had nothing to do with this purely mechanical and scientific action. That was the fond pretense. (To some extent it still is.) In the 1967 edition of his textbook, Paul Samuelson writes that the question whether high income tax rates discourage effort is "not an easy (one) to answer. For we shall see later that taxation will cause some people to work harder in order to make their million." Samuelson never demonstrates this dubious proposition (sometimes called the "income effect").

In any event the supply-siders dealt it a devastating blow simply by questioning it, and by asserting that human rationality must be a part of economic analysis. People will not work hard to further other people's ends that are both unknown and unknowable. I will not work to earn $100 if I am told that I must leave 50 of those dollars on the sidewalk for the benefit of the next person who happens to come by. Refusing to work to attain such an unknown end is not "greed" or "selfishness." It is simple rationality. Very much the same analysis applies to toiling for dollars which are to be thrown into the trillion-dollar common pool that is the federal budget.

Advocates of the free market should also insist that the individual's desire to dispose of his own earnings may well be wholly unselfish. He may, after all, want to keep his earnings so that he may give them to Mother Teresa. A man who earns money to spend on his family is likewise acting unselfishly.

There was often a kind of euphoria and excitement in those early discussions between supply-siders, as I recall from my own experience. This was before they fragmented into unseemly recriminations and rivalry in the mid-1980s.

Since then I have thought about these ideas a good deal and I have come to the conclusion that they should be restated.

Supply-siders have been on a great treasure hunt for information about Third World tax rates. These were found to be shockingly high in almost every case. The Agency for International Development was scorned for not knowing the first thing about such matters; the World Bank and the International Monetary Fund were likewise excoriated. Indeed, such agencies have tended to favor raising taxes. All this tended to confirm the idea that tax rates—particularly income tax rates—were the key to understanding the great mystery that has bedeviled development economics since World War II: Why is it that some countries have prospered, while most have stagnated (in Africa, actually declined in many instances)?

It is clear, however, that this diagnosis is inadequate. There is another way of expressing the problem, at a level of greater generality, which gives us a much better grasp of the matter. The key is not taxation but property rights: private property is (comparatively) secure in some countries, highly insecure in others, while in still others (the Communist countries) it has been abolished outright as a matter of ideology. In any country, I believe, the extent and security of private property will be found to correlate closely with economic performance there.

The necessary studies have not been undertaken, however, because it has been dogma among professional economists (except Austrians) for almost a century that private property is an "optional extra." The piece of machinery called "the economy" can come equipped with or without it. If anything, higher rates of economic growth can be achieved without it. (That is what they claim, gentlemen.) Incidentally, one reason why so many academic economists are unenthusiastic about property as an analytical tool is that it is difficult to quantify. Furthermore, it threatens to throw economics into reverse gear, back into the "political economy" of the 19th century and away from the "economic science" of the 20th.

Once we examine the "way the world works" from the vantage-point of property, however, we find that it casts new light not just on economic development but on taxation itself. It is true, of course, that all taxation is an abridgement of property rights, and the high levels of taxation encountered in all Western countries today in general impair property rights more seriously than anything else. (The property rights of certain classes of citizens, e.g., apartment owners in New York, Santa Monica, Brookline, and Berkeley are even more gravely impaired, but for the population as a whole taxation tops the list of property infringements.) This accounts for the overall accuracy of the supply-siders' prognosis a decade ago. Property was (and is) the key, but in the Western countries in which supply-side theory has primarily been tested (by reducing tax rates) it is precisely the tax code that constitutes the most serious attack on property.

In many Third World countries, however, it is not sufficient to reduce the income tax rates (as was done in the Philippines, for example). If regulations prevent the acquisition of property, or its voluntary transfer, or effectively confine it to presidential cronies, as in some Latin American countries, then reducing the progressivity of the tax code won't work magic. As for Communist countries, it is more or less meaningless to analyze economic problems in terms of taxation. They are more fundamental than that. Thus we may say that reform of the tax code is a necessary but not a sufficient condition of economic revival.

Finally, it is worth noting the economic bias that has created the system that now prevails throughout the West, in which up to one third of income property is subject to legal confiscation (more than a third, if you add in social security taxes, state taxes, and the taxation of interest on savings), but real property is secure (as long as you don't rent it out in certain jurisdictions). The effect is to promote a class system—the very evil that Karl Marx claimed a progressive income tax would eliminate. Old money is pitted against new. Those with valuable properties, acquired at a time of lower taxation and now safe from confiscation, are placed at a great competitive advantage over those who must toil to acquire income, and then surrender one third of it before they have accumulated enough to convert it into real property.

The French, interestingly enough, understood this diagnosis and actually decided to change the rules, shortly after Francois Mitterand was elected in 1981. Objets d'art and antiques inside those nice old chateaux would be assessed and taxed for a change! But somehow, the enthusiasm for this attack on the class system encountered unexpected resistance—from the socialists. It was as though all that talk about the desirable egalitarian effects of the progressive tax code was a mere

smokescreen, disguising the point that what the socialists really want is a system in which some people (the
better class of person, you understand) can lord it over
others—the uppity, bourgeois, nouveaux riches.

The Regulatory Attack on the Market

Llewellyn H. Rockwell

Ever since the October 1987 stock-market crash,
government officials have demanded more control
over the securities industry. As usual, their claim has
been bolstered by "disinterested" scientific analysis by
economists.

In its post-crash study, the Securities and Exchange
Commission blamed stock-index futures, and advocated
higher margin requirements and more regulatory powers
for itself. The New York Stock Exchange's study condemned futures, especially portfolio-insurance programs, and also advocated higher margins on stock-
index futures and more enforcement authority for the
SEC.

Reagan's stock market commission, headed by now-
Treasury Secretary Nicholas Brady, implicated portfolio
insurance, mutual fund redemptions, computers, and
unchecked price swings. It urged that the Federal Reserve be given supra-regulatory powers over stocks, futures, and options, and that price controls ("circuit-
breaker mechanisms") be instituted in case of massive
market movements.

In accord with these domestic developments, Great
Britain's Wilton Park Group—composed of regulators

from the ten major industrialized countries—called for global standards on insider trading, market shutdowns, and margin requirements, plus increased sharing of confidential financial information. In April 1988, the U.S. orchestrated an agreement between the Japanese market and the Chicago Board of Trade, and in September, between the London market and the Commodity Futures Trading Commission.

As then-SEC Chairman David Ruder noted: "I find myself voting more clearly for intervention...into all kinds of activities."

Except for 1934, when it banned all new stock issues at the behest of old-line firms and began to cartelize the securities industry, the SEC has never been more interventionist than it is today. As we know from economic theory, as well as the history of similar activities, such intervention will undermine the economic functions of the stock and futures markets.

In the academic world, most economists believe that the financial markets as a collective entity are all-knowing—not only about present events but also about the future. The markets discount everything, so there can be no profits or losses through better or poorer forecasting, only through good or bad luck. The markets are a giant gambling casino, with no real economic function.

The more accurate Austrian view sees securities markets as efficient, but also imperfect, functioning as they do in a world of uncertainty. Within the division of labor, there are more successful forecasters, and one function of the markets is to convey financial assets from the less efficient in this area to the more efficient. The far-seeing traders profit while others do not, and that serves an important economic purpose; Wall Street is not the equivalent of Caesar's Palace.

The markets also must coordinate complex price relationships among the many stages of production over time. It is a job that no regulator can perform, no matter what his intentions or how many computers he has.

The price system is like a communications network that transmits signals about possible profits and losses. Through this network, producers learn from consumers about how they value the various goods and services available, and therefore how best to make use of the available capital, land, and labor.

These signals also affect the perceived outlook for company profits, and therefore stock prices. Entrepreneurs respond to the signals by trying to outcompete their rivals in better meeting consumer demand, and thereby reap higher profits. But this communications network can only be sensitive to consumer desires and transmit undistorted signals when it is free and open.

Prices—especially in the stock and futures markets— must be allowed to reflect real market conditions. Higher stock prices, for example, signal that more capital can be raised for a particular industry or firm, and that its output can be expanded. Lower stock prices show us the less desired industries and firms, and lead to the shifting of resources into more productive endeavors.

Consumers can change their subjective valuations of goods and services because of their expectations about the future, their preference for a new product over an old, or simply changing tastes. Regardless, economic efficiency requires a price system that can accurately reflect these adjustments in changes of value on the markets.

Only the unhampered market allows entrepreneurs to efficiently meet and even anticipate consumer preferences. In the frozen world of government econometric models, all possible economic data, present and future, is known. There is no experimentation, creativity, or discovery. All consumer prices are determined by the costs of production—rather than supply and demand—and the prices of capital are "given." It is not surprising that these models show no ill effects from regulation.

In the real markets, the prices that consumers are willing to pay determine every price through the many stages of production. This "imputation" process, which enables entrepreneurs to build the long-term production processes characteristic of an advanced economy, cannot take place efficiently when there are regulatory barriers.

As in the rest of the economy, economic freedom in the stock and futures markets is essential for productivity, efficiency, and innovation. More regulation can cause only discoordination and stagnation, as the desires of regulators take precedence over the buying public.

Circuit-breaker mechanisms, for example, temporarily block this flow of information. Radical price corrections, such as the one in the 1987 crash, are just as necessary as small ones. Since they are almost always caused by Federal Reserve credit manipulation, these radical swings ("clusters of errors," as F.A. Hayek termed them) are unnatural phenomena. That is another reason why the markets must be allowed to adjust.

Higher margin requirements in the futures markets will make trading stock index-futures prohibitively expensive and reduce competition.

All the current attempts to add to the already elaborate regulatory apparatus are no service to the economy. Rather than erecting new barriers, a clear understanding of markets instead requires elimination of all the present ones.

Are Savings Too Low?

Murray N. Rothbard

One strong recent trend among economists, businessmen, and politicians, has been to lament the amount of savings and investment in the United States as being far too low. It is pointed out that the American percentage of savings to national income is far lower than among the West Germans, or among our feared competitors, the Japanese. Recently, Secretary of the Treasury Nicholas Brady sternly warned of the low savings and investment levels in the United States.

This sort of argument should be considered on many levels. First, and least important, the statistics are usually manipulated to exaggerate the extent of the problem. Thus, the scariest figures (e.g., U.S. savings as only 1.5% of national income) only mention personal savings, and omit business savings; also, capital gains are almost always omitted as a source of savings and investment.

But these are minor matters. The most vital question is: even conceding that U.S. savings are 1.5% of national income and Japanese savings are 15%, what, if anything, is the proper amount or percentage of savings?

Consumers voluntarily decide to divide their income into spending on consumer goods, as against saving and investment for future income. If Mr. Jones invests X percent of his income for future use, by what standard, either moral or economic, does some outside person come along and denounce him for being wrong or immoral for not investing X + 1 percent? Everyone knows that if they consume less now, and save and invest more, they will be able to earn a higher income at some point in the future. But which they choose depends on the rate of their time preferences: how much they prefer consuming now to consuming later. Since everyone makes this decision on the basis of his own life, his particular situation, and his own value-scales, to denounce his decision requires some extra-individual criterion, some criterion outside the person with which to override his preferences.

That criterion *cannot* be economic, since what is efficient and economic can only be decided within a framework of voluntary decisions made by individuals. For the criterion to be moral would be extraordinarily shaky, since moral truths, like economic laws, are not quantitative but qualitative. Moral laws, such as "thou shalt not kill" or "thou shalt not steal," are qualitative; there is no moral law which says that "thou shalt not steal more than 62% of the time." So, if people are being exhorted to save more and consume less as a moral doctrine, the moralist is required to come up with some quantitative optimum, such as: *when* specifically, is saving too low, and *when* is it too high? Vague exhortations to save more make little moral or economic sense.

But the lamenters do have an important point. For there are an enormous number of government measures which cripple and greatly lower savings, and add to consumption in society. In many ways, government steps in, employs many instruments of coercion, and skews the voluntary choices of society away from saving and investment and toward consumption.

Our complainers about saving don't always say what, beyond exhortation, they think should be done about the situation. Left-liberals call for more governmental "investment" or higher taxes so as to reduce the government deficit, which they assert is "dissaving." But one thing which the government *can* legitimately do is simply get rid of its own coercive influence in favor of consumption and against saving and investment. In this way, the voluntary time preferences and choices of individuals would be liberated, instead of overridden, by government.

The Bush administration has begun to propose eliminating some of the coercive anti-saving measures that had been imposed by the so-called Tax Reform Act of 1986. One was the abolition of tax-deduction for IRAs, which wiped out an important category of middle-class saving and investment; another was the steep increase in the capital gains tax, which is a confiscation of savings, and—to the extent that capital gains are not indexed for inflation—a direct confiscation of accumulated wealth.

But this is only the tip of the iceberg. To say that only government deficits are "dissaving" is to imply that higher taxes increase social savings and investment. Actually, while the national income statistics assume that all government spending except welfare payments are "investment," the truth is precisely the opposite.

All business spending is investment because it goes toward increasing the production of goods that will eventually be sold to consumers. But government spending is simply consumer spending for the benefit of the income, and for the whims and values, of government's politicians and bureaucrats. Taxation and government spending siphon social resources away from productive consumers who earn the money they receive, and away from these consumers' private consumption and saving, and toward consumption expenditure by unproductive politicians, bureaucrats, and their followers and subsidies.

Yes, there is certainly too little saving and investment in the United States, as a result of which the U.S. standard of living per person is scarcely higher than it was in the early 1970s. But the problem is not that individuals and families are somehow failing their responsibilities by consuming too much and saving too little, as most of the complainers contend. The problem is not in ourselves the American public, but in our overlords.

All government taxation and spending diminishes saving and consumption by genuine producers, for the benefit of a parasitic burden of consumption spending by non-producers. Restoring tax deductions and repealing—not just lowering—the capital gains tax, would be most welcome, but they would only scratch the surface.

What is really needed is a drastic reduction of all government taxation and spending, state, local, and federal, across the board. The lifting of that enormous parasitic burden would bring about great increases in the standard of living of all productive Americans, in the short run as well as in the future.

The "We" Fallacy

Sheldon L. Richman

I n discussions of international trade, there is no word more pernicious, more responsible for the inanities heard daily, than we: "We have a trade deficit. We are a debtor nation. We must do something about it." Reporters and commentators endlessly drone on about these things. But who is we? The people living under the jurisdiction of the U.S. government may be conveniently referred to as we, but the uncritical use of this term infects thinking about political-economic subjects. Careless aggregation is the enemy of good sense.

For example, it is said that we have a merchandise trade deficit of over $4 billion with Japan. In other words, the dollar value of the products sold by some Americans to some Japanese was $4 billion short of the dollar value of what some Japanese sold to some Americans. Who exactly suffered this deficit? Maybe I did. I probably bought some Japanese-made products that month, but I cannot recall selling anything to a Japanese person. On the other hand, there are probably Americans around who sold things to Japanese people, but didn't buy anything from them; they had a trade surplus, according to the statisticians. Although I seem to have a trade deficit with "Japan," I can't say this was any kind of disadvantage. I bought what I wanted, period. The same is true for those with a "surplus." They could have bought Japanese products had they preferred, but they didn't.

What does it mean to statistically combine all the transactions of Americans and Japanese (ignoring transactions with people in other groups) in order to determine the status of the two groups? All of us in the "deficit" group are still as happy as we were when we were considered individually. To be sure, some people wish they sold more to the Japanese than they did. But it has nothing to do with the rest of us. What they did not sell in no way offsets the benefits of what any of us bought. Lee Iacocca's failure to sell more Reliants to people in Tokyo has no great implications for "the nation," though it may mean something for a specific, identifiable group involved in producing Reliants.

But this is not the way the policymakers and news media see it. When the trade figures are reported, the increase in the "deficit" is always lamented across the land. True, American businesses had record exports, but this was said to be undercut by the larger volume of imports and thus the overall picture was reported bleak. How absurd! For any level of exports, there can always be a higher level of imports. More important, the media's analysis implies that it is better to be on the money side rather than the goods side of a transaction. Put that way, no one would believe it. But drape it in the mantle of statistics and it's time to crack down on buyers of excessive imports.

There are other ways in which the pernicious we infects people's thinking about trade. It is often said that foreigners should open their markets to "us" because "we've" opened ours to them. We do them a favor by letting them sell here? Do you buy things as a favor to the seller? I don't, and I'm sure no one else does. But if that is true, what happens when the U.S. government closes a market in the United States in retaliation for some misdeed abroad? It might be a favor to those seeking shelter from competition, but must it hurt other Americans? There is no indivisible we.

This policy of hurting some Americans to help others is known officially as strategic trade policy; it is really protectionism prettified by the claim that its motive is free trade. Not only does it play fast and loose with the right of Americans to buy what they want, but it also fails on it own terms. In the 1960s, the American government and the producers of chickens complained that European countries had barriers to chicken imports. In the name of open markets, the U.S. government imposed a 25% tariff on light trucks, which Europeans exported here. That tariff not only remains in effect today, it is applied to light trucks from Japan as well.

If the Europeans had removed their barriers to chickens, do you suppose the American producers of light trucks would say, "Okay, the chicken market is open; time to abolish the truck tariff?" Of course not. And that's the point: a nation is not made up of a single set of interests. There is no we.

As much as it might pain Lee Iacocca and his cohorts, most Americans have a harmony of interests with producers in other countries. What comes between them hurts some of us. These Americans do not necessarily benefit by everything that benefits Chrysler or USX or Harley Davidson. They certainly do not benefit when companies win political privileges, because they must come at the expense of everyone else. Anytime someone invokes patriotism to get you to buy his product ("Made in the U.S.A. It Matters!"), bolt your door and get out the shotgun.

Once aggregates are banished from discussions of trade, everything is clearer. Take foreign investment:

there is suddenly great concern that foreigners are investing in American businesses, even buying them out. This is supposed to spell danger for us. How so? All that is happening is that foreign capitalists are bringing their money here and putting it to work. The results are new opportunities and new products. Is that bad? Note that you rarely hear complaints about British or Dutch investment. The danger seems exclusively Japanese. But British and Dutch holdings combined are three times those of the Japanese. There is undoubtedly some racism at the bottom of this, and I expect the New Yellow Peril to be a major issue in the 1990s.

What about this business that America is a debtor nation? Same fallacy. Some Americans are debtors, some are creditors. America is neither. (I exclude from consideration the government's debt, which is another story.) As a matter of fact, the statistics being bandied about are misleading. Assets are recorded at book, or historic value, and the foreign holdings of Americans are older than foreigners' holdings here. Thus, it appears, falsely, that Americans' holdings are worth less than foreigners' holdings. Last year, Americans' total income from foreign assets exceeded that of foreigners' from American assets.

But even if it were true that foreigners' holdings were worth more or that they had more income, so what? Freely chosen investment here by anyone cannot possibly be bad. And if investment produces large incomes for foreigners, it must mean that it's profitable—that the goods and services being produced are popular with consumers.

Ludwig von Mises taught that we must be methodological individualists. Economic phenomena are invariably the products of individual persons acting for chosen objectives. Two persons come together for exchange if and only if each expects to come out ahead. And, assuming neither has erred, each can and does come out ahead. That is virtually all one needs to know to make sense of international trade.

U.S. Trade Law: Losing Its Bearings

Alex Tabarrok

We hear that consumers are the major victims of protectionism. This is true if we remember that businesses are also consumers, and that protectionism can hurt them as much as retail consumers. In fact, protectionism has become a major threat to American firms. For example, the "voluntary" restraint agreements in steel and semiconductors have hurt Caterpillar, General Motors, and Atari, which need steel and semiconductors to produce goods and services. These firms have lost profits and customers because their production costs have been increased by U.S. trade laws.

Most protectionism results from the lobbying activities of domestic manufacturers. A recent example is a decision by the U.S. International Trade Commission (ITC) to impose massive duties on hundreds of types of bearings and ball bearings—at the behest of an American producer. The duties are currently wreaking havoc at many American firms.

At present, the world-wide demand for commodity bearings—the mass-produced sort used in many household appliances—is extremely high. Although U.S. manufacturers are producing at capacity, they cannot begin to meet the requirements of U.S. users, so firms like Penn Fishing Tackle, Black and Decker, G.E., and many others have turned to foreign suppliers.

Penn Fishing Tackle, for example, bought from the French producer SKF because domestic firms could not deliver the bearings they needed. In one case, an order placed by Penn with a domestic supplier—Torrington Co.—took two years to deliver.

Alcoa, Dana Corp., and Xerox, among others, have also had problems with Torrington. William R. Wilson of Xerox reports that Torrington "has taken around 44 weeks to supply an initial order." When "domestic sources prove to be unreliable suppliers, as Torrington has, we have no alternative but to seek alternative suppliers abroad."

Not surprisingly it was Torrington that initiated the ITC investigation of foreign producers who were "dumping" ball bearings, i.e., selling them too cheaply. True to form, the ITC decided in favor of Torrington and imposed duties—in spite of the fact that their own survey showed that "the most common reason for purchasing imported bearings...was the inability of the domestic manufacturers to meet delivery and availability requirements."

These duties unjustly injure productive American firms. But according to the ITC, this is unimportant because duties should be imposed if "imports contribute, even minimally to [the] material injury" of the domestic producer. The ITC has found even this lax and irrational standard difficult to prove. It claims that bearing producers have been materially injured by foreign dumping—a necessary finding for the imposition of duties. However, ITC data show that the U.S. bearing industry was consistently profitable over the investigation period. Even as the ITC found injury, the U.S. bearing industry was spending more on research and development. Furthermore, ITC vice-chairman Ronald Cass, the sole dissenter in the case, points out that "capital expenditures increased dramatically from 1985 to 1987." Firms experiencing difficult times rarely invest in research and development or new plant and equipment.

While the "injury" done to the domestic bearing industry is invisible, the injury perpetrated by the duties is crystal clear. One of the most popular fishing reels produced by Penn uses a bearing that has nearly tripled in price because of the duties. Penn may have to stop making it because they are having difficulties competing with lower-priced offshore manufacturers.

Pittman, a U.S. producer of miniature motors, has also been injured by Torrington and the ITC decision. The bearings they use have risen in price by 40-50%—a burden their world competitors do not have to bear.

On the opposite end of the spectrum from commodity bearings are "super-precision" bearings. These are made from specialized materials, are very expensive, and must be produced in small batches to high tolerance levels. However, the ITC ignored all these important distinctions and imposed duties on a wide variety of super-precision bearings—even though many are not even produced in the United States!

"Tenter bearings," for example, are made to withstand extreme heat and stress. Torrington, the petitioner, doesn't produce these bearings. The 3M Company uses these bearings to produce specialty film products. Although 3M has tried to encourage U.S. producers to supply the bearings, demand is not high enough to justify the considerable investment in specialized machinery needed for their production.

It will probably take U.S. industries a year or two to build the factories and train the workers needed to make tenter bearings. In the meantime the government is forcing 3M to pay a debilitating 132% duty.

These rulings are unjust. Why should innovative companies like Penn and 3M be penalized because the government kowtows to the greed of a company that wants profits by federal fiat?

Anti-dumping laws shift resources from one set of American firms to another: from smaller, dynamic, and entrepreneurial firms to large, politically well-connected, but inefficient firms.

Retail consumers are, of course, also injured by duties. In this case they can expect large price increases on products that use bearings, from heavy-duty construction machinery to office equipment, power tools, fishing reels, and household appliances.

The ITC should stop undermining efficient American companies and consumers with this nonsense. They should start considering the harmful effects that duties impose on consumers, be they companies or individuals. But if that occurred, they would have to vote themselves out of existence.

Statistics: Destroyed from Within?

Murray N. Rothbard

As improbable as this may seem now, I was at one time a statistics major in college. After taking all the undergraduate courses in statistics, I enrolled in a graduate course in mathematical statistics at Columbia with the eminent Harold Hotelling, one of the founders of modern mathematical economics. After listening to several lectures of Hotelling, I experienced an epiphany: the sudden realization that the entire "science" of statistical inference rests on one crucial assumption, and that assumption is utterly groundless. I walked out of the Hotelling course, and out of the world of statistics, never to return.

Statistics, of course, is far more than the mere collection of data. Statistical *inference* is the conclusions one can draw from that data. In particular, since—apart from the decennial U.S. census of population—we never know all the data, our conclusions must rest on very small samples drawn from the population. After taking our sample or samples, we have to find a way to make statements about the population as a whole. For example, suppose we wish to conclude something about the average height of the American male population. Since there is no way that we can mobilize every male American and measure everyone's height, we take samples of a small number, say 500 people, selected in various ways, from which we presume to say what the average American's height may be.

In the science of statistics, the way we move from our known samples to the unknown population is to make one crucial assumption: that the samples will, in *any and all* cases, whether we are dealing with height or unemployment or who is going to vote for this or that candidate, be distributed around the population figure according to the so-called "normal curve."

The normal curve is a symmetrical, bell-shaped curve familiar to all statistics textbooks. Because all samples are assumed to fall around the population figure according to this curve, the statistician feels justified in asserting, from his one or more limited samples, that the height of the American population, or the unemployment rate, or whatever, *is* definitely XYZ within a "confidence level" of 90 or 95%. In short, if, for example, a sample height for the average male is 5 feet 9 inches, 90 or 95 out of every 100 such samples will be within a certain definite range of 5 feet 9 inches. These precise figures are arrived at simply by assuming that all samples are distributed around the population according to this normal curve.

It is because of the properties of the normal curve, for example, that the election pollsters could assert, with overwhelming confidence, that Bush was favored by a certain percentage of voters, and Dukakis by another percentage, all within "three percentage points" or "five percentage points" of "error." It is the normal curve that permits statisticians not precisely to claim absolute knowledge of all population figures, but instead to claim such knowledge within a few percentage points.

Well, what is the evidence for this vital assumption of distribution around a normal curve? None whatever. It is a purely mystical act of faith. In my old statistics text, the only "evidence" for the universal truth of the normal curve was the statement that if good riflemen shoot to hit a bullseye, the shots will tend to be distributed around the target in something like a normal curve. On this incredibly flimsy basis rests an assumption vital to the validity of all statistical inference.

Unfortunately, the social sciences tend to follow the same law that the late Dr. Robert Mendelsohn has shown is adopted in medicine: never drop any procedure, no matter how faulty, until a better one is offered in its place. And now it seems that the entire fallacious structure of inference built on the normal curve has been rendered obsolete by high-tech.

Ten years ago, Stanford statistician Bradley Efron used high-speed computers to generate "artificial data sets" based on an original sample, and to make the millions of numerical calculations necessary to arrive at a population estimate without using the normal curve, or any other arbitrary, mathematical assumption of how samples are distributed about the unknown population figure. After a decade of discussion and tinkering, statisticians have agreed on methods of practical use of this "bootstrap" method, and it is now beginning to take over the profession. Stanford statistician Jerome H. Friedman, one of the pioneers of the new method, calls it "the most important new idea in statistics in the last 20 years, and probably the last 50."

At this point, statisticians are finally willing to let the cat out of the bag. Friedman now concedes that "data don't always follow bell-shaped curves, and when they don't, you make a mistake" with the standard methods. In fact, he added that "the data frequently are distributed quite differently than in bell-shaped curves." So that's it; now we find that the normal curve Emperor has no clothes after all. The old mystical faith can now be abandoned; the Normal Curve god is dead at long last.

The Truth About Economic Forecasting

Graeme B. Littler

A strologers, palmists, and crystal-ball gazers are scorned while professional economists are heralded for their scientific achievements. Yet the academics are no less mystical in trying to predict the direction of interest rates, economic growth, and the stock market.

Forty years ago, Thomas Dewey was defeated by Harry Truman, stunning the political experts and journalists who were certain Dewey was going to win. While questions about "scientific" polling techniques naturally arose, one journalist focused on the heart of the matter. In his November 22, 1948, column in Newsweek, Henry Hazlitt said the "upset" reflected the pitfalls of forecasting man's future. As Hazlitt explained: "The economic future, like the political future, will be determined by future human behavior and decisions. That is why it is uncertain. And in spite of the enormous and constantly growing literature on business cycles, business forecasting will never, any more than opinion polls, become an exact science."

We know how well economists forecast the eighties: from the 1982 recession and the employment boom to the Crash of 1987, no major forecasting firm came close to predicting these turns in the market. And following the Crash, virtually every professional forecaster revised his economic forecasts downward, all because the historical data suggested that the stock market was a reliable barometer of future economic activity. The economy then continued to expand and the stock market eventually reached new highs.

After President Eisenhower's heart attack on September 24, 1955, the stock market experienced a massive drop. The stock market later recovered as the president recovered; like 1987, 1955 turned out to be one of the statistically best in economic history.

Despite the sorrowful record, most economists remain die-hard advocates of forecasting. Most have spent years in college and graduate school learning the tools of their trade, and can't bring themselves to admit their own entrepreneurial errors. As one investment advisor put it: "No matter how many times they fail, their self-assurance never weakens. Their greatest (or only) talent is for speaking authoritatively."

Of their errors, the forecasters contend that it's only a matter of time before they master the techniques. Though that day will never arrive, economic forecasting remains an integral part of the economics mainstream. The original motto of the Econometric Society still holds sway: "Science is Prediction."

Whether one uses a ruler to extend an economic trend into the future, or a sophisticated econometric model with dozens of equations, the problem is still the same: there are no constant relations in human affairs.

Economics, unlike the natural sciences, deals with human actions, plans, motivations, preferences, and so on, none of which can be quantified. Even if it were possible to quantify these things, changing tastes (and all the factors that affect tastes) would make the data almost instantaneously useless to the forecaster. And then there are the millions of "unimaginable" things, like Eisenhower's heart attack, which constantly crop up, influencing people in unpredictable ways.

Economic statistics (i.e., history) do not imply anything about the future. Because data show the relation between price and supply to be one way for one period of time doesn't mean that it cannot change. As Mises pointed out, "external phenomena affect different people in different ways" and "the reactions of the same people to the same external events vary."

Some economic forecasters like to argue that economic forecasting is not unlike predicting the weather (and should also be equally difficult). Not only is the nature of these two problems entirely different, but one can reasonably expect that as scientific methods become more sophisticated, weather prediction could theoretically approach perfection. This is because there are constant relations among physical and chemical events. By experimenting in the laboratory, the natural scientist can know what these relations are with a high degree of precision. However, human society is not a controlled laboratory. This fact makes the forecaster's job of accurately predicting future events impossible.

Forecasters try to get around this problem by linking events in historical chains, and randomly guessing that if one variable reoccurs, then the others will necessarily follow. But this is a sophisticated version of the logical fallacy, *post hoc ergo propter hoc* (after this, therefore, because of this). This has led major forecasters to seriously study astrological patterns and to build mathematical models that correlate weather patterns with business cycles. Once the forecaster throws out economic logic, anything could have caused anything else, and all variables in the universe are open to study. One mainstream forecasting theory for investors, for example, is based on the rate at which rabbits multiply.

Does this mean we can know nothing about the future? No, the best forecasters are successful businessmen, whose entrepreneurial judgment allows them to anticipate consumer tastes and market conditions. As Murray N. Rothbard points out: "The pretensions of econometricians and other 'model-builders' that they can precisely forecast the economy will always flounder on the simple but devastating query: 'If you can forecast so well, why are you not doing so on the stock market, where accurate forecasting reaps such rich rewards?'" Forecasting gurus, instead, tend to disdain successful entrepreneurs.

The myth that economists can predict the future is not just harmless quackery, however. Central planners use the same theories to direct the economy. Yet by setting production goals with the data collected by the planners themselves, they destroy the very process that directs free-market production.

Central planners try to overcome uncertainty by substituting formulas for entrepreneurial judgment. They believe that they can replace the price system with commands, but they miss the whole purpose of individual action on the free market. As Ludwig von Mises said, they make "not the slightest reference to the fact that the main task of action is to provide for the events of an uncertain future." In that sense, central planners are no different from professional forecasters.

Don't expect unemployment among forecasters, however. Many have cushy jobs with the Congress, the White

House, and virtually every agency of the U.S. government, and will happily issue predictions to no end.

In the Austrian view, on the other hand, economists have three functions: to further our understanding of the free market, to identify possible consequences of government policies, and to counter economic myths.

Economic forecasting has nothing to do with these objectives. In fact, by presenting itself as the only scientific dimension of economics, forecasting has helped discredit the whole discipline, and fueled an exodus of economists from the more mundane academic world to the arena of state control and coercion, to the detriment of every American.

Michael R. Milken: Political Prisoner?

Llewellyn H. Rockwell

The Dom Perignon must be flowing in the boardrooms of New York: the feds finally got the kid from Encino.

To avoid a worse fate, Michael R. Milken agreed to say he was guilty of six regulatory offenses, manufactured transgressions typical of the Alice-in-Wonderland world of big government.

Crimes are supposed to have victims. But who exactly was harmed by the dread offense of "stock parking?"

Yet Milken will pay a $600 million fine and be sentenced to prison with other "white-collar criminals." After a years-long federal envy campaign, he felt he would be convicted by a Bonfire of the Vanities jury for being rich. But he kept his brother Lowell out of jail and avoided 28 years in a federal pen where homosexual rape is the major pursuit, and AIDS, the normal blood condition.

David Rockefeller, said the New York Times, had been furious over Milken's earnings. They indicated "something unbalanced" in "our financial system." Indeed, when it comes to unbalancing the status quo that has served Rockefeller so well, Milken is guilty.

His entrepreneurial discovery was the use of high-yield bonds (called "junk" by his old-line competitors) to finance corporate takeovers. In the past, would-be raiders had to get financing from such big banks as Rockefeller's Chase Manhattan. This meant profits and control, both of which shrunk with the advent of Milken.

In the reduced competition of a regulated economy, corporate managers tend to put their own interests before the stockholders. If an entrepreneur can get financing, he can take over the company—that is, buy it from its owners—and try to improve it. Everyone benefits, except the tossed-out managers.

Managers of big corporations, not surprisingly, hate and fear this process, and they lobbied to pass the Williams Act introduced by Harrison Williams (D-NJ), later convicted as a bribe taker. This law requires anyone buying more than 5% of a company's shares to stop and announce his intentions. This raises the price of the shares, as intended, making it far more expensive to acquire control. It also gives management time to erect barriers ("greenmail" and "poison pills") to thwart the will of stockholders who might want to sell.

The Williams Act and related regulations worked all too well. For more than a decade, there were few challenges to the ensconced managements of big companies, and U.S. competitiveness nosedived. But in the early eighties, a group of outsiders like Carl C. Icahn and T. Boone Pickens were able to challenge the system, thanks to Milken.

As the London Financial Times noted, this made Milken "enemies all over corporate America." Not surprisingly, said the Washington Post, since he was an "an adversary of Wall Street's leading investment firms and blue-chip corporations."

Milken was "the ultimate outsider," working 3,000 miles away in Drexel Burnham Lambert's Los Angeles office, said the New York Times, living a "relatively modest life" while donating "hundreds of millions of dollars to charity."

But didn't he make too much money? In a free market, such a question makes no sense. Milken single-handedly raised Drexel from a third-tier firm to one of the giants. It was happy to pay for the results, although it too has been destroyed in the government's anti-Milken vendetta, with thousands of people losing their jobs.

The humiliation of Michael Milken "will send the right message to the financial community," said Assistant Attorney General John Carroll. Exactly. Don't rock the boat. And don't threaten entrenched interests.

If we had a free-market Amnesty International, Michael Milken would be listed as a political prisoner of special-interest big government.

Richard Breeden, head of the SEC, says that Milken "stood at the center of a network of manipulation, fraud, and deceit." To me, that sounds like a good working definition of Washington, D.C.

The Economic Wisdom
of the Late Scholastics

by Jeffrey A. Tucker

F ree markets are most often threatened by both economic and ethical considerations. Even if statists
grant that free markets are productive, they claim it is at
too high a price. And they say mere economic analysis is
not enough to satisfy the demands of "social justice" or
"compassion" to the poor. The answer to both criticisms
is government intervention or even socialism.

To answer these charges, new writers have begun to
show that free markets have economic and moral justification, and that these are compatible. Both Michael
Novak and Ronald Nash have shown that Christian
morality and tradition are more supportive of free markets than state coercion.

Most impressive is the work of Alejandro A. Chafuen
in bringing to light a great—if hitherto lost—tradition of
the late scholastics, a school of thought active in Spain
from the 14th to 17th century. They taught that the free
market was always practically and morally superior to
statism, and did so without compromising their emphasis on economic science.

In his groundbreaking *Christians for Freedom: Late-
Scholastic Economics* (1986), Chafuen shows that this
school was even pre-Austrian in subjective value, marginal
utility, prices, the quantity theory of money, economic
calculation, and the problems of collective ownership.

Jesuit Juan de Mariana (1535-1624) wrote that the
king may spend his own personal wealth, but he has "no
domain over the goods of the people, and he cannot take

them in whole or in part." Further, "how sad it is for the republic and how hateful it is for good people to see those who enter public administration when they are penniless grow rich and fat in public service." Mariana demanded to know, "where is this money coming from if it is not from the blood of the poor and the flesh of the business-men?"

Balanced budgets, Mariana said, should be the "main concern" so that "the republic is not entangled in more evils because of its inability to pay its debts." But taxes are not the solution to debt because, as Mariana noted, "taxes are commonly a calamity for the people and a nightmare for the government. For the former they are always excessive; for the latter they are never enough, never too much."

Writing in 1619, Fernandez Navarrete, chaplain to the king, advised him that, "The origin of poverty is high taxes. In continual fear of tax collectors, [the farmers] prefer to abandon their land, so they can avoid their vexations. As King Teodorico said, the only agreeable country is one where no man is afraid of tax collectors."

Regarding bureaucrats, Navarrete said "it is good to dismiss many of them." It is not sufficient to stop the growth of bureaucracy. Rather, "we need to...purge it of its present excess of hangers-on. People may say that this is an extreme suggestion since the court supports so many people, but the disease has become so grave and so evident that we have no excuse not to employ the remedy."

On inflation, Mariana pointed out that "if the legal value of the currency is reduced, the prices of all goods will, without fail, increase in the same proportion." He concluded that "any alteration of money is dangerous. It can never be good to debase currency or to fix its price higher than its natural valuation and common estimation." Martin de Azpilcueta, a Dominican, noted in 1553 that "other things being equal, in countries where there is a great scarcity of money, all other saleable goods, and ever the hands and labor of men, are given for less money than where it is abundant."

Another Dominican, Tomas de Mercado (1500-1575), condemned inflation because it rearranges debtor-creditor relations so that "the poor become rich and the rich poor." His solution: "the value" of money, and "even its seal and design, must be durable and as invariable as possible." Not for just a short time, but for "twenty generations, and the great-grandsons will know what they inherited from their great-grandparents and what in their goodness they increased, gained, and left to their children."

What about the common claim that scholastics from St. Thomas Aquinas forward believed in a "just price" and a "just wage" set outside the market? Chafuen shows that this is a myth. The Jesuit scholar Luis de Molina (1535-1600) captured the prevailing view: "the just price of goods depends principally on the common estimation of the men of each region. When a good is sold in a certain region or place at a certain price (without fraud or monopoly or any foul play), that price should be held as a rule and measure."

To these scholastics, the "common estimation of market" theory of pricing also applied to wages. Molina said, "if the wage that is set for him is at least the lowest wage that is customarily set in that region at the time for people in such service, the wage is to be considered just." The just wage cannot be judged on "what is sufficient for his sustenance, and much less for the maintenance of his children and family." The Dominican scholar Domingo de Soto (1495-1560) wrote that workers cannot steal from their employers "with the excuse that they are not sufficiently well paid." This is because "no injury is done to those who gave their consent." He advised workers, "if you do not want to serve for that salary, leave!"

They also understood that value is not inherent in a good; it resides in the minds of individuals who use it. Molina writes, "a price is considered just or unjust not because of the nature of the things themselves...but due to their ability to serve human utility." That is "why rats, which according to their nature are nobler than wheat, are not esteemed or appreciated by men. The reason is that they are of no utility whatsoever."

On value, Adam Smith said we could never understand why diamonds sell for a higher price than bread, even though bread is more necessary for life. Almost 400 years earlier, St. Bernardino of Siena (1380-1444) solved that problem. He said that prices are a function of relative scarcities: "Water is usually cheap where it is abundant. But it can happen that, on a mountain or in another place, water is scarce, not abundant. It may well happen that water is more highly esteemed than gold, because gold is more abundant in this place than water."

The scholastics were, of course, in favor of private property and rejected common ownership. Domingo de Soto notes in 1567 that "private interest" works where "universal love" doesn't. "Hence, privately owned goods will multiply. Had they remained in common possession, the opposite would be true."

Chafuen shows that the late scholastics found a perfect harmony between the demands of economic logic and Christian morality. By restoring the wisdom of this school, we undermine the Christian socialists and left-liberals, and renew the credibility of those who find no contradiction—indeed, a harmony—between morality and good economics.

2

DEBUNKING THE BANKERS

Bring Back the Bank Run!

James Grant

The banking dilemma seems eternal, like the monetary dilemma, the tax dilemma, and the marital dilemma. The essence of the banking dilemma, however, is that the depositors' money is not in the vault awaiting the depositors' decision to withdraw it. Instead it is out on loan or invested in the money market or in mortgage-backed securities.

Some of the money is in the vault or on deposit with the Federal Reserve—these funds are called bank reserves—but only a few cents of every dollar. Depending on the specific management, depositors, and financial markets, the average bank may be prepared to accommodate a sudden demand for repayment by a sizable minority of its depositors. Almost no bank in modern times, however, has been able to accommodate a sudden demand for repayment by a majority of its depositors.

Murray N. Rothbard, the economist and libertarian philosopher, has a forcible view on the institutions of fractional-reserve banking: It is "a giant Ponzi scheme in which a few people can redeem their deposits *only* because most depositors do not follow suit."

Some features of the modern banking dilemma are new, notably the socialization of credit risk during the Reagan years. It was decided that no money-center bank would be allowed to fail and that no depositor, even a sophisticated one, would be allowed to lose his money in a failure, if it could possibly be helped. But other problems are cyclical and still others are chronic. Reading up on the subject, one becomes fatalistic about it.

In gaslight days, before the "Too-Big-To-Fail" doctrine and other modern banking improvements, national banks were bound to hold reserves amounting to 25% of demand deposits. By our standards, this was a lavish margin of safety, even if, as Rothbard notes, capital reserves were often tied up in government bonds ("...banks were induced to monetize the public debt," he has written, "state governments were encouraged to go into debt and government and bank inflation were intimately linked").

Reserve requirements were reduced to 18% with the advent of the Federal Reserve System in 1913 and stand at 12% today. Loans as a percentage of assets are higher today than they used to be, however. And off-balance sheet liabilities—such as standby letters of credit, interest-rate swap commitments, and futures-markets trading—are higher, too.

The rise in the risks attached to banking prompts numerous questions about the nature of lending and the credit cycle. How has the regulatory and monetary climate of the 1980s affected bank lending? If, as seems obvious, it has inflated it, what will be the consequences of it?

If anything is new about banking our epoch, it is the substitution of federal guarantees for the liquidity of individual banks. It is the policy that, in the case of the 11 or so largest banks, failure will not be allowed and that, even in smaller institutions, depositors will be protected. It is this regulatory sea change that distinguishes the current debt expansion from so many earlier ones.

Years ago, when weak banks suffered runs by public depositors, instead of seizure by the Federal Deposit Insurance Corporation, a liquid balance sheet constituted a competitive advantage. When James ("Sunshine Jim") Stillman, National City's dour chairman, correctly forewarned his associates in early 1907 to prepare for a panic that fall, he was able to anticipate a competitive silver lining: "What impresses me as most important is to go into next Autumn ridiculously strong and liquid, and now is the time to begin and shape for it. If by able and judicious management we have money to help our dealers when trust companies have suspended, we will have all the business we want for many years."

If, however, one's institution is beyond failure, it hardly makes business sense to build reserves against an unpredictable day of reckoning. What it makes sense to do is lend, and so banks have lent.

Economist Rothbard has written a brief ode in prose to the bank run: "It is a marvelously effective weapon because (a) it is irresistible, since once it gets going it cannot be stopped, and (b) it serves as a dramatic device for calling everyone's attention to the inherent un-soundness and insolvency of fractional reserve banking."

The Federal Reserve Act of 1913 was hailed as a gift to the nation, in part because it seemed to promise a run-free future. Because the reserve banks would lend in times of crisis, commercial banks could afford to become a little less liquid—a little more expansive—in good times.

Things did not work out exactly that way, and the 1930s saw a marathon of bank runs. Rejecting conservative counsel, the Roosevelt administration created the Federal Deposit Insurance Corporation to furnish still more federal assurances to bankers and depositors. Over the next several decades, the conviction took root that enlightened legislation had eliminated the possibility of another national banking crisis.

The strategy has worked, and it hasn't worked. There has been no great deflation, no national bank holiday, and no prairie-fire run on the members of the New York City Clearing House Association. On the other hand, there has been the thrift snafu and the Third World crisis. Each is an emblematic event, as each has lingered for years, not months, and the cost of each is measured in the scores of billions of dollars, nothing less. It is hard to imagine a free banking system getting itself into scrapes like those in the first place.

Commenting on some of these trends some months ago was none other than the Chairman of the Federal Reserve Board. Alan Greenspan delivered an unusual speech at a remarkable time. The date was October 16, 1989, the Monday following Friday the 13th, and the audience was the American Bankers Association. Greenspan proceeded to describe the 150-year odyssey by which American banks have become more leveraged and less liquid.

What was notable was the chairman's historical perspective (even if, for professional reasons, he did not share Rothbard's view that fractional-reserve banking is a fraud). In banking and credit terms, Greenspan admitted, the 20th century has been an age of relaxation. While not deploring this trend, he did not ignore it either. "Although leverage was important in the past, as now, the amount of leverage historically was much less than we see today." Despite the addition of $14 billion in equity capital by national banks in 1988 and the first half of 1989, "capital levels for the industry remain at the low end of their broad historical range."

In other words, by historical standards, the banks are loaned up. More than that, they are stuffed (many of them) with loans that were once considered inappropriate for the balance sheet of a commercial lending institution. The most prevalent specimen of this class of dubious assets is loans against speculative commercial real estate. As banks withdrew from business lending, they turned to property.

Like Greenspan, Robert L. Clarke, Comptroller of the Currency, adopts a non-Rothbardian world view. He recently testified that "the national banking system is fundamentally sound. That conclusion is based on a substantial increase in capital levels, especially equity capital levels, relatively strong earnings, and an improvement in overall credit quality among the majority of national banks during the past 18 months."

He evidently rejects Professor Rothbard's theory that a run-resistant, semi-socialized, fractional-reserve banking system is a house of cards.

What has been lacking in American banking in recent years is the run. And when it has not been lacking—as in the rescue of Continental Illinois in 1984—it has been frightening. With the wholesale substitution of federal promises, actual or implied, for conservative banking practices, the caliber of lending has inevitably suffered. Sunshine Jim Stillman, were he to return to Wall Street for a day, would very probably wish that he hadn't.

Is the banking dilemma eternal? It doesn't have to be. We could desocialize credit risk and let the bank runs take their toll. Absent federal meddling, the bottom line would be simplicity itself. The proof that banks have created excess credit would be found in the action of markets. It would be a fascinating picture if not a pretty one.

Nick and Jim Dandy to the Rescue

Bradley Miller

Could I interest you in buying some of the external debt run up by the Mexican or Philippine government? Could I interest you in buying *anything* from the Mexican or Philippine government? And if not, how in the world am I going to get you to *lend* anything to the Mexican or Philippine government?

Such are the questions confronting Treasury Secretary Nicholas Brady as the Bush administration and creditor banks try to figure out how to collect some half a trillion bucks in outstanding debt from the Third World. And his answer is the inevitable fallback of governments unwilling, for political reasons, to call to account those responsible for messes: stick taxpayers with a sizable chunk of the bill, bank on their ignorance, and realize that if they wake up in the long run, in the long run we're all dead.

Brady wants the World Bank and the International Monetary Fund to "guarantee" repayment in exchange for reduced claims. Many think this is a swell idea. Harvard economist Jeffrey Sachs, for example, a U.N. adviser to Latin American governments, writes in the *New York Times* that "the debt load should fall by half or more." Financing the guarantee of the remaining half of the debt, Sachs says, should come not only from the World Bank and the IMF, but also from "creditor governments and from collateral provided by the debtor governments themselves."

"Government" means taxpayers. It usually means taxpayers getting stuck to make the world worse toward the end of creating a bigger and safer playpen for bankers, bureaucrats, and spendthrift politicians.

Saying the IMF or World Bank will bail out banks—or, "guarantee" their loans—is prettier than saying taxpayers will bail them out. And of course it is *American* taxpayers who are the chief bankrollers of the World Bank and IMF.

This is consistent with free-market capitalism in the same way that shrieking "Heil Hitler" on a Berlin street in 1940 is consistent with free speech.

True freedom includes the freedom to fail, just as true freedom of speech means the freedom to say offensive as well as popular things. But however popular the phrase "free market" has become in speeches, some savvy souls unburdened by excessive concern for the commonweal have had this figured out for a long time. "Freedom" in today's allegedly free American marketplace means freedom *from* failure—as long as you remember one thing: fail *big*.

If your restaurant goes under, you're a gone goose. If you renege on your $3,000 personal loan, your credit is ruined. But those who run up millions of dollars of debt manage to continue living like sultans as their creditors "carry" them forever, and indeed extend them more loans. I haven't noticed Jim and Tammy Bakker slaving in salt mines or sleeping in tents to pay back their monstrous debts. Perhaps the IMF should define Heritage USA as a Third-World country and impose austerity measures.

If your failure is big enough, the federal government itself—again, read "taxpayers"—will ride to your rescue, as it did for Chrysler and Lockheed, as it is about to do for the savings and loan industry (to the tune of more than $100 billion), and as Brady wants it to do for large commercial banks that made reckless loans to the Third World. You'd think this would make it hard for Washington's wizards to keep a straight face when they talk about the American dream and the entrepreneurial spirit.

Compassion for monstrous flops is not, of course, limited to the economic realm. Geopolitics sets the pace in this regard. Kill a gas-station clerk and you'll have the community, led by the mayor and editorial writers, howling to fry you. Commit physical and cultural genocide, as a series of Communist and Third-World government dictators have done, and dignitaries will flock to your funeral to gush about your statesmanship.

At least genocides are easier to explain. They tend to be effective in silencing political opposition. But what purpose is served by lending billions to prop up basket-case collectivist regimes, many of which specialize in oppression and anti-capitalism? What purpose is served by *taxpayer guarantees* of such loans?

The purpose is to bail out powerful special interests, i.e., the banks, by thinning the wallets of the ignorant, unorganized, and hence powerless, i.e., most taxpayers.

What's going on is a shell game designed to shield special interests from competitive risks. Fear of failure is one of the driving forces of vibrant capitalism. The government should no more bail out banks for bad loans than it should bail out restaurants for bad food.

Subsidize failure and you get more failure. Tax wealth-production and you get less wealth. That's why, if you really want to change things, it won't work simply to chant "free-market reform" while you keep the gravy train running, as Brady's predecessor James Baker tried to do (while, be it noted, ladling his own gravy through Treasury-caused stockmarket increases in his millions of dollars of big-bank stock.)

Too many Third World countries—Mexico is perhaps the most egregious case—have subsidized failure and taxed wealth so much for so long that they no longer have enough wealth left to continue the game on its own. So they turn to Uncle Sam and others almost as gullible.

"It's time [Latin American debtor nations] were introduced to the real world," growled a justly piqued Pat Buchanan. But in the real world, economic outrages lead to political profits, as the Swiss bank accounts of Mexican politicians attest. If the presidents of several free-lending U.S. banks are now on food stamps, I stand corrected.

Q&A on the S&L Mess
Murray N. Rothbard

Q. When is a tax not a tax?

A. When it's a "fee." It was only a question of time before we would discover what form of creative semantics President Bush would use to wiggle out of his "read my lips" pledge (bolstered by the Darman "walks like a duck" corollary) never ever to raise taxes. Unfortunately, it took only a couple of weeks to discover the answer. No, it wasn't "revenue enhancement" or "equity" or "closing of loopholes" this time; it was the good old chestnut, the "fee."

When Secretary of the Treasury Brady came up with the ill-fated "fee" proposal for all bank depositors to bail out the failed, insolvent S&L industry, President Bush likened it to the user fee the federal government charges for people to enter Yellowstone Park. But the federal government—unfortunately—*owns* Yellowstone and, as its owner, may arguably charge a fee for its use without it being labeled a "tax" (although even here problems can be raised since the government does not have the same philosophical or economic status as would a private owner). But on what basis can someone's use of his own money to deposit in an allegedly private savings and loan bank be called a "fee?" To *whom*, and for *what*?

No, in the heartwarming firestorm of protest that arose, from the general public, and from all politicians and political observers, it was clear that to everyone except the Bush Administration, that the proposed levy on savers looked, talked, and waddled very much like a tax-duck.

Q. When is insurance not insurance?

A. When you are trying to "insure" an industry that is already bankrupt. Sometimes, the tax that is supposedly not a tax is called, not a "fee" but an "insurance premium." When the barrage of public protest virtually sank the "fee" on savers, the Bush Administration began to backpedal and to shift its proposal to a levy on other banks that are not yet officially insolvent, this new tax on banks to be termed a higher "insurance premium."

But there are far more problems here than creative semantics. The very concept of "insurance" is fallacious. To "insure" a fractional-reserve banking system, whether it be the deposits of commercial banks, or of savings and loan banks, is absurd and impossible. It is very much like "insuring" the *Titanic* after it hit the iceberg.

"Insurance" is only an appropriate term and a feasible concept when there are certain near-measurable risks that can be pooled over large numbers of cases: fire, accident, disease, etc. But an entrepreneurial firm or industry cannot be "insured," since the entrepreneur is undertaking the sort of risks that precisely cannot be measured or pooled, and hence cannot be insured against.

All the more is this true for an industry that is inherently and philosophically bankrupt anyway: fractional-reserve banking. Fractional-reserve S&L banking is pyramided dangerously on top of the fractional-reserve commercial banking system. The S&Ls use their deposits in commercial banks as their own reserves. Fractional-reserve banks are philosophically bankrupt because they are engaged in a gigantic con game: pretending that your deposits are there to be redeemed at any time you wish, while actually lending them out to earn interest.

It is *because* fractional-reserves are a giant con that these banks rely almost totally on public "confidence," and that is why President Bush rushed to assure S&L depositors that their money is safe and that they should not be worried.

The entire industry rests on gulling the public, and making them think that their money is safe and that everything is OK; fractional-reserve banking is the only industry in the country that can and will collapse as soon as that "confidence" falls apart. Once the public realizes that the whole industry is a scam, the jig is up, and it goes crashing down; in short, the whole operation is done with mirrors, and falls apart once the public finds out the score.

The whole point of "insurance," then, is not to insure, but to swindle the public into placing their confidence where it does not belong. A few years ago, private deposit insurance fell apart in Ohio and Maryland because one or two big banks failed, and the public started to take their money out (which was not there) because their confidence was shaken. And now that one-third of the S&L industry is *officially* bankrupt—and yet allowed to continue operations—and the Federal Savings and Loan Insurance Corporation (FSLIC) is officially bankrupt as well, the tottering banking system is left with the Federal Deposit Insurance Corporation (FDIC). The FDIC, which "insures" commercial banks, is still officially solvent. It is only in better shape than its sister FSLIC, however, because everyone perceives that behind the FDIC stands the unlimited power of the Federal Reserve to print money.

Q. Why did deregulation fail in the case of the S&Ls? Doesn't this violate the rule that free enterprise always works better than regulation?

A. The S&L industry is no free-market industry. It was virtually created, cartelized, and subsidized by the federal government. Formerly the small "building and loan" industry in the 1920s, the thrifts were totally transformed into the government-created and cartelized S&L industry by legislation of the early New Deal. The industry was organized under Federal Home Loan Banks and governed by a Federal Home Loan Board, which cartelized the industry, poured in reserves, and inflated the nation's money supply by generating subsidized cheap credit and mortgages to the nation's housing and real-estate industry.

FSLIC was the Federal Home Loan Board's form of "insurance" subsidy to the industry. Furthermore, the S&Ls persuaded the Federal Reserve to cartelize the industry still further by imposing low maximum interest rates that they would have to pay their gulled and hapless depositors. Since average people, from the 1930s through the 1970s, had few other outlets for their savings than the S&Ls, their savings were coercively channeled into low-interest deposits, guaranteeing the S&Ls a hefty profit as they loaned out the money for higher-interest mortgages. In this way, the exploited depositors were left out in the cold to see their assets decimated by continuing inflation.

The dam burst in the late 1970s, however, with the invention of the money-market mutual fund, which allowed the fleeced S&L depositors to take out their money in droves and put it into the market-interest funds. The thrifts began to go bankrupt, and they were forced to clamor for elimination of the cartelized low rates to depositors, otherwise they would have gone under from money-market fund competition. But then, in order to compete with the high-yield funds, the S&Ls had to get out of low-yield mortgages, and go into swinging, speculative, and high-risk assets.

The federal government obliged by "deregulating" the assets and loans of the S&Ls. But, of course, this was phony deregulation, since the FSLIC continued to guarantee the S&Ls' liabilities: their deposits. An industry that finds its assets unregulated while its liabilities are guaranteed by the federal government may be, in the short-run, at least, in a happy position; but it can in no sense be called an example of a free-enterprise industry. As a result of nearly a decade of wild speculative loans, official S&L bankruptcy has now piled up, to the tune of *at least* $100 billion.

Q. How will the federal government get the funds to bail out the S&Ls and FSLIC, and, down the road, the FDIC?

A. There are three ways the federal government can bail out the S&Ls: increasing taxes, borrowing, or printing money and handing it over. It has already floated the lead balloon of raising "fees" on the depositing public, which is not only an outrageous tax on the public to bail out their own exploiters, but is *also* a massive tax on savings, which will decrease our relatively low amount of savings still further. On borrowing, it faces the much ballyhooed Gramm-Rudman obstacle, so the government is borrowing to bail out the S&Ls by floating special bonds that would not *count* in the federal budget. An example of creative accounting: if you want to balance a budget, spend money and don't *count* it in the budget!

Q. So why doesn't the Fed simply print the money and give it to the S&Ls?

A. It could easily do so, and the perception of the Fed's unlimited power to print provides the crucial support for the entire system. But there is a grave problem. Suppose that the ultimate bailout were $200 billion. After much hullabaloo and crisis management, the Fed simply printed $200 billion and handed it over to the S&L depositors, in the course of liquidating the thrifts. This *in itself* would not be inflationary, since the $200 billion of increased currency would only replace $200 billion in disappeared S&L deposits. But the big catch is the next step.

If the public then takes this cash, and redeposits it in the commercial banking system, as they probably would, the banks would then enjoy an increase of $200 billion in reserves, which would then generate an immediate and enormously inflationary increase of about $2 trillion in the money supply. Therein lies the rub.

Q. What's the solution to the S&L mess?

A. What the government *should* do, if it had the guts, is to 'fess up that the S&Ls are broke, that its own "insurance" fund is broke, and therefore, that since the government has no money which it does not take from the taxpayer, that the S&Ls should be allowed to go under and the mass of their depositors to lose their nonexistent funds.

In a genuine free-market economy, no one may exploit anyone else in order to acquire an ironclad guarantee against loss.

The depositors must be allowed to go under along with the S&Ls. The momentary pain will be more than offset by the salutary lessons these depositors will have learned: don't trust the government, and don't trust fractional-reserve banking. One hopes that the depositors in fractional-reserve commercial banks will profit from this example and get their money out posthaste.

All the commentators prate that the government "has to" borrow or tax the funds to pay off the S&L depositors. There is no "has to" about it; we live in a world of free will and free choice.

Eventually, the only way to avoid similar messes is to scrap the current inflationist and cartelized system and move to a regime of truly sound money. That means a dollar defined as, and redeemable in, a specified weight of gold coin, and a banking system that keeps its cash or gold reserves 100% of its demand liabilities.

Inflation Redux

Murray N. Rothbard

I nflation is back. Or rather, since inflation never really left, inflation is back, with a vengeance. After being driven down by the severe recession of 1981-82 from over 13% in 1980 to 3% in 1983, and even falling to 1% in 1986, consumer prices in the last few years have begun to accelerate upwards. Back up to 4-5% in the last two years, price inflation finally drove its way into public consciousness in January 1989, rising at an annual rate of 7.2%.

Austrians and other hard-money economists have been chided for the last several years: the money supply M-A increased by about 13% in 1985 and 1986; why didn't inflation follow suit? The reason is that, unlike Chicago School monetarists, Austrians are not mechanists. Austrians do not believe in fixed leads and lags. After the money supply is increased, prices do not rise automatically; the resulting inflation depends on human choices and the public's decisions to hold or not to hold money. Such decisions depend on the insight and the expectations of individuals, and there is no way by which such perceptions and choices can be charted by economists in advance.

As people began to spend their money, and the special factors—such as the collapse of OPEC and the more expensive dollar—began to disappear or work through their effects in the economy, inflation has begun to accelerate in response.

The resumption and escalation of inflation in the last few years has inexorably drawn interest rates ever higher in response. The Federal Reserve, ever timorous and fearful about clamping down too tightly on money and precipitating a recession, allowed interest rates to rise only very gradually in reaction to inflation. In addition, Alan Greenspan has been talking a tough line on inflation so as to hold down inflationary expectations and thereby keep down interest yields on long-term bonds. But by insisting on gradualism, the Fed has only managed to prolong the agony for the market, and to make sure that interest rates, along with consumer prices, can only increase in the foreseeable future. Most of the nation's economists and financial experts are, as usual, caught short by the escalating inflation, and can make little sense out of the proceedings. One of the few perceptive responses was that of Donald Ratajczak of Georgia State University. Ratajczak scoffed: "The Fed always follows gradualism, and it never works. And you have to ask after a while, 'Don't they read their own history?'"

Whatever the Fed does, it unerringly makes matters worse. First it pumps in a great deal of new money because, in the depth of recession, prices go up very little in response. Emboldened by this "economic miracle," it pumps more and more new money into the system. Then, when prices finally start accelerating, it tries to prolong the inevitable and thereby only succeeds in delaying market adjustments.

Apart from a few exceptions, moreover, the nation's economists prove to be duds in anticipating the new inflation. In fact, it was only recently that many economists began to opine that the economy had undergone some sort of mysterious "structural change," and that, as a result, severe inflation was no longer possible. No sooner do such views begin to take hold, than the economy moves to belie the grandiose new doctrine.

Ironically, despite the gyrations and interventions of the Fed and other government authorities, recession is inevitable once an inflationary boom has been set into motion, and will occur after the inflationary boom stops or slows down. As investment economist Giulio Martino states: "We've never had a soft landing, where the Fed brought inflation down without a recession."

We can see matters particularly clearly if we rely on M-A (for Austrian), rather than on the various Ms issued by the Fed which are statistical artifacts devoid of real meaning. After increasing rapidly for several years, the money supply remained flat from April to August 1987, long enough to help precipitate the great stock market crash of October. Then, M-A rose by about 2.5% per year, increasing from $1,905 billion in August 1987 to $1,948 billion in July 1988. Since July, however, this modest increase has been reversed, and the money supply remained level until the end of the year, then fell sharply to $1,897 billion by the end of January 1989. From the middle of 1988, then, until the end of January 1989, the total money supply, M-A, fell in absolute terms by no less than an annual rate of 5.2%. The last time M-A fell that sharply was in 1979-80, precipitating the last great recession.

This is not an argument for the Fed to expand money again in panic. Quite the contrary. Once an inflationary boom is launched, a recession is not only inevitable but is also the only way of correcting the distortions of the boom and returning the economy to health. The quicker a recession comes the better, and the more it is allowed to perform its corrective work, the sooner full recovery will arrive.

Faustian Economics

John V. Denson

One expects to be warned by good economists that inflation must result if the issuance of paper money is not limited by its redeemability in gold. However, it's a pleasant surprise to find such advice in one of the classics of world literature: J.W. von Goethe's philosophical poem, *Faust*.

During Goethe's long life he achieved an Olympian status with achievements not only in literature and poetry, but also in science and government (as well as his much publicized love life!). He also practiced law (although not very successfully) and studied medicine. In 1775, he became an administrator in the small German state of Weimar and later its major official, supervising natural resources, mining, finances, arms, and education. During this time, Goethe abandoned literature, but became very knowledgeable about how government works. Or doesn't work.

Goethe was writing *Faust* during the French Revolution, when the government issued paper assignats allegedly redeemable in real estate rather than gold. He also witnessed the resulting hyperinflation and misery of the French people, which might have been his inspiration for the warning in *Faust* that governments should not issue paper money that cannot be redeemed by gold.

The legend of Faust was well known to the German people before Goethe began his version. It described the erudition of Faust and his pact with the demon, Mephistopheles, to receive power and pleasure in return for agreeing that his soul would go to Hell after a long, full life on earth.

Goethe's warning about inflation is one of his additions to the myth. It all begins in his poem at a meeting of the State Council. Mephistopheles appears as the new court fool and suggests that mining for hidden gold will solve all the political problems of the state. The Emperor then signs a proclamation to issue inflationary paper money:

Chancellor:
"To all whom it concerns, let it be known:
Who hath this note, a thousand crowns doth own.
As certain pledge thereof shall stand
Vast buried treasure in the Emperor's land.
Provision has been made the ample treasure,
Raised straightway, shall redeem the notes at pleasure."

Emperor:
"I sense a crime, a monstrous, cheating lure!
Who dared to gorge the Emperor's signature?
Is still unpunished such a breach of right?"

Treasurer:
"Remember, Sire, yourself it was last night
That signed the note. You stood as might Pan,
The Chancellor came and spoke in words that ran:
'A lofty festal joy do for thyself attain:
Thy people's weal—a few strokes of the pen!'
These did you make, then thousand-fold last night
Conjurors multiplied what you did write;
And that straightway the good might come to all,
We stamped at once the series, large and small;
Tens, twenties, thirties, hundreds, all are there.
You can not think how glad the people were.

Behold your city, once half-dead, decaying,
Now full of life and joy, and swarming, playing!
Although your name has blessed the world of yore,
So gladly was it never seen before.
The alphabet is really now redundant;
In this sign each is saved to bliss abundant."

Emperor:
"My people take it for good gold, you say?
In camp, in court, sufficient as full pay?
Although amazed, still I must give assent."

Steward:
"The flight of notes we could nowise prevent;
Like lightning notes were scattered on the run.
The changers' shops open wide to everyone;
And there all notes are honored, high and low,
With gold and silver at a discount, though
From there to butcher, baker, tavern hasting,
One-half the world seems thinking but of feasting,
The other in new raiment struts and crows;
The draper cuts the cloth, the tailor sews.
In cellars 'Long live the Emperor!' is the toasting;
There platters clatter, there they're boiling, roasting."

The people are ecstatic with their new found "wealth" of unlimited paper money, which causes a spending frenzy and drastic price increases. As expected, the joy eventually turns to grief and financial destruction of the Emperor's kingdom.

While this work of art became a part of German culture, it did not prevent the massive paper money explosion of 1923. One wonders how and when this wisdom concerning inflation, paper money, and gold will become a part of the common sense of the common man, rather than the statement of genius in literature or the province of good economists.

A Gold Standard For Russia?

Murray N. Rothbard

In their eagerness to desocialize, the Soviets have been calling in Western economists and political scientists—trying to imbibe wisdom from the fount of capitalism. In this search for answers, the host of American and European Marxist academics have been conspicuous by their absence. Having suffered under socialism for generations, the East Europeans have had it up to here with Marxism; they hardly need instruction from starry-eyed Western naifs who have never been obliged to live under their Marxist ideal.

One of the most fascinating exchanges with visiting Western firemen took place in an interview in Moscow between a representative of the Soviet Gosbank (the approximate equivalent of Russia's Central Bank) and Wayne Angell, a governor of the Federal Reserve Bank in the U.S. The interview, to be published in the Soviet newspaper *Izvestia*, was excerpted in the *Wall Street Journal*.

The man from Gosbank was astounded to hear Mr. Angell strongly recommend an immediate return of Soviet Russia to the gold standard. It would, furthermore, not be a phony supply-side gold standard, but a genuine one. As Angell stated, "the first thing your government should do is define your monetary unit of account, the ruble, in terms of a fixed weight of gold and make it convertible at that weight to Soviet citizens, as well as to the rest of the world."

Not that the Gosbank man was unfamiliar with the gold standard; it was just that he had imbibed conventional Western wisdom that the gold standard only be restored at some indistinct point in the far future, after all other economic ills had been neatly solved. Why, the Soviet financial expert asked Angell, should the gold standard be restored *first*?

Wayne Angell proceeded to a cogent explanation of the importance of a prompt return to gold. The ruble, he pointed out, is shot; it has no credibility anywhere. It has been systematically depreciated, inflated, and grossly overvalued by the Soviet authorities. Therefore, mark or even dollar convertibility is not enough for the ruble. To gain credibility, to become a truly hard money, Angell explained, the ruble must become what Angell, with remarkable candor, referred to as "honest money."

"It is my belief, " Angell continued, "that without an honest money, Soviet citizens cannot be expected to respond to the reforms," whereas a "gold-backed ruble would be seen as an honest money at home and would immediately trade as a convertible currency internationally."

With the ruble backed solidly by gold, the dread problem of the inflationary "ruble overhang" would wither away. The Soviet public is anxious to get rid of ever-depreciating rubles as soon as consumer goods become available. But under a gold standard, the demand for rubles would greatly strengthen, and Soviets could wait to trade them for more consumer goods or Western products. More goods would be produced as

Soviet workers and producers become eager to sell goods and services for newly worthwhile rubles.

Without gold, however, Angell warned that the Soviet reform program might well collapse under the blows of rampant inflation and a progressively disintegrating ruble.

The man from Gosbank was quick with the crucial question. If the gold standard is so vital, why don't the United States and other Western countries adopt it? Angell's reply was fascinating in its implications: that the dollar and other Western currencies "have at least a history of gold convertibility" which enabled them to continue through the Bretton Woods system and launch the present system of fluctuating fiat currencies.

What, then, is Mr. Angell really saying? What is he really telling the Soviet central banker? He is saying that the United States and other Western governments have been able to get away with imposing what he concedes to be *dishonest* money because of the remnants of association these currencies have had with gold.

In contrast to the ruble, the dollar, the mark, etc., have still retained much of their credibility; in short, their governments are still able to con their public, whereas the Soviet government is no longer able to do so. Hence, the Soviets must return to gold, whereas Western governments don't yet need to follow suit. *They* can still get away with dishonest money.

It would have been instructive to ask Mr. Angell about the myriad of Third World countries, particularly in Latin America, who have been suffering from severe currency deterioration and hyperinflation. Aren't those currencies in nearly as bad shape as the ruble, and couldn't those countries use a prompt return to gold? And perhaps even we in the West don't have to be doomed to wait until we too are suffering from hyperinflation before we can enjoy the great benefits of an honest, stable, noninflatable, money?

The Source of the Business Cycle

Jeffrey A. Tucker

Policy makers at the Federal Reserve sometimes find themselves in the public-policy equivalent of a cleft stick. When interest rates and inflation are rising, and the economy is sliding into recession, the Fed's policy options are drastically limited. How can the Federal Reserve keep the economy out of recession and tame price inflation at the same time? This is the problem of "stagflation," the one most economists found so baffling in the mid-1970s.

The experts don't even agree on the root cause of inflation. Is inflation caused by an "overheating economy," as the media like to say? If so, how could we see rising prices even while the economy is "slowing down" into a recession? Others blame the deficit. But big deficits are commonplace in U.S. policy. Why are their alleged inflationary effects so rarely seen?

With confusion like this, everybody's a potential target for political scorn: selfish workers, greedy capitalists, speculators, corporate raiders, and the over-consuming public. Yet these endless disputes are a distraction. They overlook the *monetary origins* of business cycles and inflation.

The Austrian school gained early recognition for its business cycle theory, which points to credit expansion as a necessary and sufficient cause of inflation and the boom-bust cycle. And despite the theorists that proclaim the "End of Economics," the theory explains as much today as it did in 1912, when Ludwig von Mises wrote *The Theory of Money and Credit*.

All during the 1920s, Mises wrote and lectured on business cycle theory, and he established the Austrian Institute for Business Cycle Research in Vienna, appointing his student F. A. Hayek as the director because, according to one AIBCR secretary, Mises "wanted to help Hayek find the right start in life."

By the time Mises published his *Monetary Stabilization and Cyclical Policy* in 1928, he had already become, Hayek writes, "the most respected and consistent exponent of the monetary theory of the Trade Cycle" in the German-speaking world. Unfortunately, this book, along with other early works on monetary theory, were inaccessible to English-speaking academic audiences as late as 1978.

Hayek also wrote a series of scholarly studies on the business cycles beginning in 1928 with *Monetary Theory and the Trade Cycle*. In that book, he argued that business cycles find their origin in monetary phenomenon, especially central-bank credit expansion. This and other books won him fame and four years later, Hayek became a professor of economics at the London School of Economics (LSE).

While at the LSE, Hayek developed a cadre of followers, including then-Misesian Lionel Robbins, who later became a famous Keynesian. Robbins arranged the English translation and publication of *Monetary Theory and the Trade Cycle* in 1933. This book and Hayek's *Prices and Production* became the leading volumes on the Austrian business cycle theory in the English-speaking world.

In the late 1930s, however, the Keynesian revolution swept all opposition from its path, as the industrialized world fell to fascist and socialist ideologies and centralized control. This environment was hardly conducive to a business-cycle theory that blames money and credit inflation, and the Austrian theory was ignored, although never refuted.

The climate changed, however, in 1974 when Hayek won the Nobel Prize for his work on the monetary origins of the business cycle. For a small, largely unrecognized group of Austrian economists, it was an exciting event, and it led to a revival in Austrian thought. A new generation of economists sought out the perspective of Austrian school economists such as Carl Menger, Eugen von Böhm-Bawerk, F.A. Hayek, and Hayek's teacher and mentor, Ludwig von Mises.

Hayek's 1928 book, *Monetary Theory and the Trade Cycle*, remains a reasoned, readable, and persuasive account that points to problems in other theories of cyclical economic behavior and presents a coherent, alternative explanation. Non-monetary theories of the business cycle postulate, for example, that the business cycle can be explained by psychological factors, by a failure in the level of saving or investment, or by a failed type or method of production. Unanswered in all these theories is the question of how the economy comes to fail in its ability to *coordinate* consumer's preferences with production decisions.

When the price system is working properly, Hayek shows, the "structure of production" allows for "intertemporal coordination," that is, the fulfillment of producer's and consumer's plans over a long period of time. It is the institution of money that makes this possible by allowing calculation to take place through time. Business cycles, then, must have originated as a failure in the monetary system.

Central-bank credit expansion sends incorrect pricing signals to entrepreneurs by artificially lowering the rate of interest. This leads entrepreneurs to make unwarranted investments, mainly in the capital sectors, errors which later become evident when the central bank stops expanding credit. The malinvestment created by distorted interest rates "corrects" and the economy enters a downturn. This is the essence of the business cycle.

Hayek rejects the idea that the goal of monetary policy should be "stable prices," a theory popular in the 1920s that made a comeback in the 1980s. He shows that prices can be stable even while credit expansion does unseen damage to the structure of production, that is, the market relationship between consumption goods and production goods. Prices were stable all throughout the twenties, but the damage done by credit expansion led to the Great Depression.

The world economy has seen a recession since the early eighties. The opening of Eastern Europe and the Soviet Union, and the innovations in financial instruments, may postpone one even longer. But if Hayek and Mises are right, the business cycle has not been permanently shelved. We cannot know its timing, what sectors it will most affect, or how long it will last. We only know that "So long as we make use of bank credit as a means of furthering economic development," as Hayek says, "we shall have to put up with the resulting trade cycles." The only answer to this problem is to end the distortions caused by central banking, a goal which may be decades away. But a new recession, and a new look at Mises's and Hayek's work, can create the right intellectual climate.

The Key to Sound Money

Edwin Vieira, Jr.

Every thinking American knows that our country lacks "sound money" and "honest banking." And there is no shortage of good books that explain the economic, political, and moral justifications for free-market money, and catalog the objectives all Americans committed to monetary freedom should strive to achieve. These include a return to silver and gold coinage, an end to central banking and fraudulent fractional-reserve banking schemes, and so on.

Confusion arises, however, as to *how* we can restore sound money and honest banking. A recurrent theme seems to be that government is responsible for irredeemable fiat currency, the inherently fraudulent Federal Reserve System, abusive legal-tender laws, and the other paraphernalia of the present system. One author, for example, tells us that "sound money" and "honest banking" are "not impossible; they are merely illegal." This kind of thinking assumes a great deal: specifically, that whatever those in temporary control of public offices may do is "the law." But nothing could be further from the truth.

Strictly speaking the "government" of the United States (or of any state or locality) is a kind of "legal fiction." It is not the individuals elected or appointed to office, the physical buildings they occupy, or the actions they take per se. Rather, the government, rightly understood, is the actions duly elected or appointed officials take consistent with the Constitution. If an action is inconsistent with the Constitution, it is unlawful and nongovernmental by definition. Such an unconstitutional action may be defined as "usurpation" or "tyranny," but never as a truly governmental function. Simply put, our government has no authority to act outside of or against the Constitution; and when public officials do so, they are not acting as agents of government, but as lawbreakers or outlaws.

For that reason, before we assume that sound money and honest banking are illegal today, we had better first determine what the constitutional powers of government are with respect to money and banking, and whether the present system has any constitutional validity. When we do this, we immediately see that, if sound money and honest banking are illegal today (in the sense that public officials say they are), it is not because the Founding Fathers licensed government in the Constitution to foist unsound money, monopolistic central banking, and chronic inflation upon the American people. To the contrary, the United States now suffers from the ravages of a monetary system based on irredeemable, legal-tender Federal Reserve notes and unlimited central-bank credit expansion precisely because, during the past century, every branch of the national government has neglected to enforce, or knowingly violated, the Constitution in the monetary and banking fields.

Themselves eye-witnesses to the economically catastrophic inflation that followed emission of the paper Continental currency during the War of Independence, the Founding Fathers carefully structured the Constitution to prevent the repetition of such a calamity. They established as the nation's money a parallel system of silver and gold coinage, based on the silver dollar as the unit of account; outlawed any form of legal tender other than silver and gold coin; and deprived the government of the abusive power to issue paper money of any kind.

Indeed, under the Constitution as written, and as the Founders and their immediate descendants unerringly applied it until the Civil War, every objective of a sound monetary system that free-market economists recommend is not only attainable, but also mandated.

Rightly understood, the Constitution authorizes—and, indeed, requires—the government to mint silver and gold coins denominated only by weight and fineness, but denies it any power to emit paper money (Article I, Sec. 8, cls. 2 and 5; Article I, Sec. 10, cl. 1). It denies the government any power to enact legal-tender laws (except for "gold and silver Coin"), or laws preventing specific performance of private contracts (Article I, Sec. 8, cl. 5; Article I, Sec. 10, cl. 1; Amendments V and XIV). It permits private banks to issue their own nonfraudulent monetary notes, and deal honestly in deposits denominated in silver, gold, or foreign currencies (Article I, Sec. 8, cl. 3; Amendments IX and X). It permits free entry into private banking, throughout the United States (Article I,

Sec. I, cl. 3; Article IV, Sec. 2, cl. 1; Amendments V, IX, X and XIV). It outlaws any governmentally sponsored banking monopoly or banking cartel, such as the present-day Federal Reserve System (Amendments V and XIV). And it disables the government from levying discriminatory taxes on privately issued money (Amendments V and XIV).

Thus, in the most fundamental sense, the United States needs no reform law, or restoration law, to return to sound money. For the necessary law already exists, in the Constitution itself. What stands in the way of monetary freedom—and of all forms of individual freedom that our Constitution guarantees under the phrase "the Blessing of Liberty"—is not law, but lawlessness. In a free society, government must be fully subject to the constraint of law—to constitutional limitations on its powers. Where public officials disregard these limitations, they render their own acts illegitimate, immoral, and unworthy of popular allegiance.

Therefore, sound money and free banking are not illegal in the contemporary United States; for what the Constitution guarantees, no congressional statute, presidential order, or court decision can lawfully nullify, set aside, overrule, or condemn to obsolescence. Yet, history teaches the sad lesson that "public servants" will impose upon the citizenry as much tyranny as the people are willing to bear. So, ultimately, what freedoms the Constitution guarantees—in the monetary field as in every other—are only those freedoms that the American people force their elected and appointed officials to respect.

Money and banking are in the best condition when they enjoy the greatest degree of liberty. But money and banking are no different or separable from all other aspects of a free society. And no society can be free, in any aspect, where its laws do not recognize the value of freedom, where its public officials do not enforce the preconditions for freedom, and where its people do not exercise the vigilance in defense of freedom that led our forbearers first to take up the sword to wrest their liberties from the clutches of tyrants, and then to take up the pen to secure those liberties in the fundamental law of the Constitution.

This country will enjoy a rebirth of monetary freedom if and when it experiences a revitalization of constitutionalism, in the broadest sense: namely, the recognition that there are inherent, ineluctable limits on governmental action beyond which lie economic, political, social, and moral disaster. When that day comes, the people will know where to look for the legal formula necessary to restore sound money and honest banking—to the Constitution, where it has always been, and is now, for those with eyes to see.

Foreclose on the World Bank

R. Cort Kirkwood

There are a bunch of capitalists [there] taking steps in the right direction." That's how a World Bank official described Ethiopia a day after the *New York Times* reported that its communist government drove 350,000 people from their homes during an offensive that included napalm and cluster bombs.

The baffling mindset that gives rise to statements like that about Ethiopia demonstrates why U.S. taxpayers should not be forced to "contribute" their hard-earned income to the World Bank's coffers. The Bank does not provide any tangible benefits to the recipients of its largesse or to those whose taxes are confiscated to support its operations. First, in distributing loans to developing countries, the bank supports socialism. Second, it steadfastly refuses to reform its lending practices and divulge the terms upon which its loans are made and evaluated. Third, its chief beneficiaries are American corporations, whose products are purchased by countries using World Bank loans.

An examination of each of these problems shows why the United States should not be a member of the World Bank.

Reason 1: The World Bank Supports Socialism

Ethiopia is the principal example of the World Bank's abysmal failure to fulfill its mandate. At the height of Col. Mengistu Haile Mariam's forced resettlement program, which by conservative estimates killed 100,000 people, the World Bank provided his communist regime with nearly $150 million. Ignoring his new plan to resettle 350,000 hapless Ethiopians in 1989, the World Bank dished out another $103 million during the fiscal year. Mengistu's collectivist farm policies have continued with increasing assistance from the World Bank.

The World Bank's International Finance Corporation, which is supposed to promote private sector development, has invested in government-controlled enterprises in Zambia, Zimbabwe, Ghana, and Pakistan. The IFC's fastest growing beneficiary is the Soviet Union and Eastern Europe. And half of all IFC loans go to state-owned enterprises, which helped to forestall the collapse of socialism in those countries.

Obviously, the World Bank energizes statism and retards private-sector development.

Part of the reason the bank does so much harm in places like Ethiopia is that its "population experts" accept at face value the hoary socialist canard that high population growth in the Third World inhibits economic growth, spreads poverty, and blunts the effectiveness of World Bank loans. "I realize that population policy touches upon sensitive cultural and religious values," World Bank president Barber Conable said at the recent World Bank-IMF conference in West Berlin. "But the societies in which population is growing so fast must accept that many—perhaps most—of these new lives will be miserable, malnourished, and buried. With today's population growth, badly-needed improvement in living standards cannot be achieved, public resources for necessary services are overstretched and the environment is severely damaged."

Mr. Conable's words reflect a bogus economic theory dating to Thomas Malthus. In fact, population growth leads to economic development. Indeed, the facts show that many countries with high population densities are economically prosperous, while those with low population densities are squalid dungeons of economic despair.

Red China's population density is 110 people per square mile, while Taiwan's is 1,396; but the PRC's per capita income is $273 annually, whereas Taiwan's is $6,010. Ethiopia has only 95 people per square mile with a per capita income of $117. Yet Singapore, with 10,357 people per square mile, has a per capita income exceeding $7,286. A similar picture emerges in comparing the two Koreas. The salient difference in the two sets of figures lie in the fact that Taiwan, Singapore, and South Korea have freer economies, whereas Red China, Ethiopia, and North Korea are Communist countries.

In collaborating with the Communist world in promulgating the population growth myth, Mr. Conable is providing prestigious cover so its entrenched despots can avoid admitting their policies are by nature totalitarian, visiting economic and social misery upon their subjects.

Reason 2: There is no hope for reform.

The World Bank's new Multilateral Investment Guarantee Agency (MIGA) would provide insurance for companies operating in less-developed countries, which will promote increased investment in LDCs by shielding Third World Marxists from the consequences of nationalizing foreign-owned industries, which of course discourages new investment. The top recipients of structural adjustment loans are countries that don't need them like Turkey ($2.5 billion), while others like Argentina ($850 million) keep getting loans on the collateral of flimsy promises to reform their economies. In Berlin, World Bank President Barber Conable promised $1.25 billion to Argentina (which received $626.5 million in fiscal 1988), just enough to keep stoking the boilers on its ill-managed state-owned railroads.

The bank's documentation for its loans are "classified" from the appraisal to evaluation stages on the grounds that divulging such information would compromise the ability of the bank to carry out its operations.

Reason 3: American taxpayers don't benefit from U.S.
      membership in the World Bank.

At the urging of the Reagan Administration, Congress
approved a $14 billion taxpayer bailout for the World
Bank in the form of a general capital increase (GCI). It
would be enlightening to ask what U.S. taxpayers got for
their $14 billion and how many of them support contin-
ued U.S. membership. The answers are not something
the World Bank's myrmidons in Washington would want
to hear.

Sure, there may be few Congressman genuinely concerned about development in poverty-stricken countries,
which is laudable even if their policies for development
are misguided. But the evidence suggests that congressional support for the World Bank exists only to the
degree that it subsidizes U.S. exports. In fiscal 1987, at
least 915 U.S. companies (IBM, Dresser Industries,
Monsanto, Exxon, and Ingersoll Rand, to name a few)
earned more than $1.7 billion from the World Bank. This
makes it easy for Congress to say that Bank's loans
"create" jobs and "boost" exports.

In reality, taxpayers pay for the whole kit and caboo-
dle: the loans, exports, jobs, and bureaucrats that make
them happen. The money merely goes on a round trip to
Kwanda or Zambia to make it look like something legitimate is going on.

Indeed, it seems like the only people who support the
World Bank are big businessmen operating through
fronts like the Bretton Woods Committee, which boasts
a membership list of luminaries from soy-bean tycoon
Dwayne Andreas to money magnate David Rockefeller.

(Not coincidentally, the GCI appropriation language requires the United States to "initiate discussion" about the possibility of extending loans to countries so they can make payments on unsound loans from big U.S. banks.)

The World Bank is supposed to spur development in less-developed countries. It has not fulfilled that mandate. It is not a bank in the usual sense; it is an international welfare agency manned by government bureaucrats (whose high salaries are exempt from all taxes) whose purpose is to increase their "lending" portfolio to whatever country they work with. Their success isn't measured by the profitability of the loans they make, but by the amount of money they "lend" and the amount of power they accrue. In this respect, they are like government bureaucrats everywhere.

The World Bank is only a slick way for fat cats in the United States and corrupt despots in the Third World to fleece American and Western taxpayers under the guise of promoting economic development. Instead of expanding funding for the World Bank, as Secretary of State James Baker urges, the United States should get out.

3

UNMASKING THE BUREAUCRATS

Why Bureaucracy Must Fail

Llewellyn H. Rockwell

Washington loves a scandal. Politicians can attack the other party, pretend they're cleaning up the mess, and get lots of publicity.

All is great fun so long as the scandal can be contained, for no crime can be allowed to reflect on government itself. Any infamy, no matter how institutionalized, must be portrayed as an aberration.

That is the official line on the Department of Housing and Urban Development and its billions of dollars in graft. But despite the Democrats' attempt to portray Samuel Pierce, James Watt, Deborah Dean, and all the other Republican officials and consultants as the source of the problems, they are not—as despicable as their actions were.

The real scandal is the continued existence of HUD, an unconstitutional Great Society relic that both Republicans and Democrats want to continue to fund. While damaging the poor with crime-infested government housing, HUD has enriched politically-connected builders with our tax money under every administration since LBJ's.

Nor is HUD unique. Pick any government department that redistributes our hard-earned money to the politically powerful—Commerce, Education, Energy, HHS, Interior, Labor, Transportation, etc.—audit it rigorously, and we would find the same thing. Corruption, fraud, waste, and abuse are endemic to bureaucracy, and must be, since all spending decisions are made politically and not economically.

Mainstream economists have only recently and reluctantly begun to examine the inherent flaws of bureaucracy. As Keynesians and quasi-Keynesians, they see market failure everywhere, to be corrected by beneficent government with themselves in high-paying federal jobs doing the correcting.

The mainstream claim about "market failure" is nonsense, of course. It is *government* failure that plagues us. Yet there are relatively few mainstream economists who understand what Misesians have always known: it is economically impossible for bureaucracy to do the job assigned it.

Even before Mises, Lord Acton and Richard Simpson, in a prescient 1891 essay called "Bureaucracy," wrote that in "all governments there may be odious tyranny, monopolies, exactions, and abominable abuses of nearly all kinds." Yet "the idea of bureaucracy is not fulfilled till we add the pedantic element of a pretense to direct our life." Bureaucrats claim "to know what is best for us, to measure out our labour, to superintend our studies, to prescribe our opinions, to make itself answerable for us, to put us to bed, tuck us in, put on our nightcap, and administer our gruel."

On the eve of an Anglo-American explosion in the size of government, they warned that "a bureaucratic system" can "arise gradually under every form of policy, and it renders every form of government despotic."

Anticipating an Austrian insight, Acton and Simpson discerned that "We shall never be safe from bureaucracy till we have exorcised from our public men" the philosophy of "positivism which treats man statistically and in the mass, not as individuals." We must "be always suspicious of any school which treats men as so many ciphers to add up, subtract, divide, multiply, and reduce to vulgar fractions."

German sociologist Franz Oppenheimer, writing in 1914, also attacked "officialdom." Since the bureaucracy is "paid from the funds of the state," it is supposed to be "removed from the economic fights of conflicting interests." But the civil servant ideal is a myth. "The officials do not cease being real men" who are "subject to pressure by enormous economic interests." Bureaucracies also have their own internal incentive structure, which has nothing to do with advancing the public good, but only the relative position of the bureaucracy.

Oppenheimer implies that we should be doubly suspicious when politicians claim to help the poor through bureaucracy. The poor haven't the resources to advance themselves economically, much less secure a HUD grant for their neighborhood. The politically well connected will always reap the benefits.

Yet the perverse economic incentives of bureaucracy are only part of the problem, as Ludwig von Mises argued in his pioneering 1944 book *Bureaucracy*. In private markets, Mises said, prices tell us how acting individuals value competing goods and services. Using prices as a guide, market participants can direct goods and services to their most highly-valued uses. Free prices therefore make possible productivity, creativity, entrepreneurship, and efficiency. Without a market price mechanism, there must be irrationality and chaos.

As Mises was the first to show, socialism is doomed to fail because there are no market prices for the means of production. And that is also part of the reason bureaucracies can't work. "People are sometimes shocked by the degree of maladminstration" but it isn't due simply to "culpable negligence or lack of competence." In government, he noted, the products can neither be bought nor sold. There is no free-market demand for bureaucratic services, or at least none that can be expressed, so bureaucrats cannot allocate resources rationally, even without the ever-present political pressure.

In a profit-driven business, the wages of each employee tend to reflect his contribution to total output. But incomes in a bureaucracy are based on a non-market, government-wide grading system. The only way for the bureaucrat to increase his income is through longevity and promotion, which come through passivity and obedience, not innovation or productivity.

Mises also explained that bureaucrats cannot rationally cut costs even if they want to. With the best intentions, a bureaucrat can't know what is waste and what is not because he doesn't know what's economically desirable in the first place. Are salaries too high? Are there too many offices, publications, researchers, secretaries, copiers, file clerks? The government manager can't know.

Furthermore, Mises points out, it is futile to recommend that a bureaucracy be run like a business. "No reform could transform a public office into a sort of private enterprise."

Cost-benefit analyses are also pointless. There is no way to measure the "costs" because no one knows the potential alternative uses for the resources. Nor can the "benefits" be known, since there is no consumer market for the good or service in question. And since the bearers of the costs and the receivers of the benefits are not the same—unlike in the private sector—the process is morally flawed.

Despite Jack Kemp's promises of HUD rehabilitation, the only effective reform is abolition. For the sake of the poor, the taxpayers, and the Constitution, we need to let one last HUD contract—to a demolition firm.

Your Visit to Our Nation's Capital

Llewellyn H. Rockwell

On trips to Washington, most tourists visit only the government's monuments to itself. Interesting as these are, it's also instructive to see the memorials to your tax money: Congress and the federal bureaucracies.

Congress—as an elected body—is still accessible, but the federal agencies have recently been put off-limits to taxpayers, thanks to the alleged threat of terrorism. If some pathological enemy of the United States decided to bomb the Department of Health and Human Services, massive police protection will make sure he fails so the welfare checks can still go out. In case you were worried.

While in D.C., a city whose informal slogan is "A Work-Free Drug Place," visit your Congressman and at least one of your Senators, and tell them what you think about the pay raise and other issues. Also ask one of them to arrange a visit to a bureaucracy.

I once walked the halls of the Department of Housing and Urban Development, years before the scandals, and found it outrageous and funny, predictable and chilling—a sort of cross between Eddie Murphy and the Hillside Strangler.

There were acre after acre of offices full of over-paid, shifty-eyed drones, filing their nails, reading novels (those who could), or chatting in the halls. In spooky corridor after corridor, there wasn't one person you would want to leave alone with your wallet. And here they were with *everybody's* wallet.

When the HUD scandal became public, I was surprised only that it had become public. Rest assured, what we heard is just the scum floating on top of the pond. And that stagnant water is mighty deep.

Such agencies do not exist for their stated purposes. LBJ erected HUD not to supply housing to the poor, but to funnel tax money to politically connected builders and power to the government. Who can be surprised that there is fraud and theft? Even the official purpose is unconstitutional and immoral.

Scandals serve a healthy purpose, however. HUD, the Keating Five, and Congressional sex crimes diminish Washington's prestige, and therefore its ability to regulate, subsidize, tax, spend, and borrow.

Knowing this, and knowing there are other scandals yet to come, the Congress decided to deliver a sucker punch to the taxpayers, in hopes that we will have forgotten it by next November: they voted themselves a massive pay raise—more money, just for their raise, than the average non-government American earns in a year. And they snuck it through so fast that the opposition, led by Ralph Nader, couldn't organize.

In case we hadn't forgotten by November 1990, the Republicans and Democrats formed a cartel to punish any challenger who used the pay raise against an incumbent. Already, the Democrats have defunded a candidate who planned to attack Newt Gingrich (R-GA), one of the engineers of the pay raise, and they removed Gingrich from their list of targeted opponents, virtually ensuring his reelection. After all, some issues are too important to be made into political footballs.

Our answer must be to pretend that the Congressmen who voted for this outrage are political footballs, and kick them out of office.

Amidst all these scandals and fearing more, the Bush administration asked the inspectors general of various federal agencies to report on any little items that might embarrass the White House. Some of the results are in, and here are the lowlights:

The Department of Veteran's Affairs, the new cabinet department created by the Reagan administration, says there is loads of fraud in the $150 billion home-loan guarantee program; hundreds have been indicted this year alone.

The Department of Agriculture reports the wrong group of exporters got $170 million in taxpayer-backed loans. The well-acronymed DOA says $66 million was handed out to farmers who beat the regulations. One farmer created 51 trusts so he could receive the maximum $50,000 payment per "person," for a total of $2.55 million. Another did the same to get $1.69 million.

The Department of Education spends more than $10 billion a year on college loans, grants, and work-study programs fraught with abuse. Students get year-long scholarships for four-month courses and trade-school trainees stretch their programs out to ten years to stay at the federal trough.

At the Bureau of Indian Affairs, which a Senate panel recently said ought to be dismantled because of fraud, $17 million is missing.

And these are abuses that the bureaucrats report on themselves! Unmentioned are the S&L bailout, the coming bank bailout, the Pentagon, etc.

Under the best of conditions, bureaucracies are in disarray. As Ludwig von Mises demonstrated, bureaucracies must be inefficient. There is no consumer demand for their "services," they have no profit and loss system to check efficiency, and there is no consuming public to hold them accountable.

In Washington, the "consumers" are Congressmen and pressure groups with their hands in our wallets. That's why Mises argued, in the tradition of the Founding Fathers, that bureaucracy must be drastically limited.

Abolishing HUD and all the rest of Washington's unconstitutional agencies, and trimming the rest to a proper level, would cut the federal budget by 75%. Sounds like a good start to me.

The Case against NASA

Sheldon L. Richman

The most sacred of cows in the federal government is the National Aeronautics and Space Administration. Since it was founded, after the Soviets burst into space with Sputnik and a manned mission, NASA has been the darling of nearly everyone. Criticizing it takes more audacity than criticizing the Brownies. How could anyone deny that it was America's manifest destiny to conquer space?

Some of the sheen came off NASA in 1986 when the space shuttle *Discovery* crashed less than two minutes after it was launched. Suddenly people began to think the previously unthinkable: that NASA was inefficient and perhaps corrupt. For the first time, magazines, newspapers, and television anchormen suggested that it was a government bureaucracy like any other.

The skepticism did not last. Even at its height, the hard-boiled newsmen could hardly contain their grief at the interruption of the space program and fervently hoped for its resumption. When it was finally resumed, they did not try to hide their joy. "America is back," they declared on the day the first post crash shuttle launched.

No one should have expected any real examination of NASA and its underlying premises in the wake of the disaster, because the problem with NASA is only indirectly related to shoddy engineering and rushed launch schedules. The problem goes to the very idea that government should be sponsoring the exploration and industrial development of space. The idea is taken for granted. To even question its validity is, in most circles, to reveal oneself as a boor. But as Will Rogers said, "it's not what we don't know that hurts us; it's what we know that ain't so."

Government exploration of space is a bad idea. It is especially unsound economically. To see this, we must unravel the various justifications for the space program. Leaving aside military reasons, there are two broad justifications: national prestige and economic benefits, the spiritual and material.

Unfortunately, people are easily gulled into boondoggles on the grounds of national prestige. Throughout history the greatest waste of lives and treasure has been brought about for the glory of the nation or state. It shows no signs of abating. National glory (*government* glory) is a cheap substitute for freedom and prosperity, exactly the things sacrificed to achieve the junk-jewelry of prestige.

The economics of the state's space program is no better. Yet many people who would reject national prestige as a reason for the program heartily embrace it for the material benefits. Think of the industrial, scientific, and medical potential, they exhort. Think of the benefits we've had so far: digital watches, pocket calculators, *Tang*!

But such appeals ignore economic basics. Before costs are incurred to achieve something, more must be demonstrated than the abstract desirability of the thing in question. To want something is to prefer it to something else. Acting man is always choosing A over B. To make a choice oblivious of the alternatives foregone is an absurdity. This is the concept of subjective opportunity cost.

In some general sense, exploration of space is desirable. But it is not a free good. To get it, someone has to give up something. The key questions are who is the someone, and what is the something. These are precisely the questions that the government would like us to forget with regard to the space program (and everything else it does).

The *who* are the coerced taxpayers, even those who don't give a hoot for space. The *what* is their hard-earned money, which they have no choice but to turn over to the state. The amount is a politically determined matter that bears little relation to what it would be were space exploration left to the free market.

In the marketplace, entrepreneurs must keep their costs within the constraints set by consumers in their valuation of final products. If a businessman's outlays are greater than he can recoup from customers, he eventually goes out of business. Because of this constant threat, businessmen are driven to minimize outlays through innovation. There is no one way to do anything, so entrepreneurs are always looking for the lowest-cost way of producing their products consistent with the interests of their customers.

The government faces a different constraint. It doesn't go out of business when outlays exceed income (ain't that the truth!). Its constraints are more elastic. They can be expanded (though not infinitely) by the right combination of public relations and political intrigue. Unlike the businessman, the bureaucrat doesn't have to please customers by delivering a concrete product that they will use and reject if they don't like it. The bureaucrat must merely persuade the citizens and members of Congress that space exploration is vaguely good.

Since the taxpayers pay for the program indirectly and along with the rest of their tax bill, they do not, and perhaps cannot, submit the space program to the kind of consumer test to which they put market products. In other words, most people don't know what the space program costs them individually, and they don't relate the costs to the "benefits."

Because of this, the program is run in a way that would be entirely inappropriate in the market. That is, by definition, it is wasteful. A government program offering such abstract "benefits" constantly faces budget cuts or elimination if it doesn't maintain a high profile and public excitement. The production method that achieves those ends, however, is not necessarily the economically rational method. For example, NASA from the beginning has committed itself to manned space missions. These are more expensive than unmanned missions, and much expert opinion, in and out of the government, believe that manned missions are an unnecessary extravagance.

Why does NASA persist in sending people into space? It's simple and readily acknowledged by NASA people: unmanned missions are boring. No one watches them on television because when you've seen one rocket launched, you've seen them all. If all the launches are unmanned the public will stop caring about space. And when they stop caring, the congressmen on the budget committees will think that NASA's money could be spent on things that taxpayers care more about. So an exclusively unmanned space program threatens the existence of the program.

That's why we have manned missions. But that's not the end of it. The public's attention on any one thing is limited. The more that the manned missions go off without a hitch, the harder it is to keep public attention trained on them. After a few successful space shuttle launches, people lost interest. The program was a victim of its own success.

NASA had to find public-relations methods to regain attention. So NASA heralded a series of "firsts" in space: the first woman, the first black man, the first senator (Jake Garn), and, finally, the first public-school teacher. These firsts had no inherent relationship to the missions. They were cynical tricks designed to get people to tune in. They worked, but the Challenger explosion that killed Christa MacAuliff ended, for a long time, plans to send civilians into space. Ironically, it also did much to renew the attention that was waning.

The same kind of stupidity found in the shuttle program can be found in the $25 billion moon-landing program and will be found in the $30 billion space-station program. The upshot is the political management, as Mises points out in *Bureaucracy*, is inherently irrational because it has neither the necessity nor means to engage in market-style economic calculation.

Instead of seeking a product that people want and producing it at the lowest price, the bureaucratic managers are more interested in building their own power bases. (NASA's budget is up to about $12 billion). Moreover, people in the nominally private sector get a whiff of the gravy train and go to great lengths to hop aboard. Not only do people seek employment with NASA, but diverse interests throughout the economy—in industry, science, and academia—turn their efforts toward getting government grants and contracts. This not only gives these people a vested interest in the problem, it also diverts scarce resources from serving consumers to serving the bureaucratic agenda.

It is likely that exploration of space would benefit society. But whether those benefits are greater than what it would cost to attain them is something that only the free market can determine. To put it another way, right now we cannot know if space exploration is a good thing because the government won't let us find out.

Kemp at HUD: Should Free-Marketeers Be Optimistic?

Greg Kaza

The Department of Housing and Urban Development is a glaring example of government waste. It robs the taxpayer, promotes special interests, and hurts the poor.

And despite his conservative reputation, Jack Kemp's tenure as secretary of HUD has already increased, rather than decreased, HUD's damaging role in the U.S. economy.

HUD was founded in 1965 as part of President Lyndon Johnson's statist Great Society. Since then, more than $150 billion has disappeared down the HUD rathole. HUD bureaucrats have presided over the bulldozing of countless private buildings, while constructing expensive "model city" and "new community" public housing projects. Badly designed and poorly managed, they have quickly fallen into disrepair, acting as breeding grounds for crime and despair.

HUD spending has increased under both Democrats and Republicans. Budget outlays were $2.4 billion in 1970 under Richard Nixon, but had grown to $12.7 billion by the time Jimmy Carter left office in 1980. Under Ronald Reagan, HUD budget outlays increased from $14 billion in 1981 to $18.6 billion his last year. Even after all the scandals, George Bush gave HUD a 29% raise after his first year in office.

Typical of HUD waste are the Carter-created Community Development Block Grant (CDBG) and Urban Development Action Grant (UDAG) programs. Both programs resemble federal revenue sharing, launched as a pork-barrel project by Nixon but later abolished.

CDBGs and UDAGs were allegedly started to help the poor, but in fact exist to enrich politically powerful developers. HUD grants the money to community governments, whose officials steer it to pet builders of "infrastructure" projects and other boondoggles. Communities receiving CDBGs include some of the wealthiest in the nation, among them Beverly Hills and Palm Springs, California, Grosse Pointe Shores and Bloomfield Hills, Michigan, and Scarsdale, New York.

In another case, whistleblower David Stith, former manager of HUD's Manpower Economic Development Program in Greensboro, North Carolina, told about bribes being exchanged for HUD grants. Stith's charges were substantiated, but not before he was investigated and fired by his HUD superiors.

Jack Kemp is in charge of HUD, but don't count on progress toward the free market. Rather than challenge the institution, Kemp has proposed only marginal changes, none of which show much promise. They include enterprise zones, housing vouchers, and tenant management.

Enterprise zones are supposed to reduce regulations, taxes, and other government burdens in depressed urban areas. But the real purpose could be more spending. Designation as an enterprise-zone means HUD will give special financial assistance "to the maximum extent possible" with "priority funding" and possible UDAG grants, set asides, and "technical assistance."

Kemp also wants housing vouchers that poor and low-income families could spend on government-approved housing. This is hardly a free-market solution, since it would guarantee housing for some at the expense of others, and increase, not reduce, government involvement in the nation's housing market.

Kemp also advocates "tenant management" in public housing. But the tenants would be under bureaucratic supervision, and the problem is not lack of management, but lack of ownership. A far better idea would be tenant ownership, as undertaken by Margaret Thatcher in England. That means the ability of the owners to buy and sell their homes at will, which Kemp's reforms do not allow.

Gone are the days when conservatives criticized the waste, fraud, and corruption synonymous with HUD. Many seem to agree with Kemp's statement to the *Wall Street Journal*: "I've never understood why conservatives positioned themselves against the government."

Says Kemp: "I'm going to be an advocate" and will "throw out ideology." As to budget cuts, "I can assure you that I am going to do everything I can to make sure that there is adequate funding." And he has.

The National Taxpayers Union scores lawmakers on a spending scale of 0 to 100. For example, when the Mises Institute's Distinguished Counsellor, Ron Paul (R-TX), was in office, he scored from 91 to 99. Wisconsin Democrat Bill Proxmire always scored in the low eighties. Yet in the last legislative session, Jack Kemp (R-NY) got only 44, while liberal Pat Schroeder (D-CO) beat him with a 47.

Appointing people who are associated, even wrongly, with free-market views quiets potential critics on the Right, but the ultimate effect is to discredit the free market.

The classic case is former Education Secretary William Bennett, appointed by a president who promised to abolish the department. Bennett presided over a 51% budget increase and a vast enlargement of federal involvement in education. The *Washington Post* and *New York Times* editorialized on his departure that even though they often disagreed with him, they approved the

expanded federal role he engineered. Bureaucrat Lauro
F. Cavazos heads the department, which is stronger and
more supportive of the National Education Association
than ever. Similarly, the effect of Kemp's tenure will be
to reform the image (but not the substance) of HUD,
making it all the more powerful.

The Kemps and Bennetts help disguise the fact that
with agencies like the Departments of Education, Energy, and Housing and Urban Development, there is no
acceptable free-market solution short of abolition.

Government and Hurricane Hugo:
A Deadly Combination

Murray N. Rothbard

Natural disasters, such as hurricanes, tornadoes,
and volcanic eruptions, occur from time to time,
and many victims of such disasters have an unfortunate
tendency to seek out someone to blame. Or rather, to pay
for their aid and rehabilitation. These days, Papa Government (a stand-in for the hapless taxpayer) is called
on loudly to shell out. The latest incident followed the
ravages of Hurricane Hugo, when many South Carolinians turned their wrath from the mischievous hurricane
to the federal government and its FEMA (Federal Emergency Management Agency) for not sending far more aid
more quickly.

But why must taxpayers A and B be forced to pay for
natural disasters that strike C? Why can't C—and his
private insurance carriers—foot the bill? What is the
ethical principle that insists that South Carolinians,

whether insured or non-insured, poor or wealthy, must be subsidized at the expense of those of us, wealthy or poor, who don't live on the southern Atlantic Coast, a notorious hurricane spot in the autumn? Indeed, the witty actor who regularly impersonates President Bush on *Saturday Night Live* was perhaps more correct than he realized when he pontificated: "Hurricane Hugo—not my fault." But in that case, of course, the federal government should get out of the disaster aid business, and FEMA should be abolished forthwith.

If the federal government is not the culprit as portrayed, however, other government forces have actually weighed in on Hugo's side, and have escalated the devastation that Hugo has wreaked. First, local government. When Hurricane Hugo arrived, government imposed compulsory evacuation upon many of the coastal areas of South Carolina. Then, for nearly a week after Hugo struck the coast, the mayor of one of the hardest-hit towns in South Carolina, the Isle of Palms near Charleston, used force to prevent residents from returning to their homes to assess and try to repair the damage.

How dare the mayor prevent people from returning to their own homes? When she finally relented, six days after Hugo, she continued to impose a 7:00 pm curfew in the town. The theory behind this outrage is that the local officials were "fearful for the homeowners' safety and worried that there would be looting." But the oppressed residents of Isle of Palms had a different reaction. Most of them were angered; typical was Mrs. Pauline Bennett, who lamented that "if we could have gotten here sooner, we could have saved more."

But this was scarcely the only case of a "welfare state" intervening and making matters worse for the victims of Hugo. As a result of the devastation, the city of Charleston was of course short of many commodities. Responding to this sudden scarcity, the market acted quickly to clear supply and demand by raising prices accordingly: providing smooth, voluntary, and effective rationing of the suddenly scarce goods. The Charleston government, however, swiftly leaped in to prevent "gouging"—grotesquely passing emergency legislation making the charging of higher prices post-Hugo than pre-Hugo a crime, punishable by a fine up to $200 and/or 30 days in jail.

Unerringly, the Charleston welfare state converted higher prices into a crippling shortage of all the scarce goods. Resources were distorted and misallocated, long lines developed as in Eastern Europe, all so that the people of Charleston could have the warm glow of knowing that if they could ever *find* the goods in short supply, they could pay for them at pre-Hugo bargain rates.

Thus, the local authorities did the work of Hurricane Hugo—intensifying its destruction by preventing people from staying at or returning to their homes, and aggravating the shortages by rushing to impose maximum price control. But that was not all. Perhaps the worst blow to the coastal residents was the intervention of those professional foes of humanity—the environmentalists.

Last year, reacting to environmentalist complaints about development of beach property and worry about "beach erosion" (do beaches have "rights," too?), South Carolina passed a law severely restricting any new construction on the beachfront, or any replacement of damaged buildings. Enter Hurricane Hugo, which apparently provided a heaven-sent opportunity for the South Carolina Coastal Council to sweep the beachfronts clear of any human beings. Geology professor Michael Katuna, a Coastal Council consultant, saw only poetic justice, smugly declaring that "Homes just shouldn't be right on the beach where Mother Nature wants to bring a storm ashore." And if Mother Nature wanted us to fly, She would have supplied us with wings?

Other environmentalists went so far as to praise Hurricane Hugo. Professor Orrin H. Pilkey, geologist at Duke who is one of the main theoreticians of the beach-suppression movement, had attacked development on Pawleys Island, northeast of Charleston, and its rebuilding after destruction by Hurricane Hazel in 1954. "The area is an example of a high-risk zone that should never have been developed, and certainly not redeveloped after the storm." Pilkey now calls Hugo "a very timely hurricane," demonstrating that beachfronts must return to Nature.

Gered Lennon, geologist with the Coastal Council, put it succinctly: "However disastrous the hurricane was, it may have had one healthy result. It hopefully will rein in some of the unwise development we have had along the coast."

The Olympian attitude of the environmentalist rulers contrasted sharply with the views of the blown-out residents themselves. Mrs. Bennett expressed the views of the residents of the Isle of Palms. Determined to rebuild on the spot, she pointed out: "We have no choice. This is all we have. We have to stay here. Who is going to buy it?" Certainly not the South Carolina environmental elite.

Tom Browne, of Folly Beach, S. C., found his house destroyed by Hurricane Hugo. "I don't know whether I'll be able to rebuild it or if the state would even let me," complained Browne. The law, he pointed out, is taking property without compensation. "It's got to be unconstitutional."

Precisely. Just before Hugo hit, David Lucas, a property owner on the Isle of Palms, was awarded $1.2 million in a South Carolina court after he sued the state over the law. The court ruled that the state could not deprive him of his right to build on the land he owned without due compensation. And the South Carolina environmentalists are not going to be able to force the state's taxpayers to pay the enormous compensation for not being allowed to rebuild all of the destruction wrought by Hurricane Hugo.

Skip Johnson, an environmental consultant in South Carolina, worries that "it's just going to be a real nightmare. People are going to want to rebuild and get on with their lives." The Coastal Council and its staff, Johnson lamented, "are going to have their hands full." Let's hope so.

Big Government: An *Unnatural* Disaster
Llewellyn H. Rockwell

The California earthquake should teach "individualistic Americans" that they are "utterly dependent on government," says Washington columnist George Will. It proves that "big government is the solution, not the problem," adds Christopher Matthews of the *San Francisco Examiner*.

As someone on the front line, I draw a different moral.

Most of the heroes were volunteers. Unlike the bureaucrats, they went to work immediately after the earthquake when people's lives could be saved, and before the government lumbered in to shut off private rescue efforts and violate property rights.

Within an hour after the earthquake, thousands of individuals were directing traffic, rescuing the trapped, treating the injured, and trying to salvage property. Soon the St. Vincent de Paul Society, the Salvation Army, and the Red Cross had centers all across the Bay Area to aid the victims.

By the next day, thousands had called these three agencies to make donations. Contributions also poured into Church World Services, Direct Relief International, Feed the Children, Operation California, the Bishop's Fund of the Episcopal Church, and World Relief. A man dropped by a local TV station and donated his lottery winnings of $10,000. Appeals for blood were so successful that the Red Cross had to turn people away.

Once again, Americans showed themselves a generous and courageous people—long before the Federal Emergency Management Agency (FEMA) was in operation, long before Transportation Secretary Skinner was dispatched, long before Vice President Quayle visited, and long before FEMA and local officials were blaming each other for any shortcomings.

As Nobel laureate F. A. Hayek pointed out in *The Road to Serfdom*, "the worst rise to the top" in government. Most officials fall into two categories: smart and despicable, and stupid and despicable. An emergency gives us the chance to pull back the curtain and see these Wizards of Ooze for what they really are.

In the Bay Area, we could turn on the TV and watch San Francisco's frenetic Mayor Art Agnos and our other rulers hog the cameras and fight over the microphones. We could listen to them babble the obvious, issue irrelevant orders, and announce a Master Plan worthy of Moscow. It would have been funny if not for the suffering...and the spooky look in all those elected and appointed eyes. The little dictators were actually enjoying it.

After Hurricane Hugo, it took FEMA a week to open an office. Bothered by criticism that it acted too slowly, this time it moved more quickly. But to what end?

Grant Peterson, a top FEMA bureaucrat, said on NBC that the agency had "opened our crisis center in Washington to issue emergency guidelines according to official processes." In other words, it was pushing paper. Days later, as after Hugo, FEMA snoozed while private agencies worked around the clock.

FEMA—described by Sen. Ernest Hollings (D-SC) as "bureaucratic jackasses"—was still looking for San Francisco office space, in *suitable* buildings of course, while private agencies were running hundreds of relief stations on the streets. But, claimed Peterson, FEMA had to find suitable temporary employees: "retired federal employees and public school teachers" who know how to deal with the public!

Government did move fast, however, to stop "unauthorized relief." The night of the earthquake, volunteers pleaded to be allowed to keep rescuing people from the collapsed I-880 freeway. A concrete worker called the government "paralyzed"; why, he wanted to know, were they also "handcuffing volunteers?"

About the only thing *un*paralyzed was spending, as people from the rest of the country will be forced to bail out the politically connected in Northern California. (As with all welfare programs, the poor may be the justification, but never the prime recipients.)

Such redistributive spending is not only economically harmful, it strengthens the welfare state, chokes off real charity, and undermines the family and community; far from being kinder and gentler, it's the tax man and the social worker writ large.

A century and a half ago, Congressman Davy Crockett argued against federal relief for a fire in Georgetown. The Constitution grants no such authority, he said. More to the point, he told his colleagues, the money "is not yours to give." But he was making a contribution himself; why didn't the others join him? Then as now, however, Congress was interested only in spending *other* people's money.

In the less-severe Armenian earthquake, more than 25,000 people died in the collapse of socialist housing. In California, most of the deaths occurred when a government highway pancaked onto the road below, when a government bridge broke, and when government water pipes cracked, letting fires burn unchecked.

Then, in an act of mass victim abuse, officials denied people entry into their own damaged homes and businesses. Some San Franciscans were refused permission to recover their few possessions before the government bulldozed their houses. Adult property owners could not be allowed to make their own decisions. Government knows best.

It also knows a main chance. Like con men who target the bereft, politicians use adversity to increase taxes. Rep. Don Edwards (D-CA) wants California's tax-limiting Prop 13 repealed and Republican Governor George Deukmejian is calling for higher state taxes. The President refused to rule out a tax increase.

Big government—arrogance and waste incarnate— should get *more* of our money because now we have *less*? Taxpayers, not to speak of the country, are far better off when they send their dollars to private agencies instead of do-nothing bureaucrats.

The earthquake does not teach us the lesson of Messrs. Will and Matthews, but rather the opposite: churches and charities succor; businesses rebuild; government botches.

The Northern California quake was over in 15 seconds, but the politicians will be exacerbating its effects for years. There's no Richter for big government, but on the Rockwell Scale, it's a constant 7.1.

In Defense of Congress

Llewellyn H. Rockwell

Many of my friends in the conservative movement are denouncing the "Imperial Congress" these days. Joining statist Republicans like Newt Gingrich, they seek to strengthen the Presidency as against the Congress. *National Review*, the *Wall Street Journal*, and other conservative publications cheer them on.

All over the Right, we hear worries about slipping Presidential prerogatives, or denunciations of Congress's "meddling" in foreign policy, supposedly a Presidential preserve.

But this is exactly wrong. It is the Imperial Presidency—as the conservative heroes of my youth like *National Review* co-founder Frank Meyer knew—that threatens our freedom.

Too often, Congress simply lays down in front of the Executive steamroller. When it attempts to recover a crumb or two of its Constitutional prerogatives—with the Boland Amendment or the War Powers Act, for example—the Legislature is condemned for treading on alleged Presidential territory.

Some conservatives—who on other days pooh-pooh Republican budget deficits as meaningless—even make a cause out of the size of Congress's budget, which totals .08% of federal outlays.

Given the gargantuan government we have—which also violates the Constitution, of course—it is in our interest for Congress to have sufficient staff, if only to throw a few roadblocks in the way of the Executive behemoth. We should also remember that all the congressional staffs put together don't equal one bureau in HHS.

The Founders, steeped in the English parliamentary tradition, knew that liberty is threatened by kings and dictators, not legislators. They saw the progress of representative government as the wresting of power from the Executive. That's why they wrote the Constitution as they did.

Article I vests "all [all] legislative power" in the preeminent branch of government: Congress. Congress alone has power to: raise and spend taxes; borrow; regulate commerce; coin money; declare war; create federal courts and determine their jurisdiction; and establish an army and navy.

Article II admonishes the president to carry out the laws passed by Congress. He may veto those laws, but his veto can be overridden by Congress, the final authority.

The president may also recommend legislation, but as Frank Meyer wrote in *National Review* in 1964, "Recommend means *recommend*, not demand, not pressure, not go to the people to arouse demagogic pressures against the Congress." The president is also commander-in-chief of the armed forces; he may appoint ambassadors and judges, *with the consent of the Senate*; and he may negotiate treaties, *with the consent of the Senate*.

There is no mention of foreign policy as a presidential entitlement. And his role as head of the armed forces has a foreign policy dimension only when Congress has declared war (the Founders not having envisioned Uncle Sam as global gendarme).

Article III shows the Judiciary, despite Warren Court imperialism, as the "least-equal" branch. Not only does the Constitution mandate that Congress can establish (or abolish) all federal courts except the Supreme Court, Congress can also—except in certain narrow areas such as lawsuits between states—determine the jurisdiction of the Supreme Court and all other federal courts.

For example, Congress could, by simple majority vote, take abortion cases out of the hands of the Supreme

Court and lower federal courts, and leave this question to the states. That such a simple and Constitutional solution to Roe v. Wade occurs to no one is ample proof of a shriveled Congress and a swollen Presidency and Judiciary.

To argue that the Framers intended Congress to be the paramount branch of government is not to defend our present Representatives and Senators, however. With very few exceptions, today's Members of Congress represent a sort of reverse evolution from 1789. Men have turned into monkeys, albeit with law degrees.

Nonetheless, Congress remains the branch of government closest to the people. As their retreat on the pay raise showed, they can be influenced. A whiff of popular opposition makes them sit up and take notice. The merest hint of possible defeat can make them do anything, even the right thing.

The Armand Hammers of the world can sway the Presidency or the Judiciary. Working Americans cannot. That's why believers in a limited constitutional republic must not join the anti-Congress bandwagon. Institutionally, Congress is the bulwark of our freedom. Its enemies would, in Frank Meyer's words, "substitute the uncontrolled power of a President elected with a specious quadrennial 'mandate.'"

If we want to recover our freedom—so diminished in this century by despotic Presidents, bureaucrats, and judges—we must curb the Executive and the Judiciary, and Congress is our only weapon. The Founders gave us that weapon in the Constitution. But it is up to us to use it.

Exxon: Biggest Victim of the Alaskan Oil Spill

Llewellyn H. Rockwell

From the hysteria, one would think that Exxon had deliberately spilled 180,000 barrels of oil off Prince William Sound, Alaska. In fact, Exxon is the biggest victim. Through apparent employee negligence, the company has lost valuable oil, a giant tanker, and hundreds of millions of dollars to compensate fishermen and clean up the mess.

Yet night after night on television, we were treated to maudlin coverage of oily water and animals, and fervid denunciations of Exxon and oil production in "environmentally sensitive" Alaska. Why is it more sensitive than, say, Texas? Because there are so few people in Valdez, Alaska, and that represents the radical environmentalists' ideal.

From the snail darter to the furbish lousewort to billions of acres of wilderness—all supposedly need government protection from the production of goods and services for mankind.

Extreme environmentalism holds that nature was in perfect balance before the arrival of modern man, whose crime was economic progress through capitalism. "The only really good technology is no technology at all," says the organization manual of Friends of the Earth. Economic development is "taxation without representation imposed by an elitist species [that's us] upon the rest of the natural world."

David Brower, former director of the Sierra Club, says: "We've got to march back to our last known safe landmark. I can't say exactly where it is, but I think it's...at the start of the Industrial Revolution."

Ralph Nader told *Rolling Stone* that we ought to consider abolishing the entire petrochemical industry. Since he also believes in outlawing nuclear power, what would we use for energy? "Trees, cornhusks, manure, the sun, the wind."

Trees? In the Pacific Northwest, terrorists drive long metal spikes into trees to splinter and kill any logger who tries to cut them down.

While I enjoy the image of Nader's fireplace full of cornhusks and manure, how would the rest of us heat or cool our homes, fuel our cars and businesses, or create new jobs? The environmentalist ultras reject that question, however, because they seek the undoing of industrial civilization. "That this would mean the starvation of most of the human race seems not to figure in their calculations," says Murray N. Rothbard.

When the nuclear fusion experiment was announced, top environmentalists Jeremy Rifkind and Paul Ehrlich told the *Los Angeles Times* that a cheap, nearly inexhaustible, non-polluting energy source would be a "disaster." It would allow more economic development, and worst of all, make it possible for more people to live on the earth.

Pantheistic environmentalism holds that man is simply a part of nature—no more important than sticks or stones or rocks or trees. The Judeo-Christian tradition, on the other hand, teaches that God gave man dominion over the earth and all its resources. They exist for man, and not the reverse. And the free-market, private-property order imparts the same lesson.

It is anti-human to advocate more government intervention and less economic development, i.e., more poverty, as the rabid environmentalists do. It's no coincidence that environmental activists tend to be high-in-
come types who disdain the little guy striving to better
himself. The socialized national parks transfer wealth from
the majority who are made poorer to the minority who
backpack. Public lands and resources also enable the
government to hand out concessions to politically favored
special interests, who form a wooden triangle with environmentalists and bureaucrats against the public.

There is, of course, nothing wrong with backpacking
in the outdoors. I love it myself. But we the backpackers
should pay for it. The federal government already owns
more than a third of the United States, including most
of Alaska. Selling these federal lands would pay off the
national debt, end this gigantic misuse of resources, and
raise the average American's standard of living, which
has been declining in real terms since 1973 thanks to
big government.

I too love the New Hampshire forests, the Rocky
Mountains, and the California desert. But I also remember that modern man cherishes wilderness only from the
safe standpoint of industrial civilization. As Robert
Tucker points out, before capitalism, the forest was
feared as what the Pilgrims called a "desolation of wilderness" filled with "savage beasts and savage Indians." A
15th-century travel writer called the Alps the place
"where God had swept up all the debris of Europe to
create the plains of Lombardy."

Our view is what it is thanks only to capitalism, and
before we allow ourselves to be pushed backwards, we

ought to examine closely all the environmental crises promoted by federal scientists, politicians, and others with a vested interest in big government. Is there really too little ozone in the upper atmosphere or too much at street level? Should we really worry that the earth is supposedly a degree warmer—or cooler—than a hundred years ago? How do these people know the optimum temperature? Is it really so bad that Brazilian peasants cut down trees in the rain forests to engage in agriculture? Or should they be permanently sentenced to indentured mildewtude?

Any call to expand big government's parasitical control over our lives has to be opposed, no matter what the alleged justification. The real danger is always and everywhere, Washington, D.C., not the fluorocarbons released by cans of hairspray.

Does that mean we should not be concerned about accidents like the one at Valdez? No, but we should not forget the 8,800 tankers that have safely negotiated those waters since 1977, bringing the world 6.8 billion barrels of oil. Nor should we forget that oil is, in the environmentalists' lingo—natural, organic, and biodegradable. It will be gone in 12 to 18 months at the most.

When logging takes place in the so-called national forests, the trees are clearcut and the land erodes. When private timber companies harvest trees, they are careful to replant, to grow more trees and prevent erosion. But since no one owns the federal lands, no one cares for them. No private firm would have let Yellowstone Park burn because a forest fire is "natural."

In England, there is no municipal or industrial pollution of rivers and streams because the common law correctly holds that someone dumping filth upstream of someone else's land violates his property rights. In the United States, with nationalized waterways, no such prohibition holds, and water pollution is rampant.

As even Mikhail Gorbachev would admit, socialism is not an efficient method of economic organization. That's true for the Soviet Union, it's true for the U.S. Bureau of Land Management and Forest Service, and its true for the Mississippi River.

Now that socialism is intellectually dead, however, we can expect the special interests who want to control and live off the rest of us to dress up big government in different guises. One is environmentalism.

That—along with what one environmentalist gleefully told me was the "fantastic PR opportunity of the Exxon Valdez"—accounts for the hysteria directed at Exxon, including the claim that it used the oil spill to raise prices.

But prices are not set by the benevolence or malevolence of businessmen. They are set by supply and demand. And after the oil spill, market participants realized it would be used to further suppress energy production in Alaska, California, and other areas of the U.S., making all present resources instantly more valuable. An immediate price increase was the just and rational response.

Environmentalists are cutting up their Exxon credit cards and calling for a boycott of Exxon, itself the main victim of the oil spill. The boycott won't affect Exxon much, but it has already harmed gas station owners and their employees. But then environmental extremists have never minded harming innocent people, especially working people.

Amidst what is essentially an anti-human crusade, I am going out of my way to buy Exxon products. If the radical environmentalists win, the rest of us will lose.

"Afraid to Trust the People With Arms"

Stephen P. Halbrook

On April 5, 1989, at the instigation of drug shah William Bennett, the Bush administration violated its campaign promise against further gun control by arbitrarily decreeing a ban on the importation of most semiautomatic rifles. The same day, the House of Representatives held hearings on the Stark bill, which would impose as much as 80 years imprisonment for mere possession, by a law-abiding citizen, of a semiautomatic firearm.

There are some 70 million gunowners in the United States, and roughly one-third of all new guns are semiautomatics. Semiautomatic firearms, which require a separate pull of the trigger for each shot fired, have been in common use for about a century. And despite media doubletalk, semiautomatic rifles are not "assault weapons," a term exclusively reserved for machine guns.

The frenzy to ban semiautomatics began when Patrick Purdy gunned down elementary school children in Stockton, California. Yet this case better illustrates the failure of the criminal justice system. The only reason Purdy was roaming the schoolyard, instead of the penitentiary yard, was that prosecutors had allowed him to plea bargain away robberies and other felonies. A judge gave him a few days instead of a few years to serve in jail.

Politicians who favor no punishment for violent criminals saw the Purdy incident as a way to divert blame onto the millions of law-abiding gunowners of America.

The same politicians have also sought to blame gunowners for the violence between drug pushers. Yet this violence is the inevitable result of the New Prohibition on drugs. The same happened in the 1920s, when the Old Prohibition of alcohol led to wars between bootleggers fighting over turf. Then, the alcohol prohibitionists tried to blame the violence on law-abiding citizens who owned firearms.

FBI data show that semiautomatic rifles are only rarely used in crime and are used less frequently even than sporting shotguns. Yet firearm prohibitionists have initiated a Big Lie campaign depicting such rifles as the favorite tool of drug pushers.

Under the Gun Control Act of 1968, Congress severely restricted firearm imports. It was a protectionist measure sponsored by Senator Thomas Dodd of Connecticut— home of the domestic firearms industry. Even so, the Act required the federal Bureau of Alcohol, Tobacco, and Firearms (BATF) to authorize imports of firearms generally recognized as particularly suitable for sporting purposes.

Every one of the rifles banned from importation on April 5th had for several years been classified as sporting and the BATF allowed their importation. These rifles include the AKS, which has the cosmetic appearance of an AK-47 machine gun, but is redesigned internally so as not to be convertible to fully automatic. The Uzi, FN FAL, and AUG are similar examples of guns that have a military appearance, but which functionally are no different than typical hunting rifles.

Drug kingpins have no use for these sporting rifles, when they have their choice of millions of AK-47 and M-16 machine guns available on the black market from south of the border. Nor would a ban on rifles possessed by sportsmen affect successful narcotics smugglers.

Proponents of firearms bans—like King George III before the Revolution—simply do not trust the American people with arms. James Madison, arguing for adoption of the federal Constitution in *The Federalist* No. 46, spoke of "the advantage of being armed, which the Americans possess over the people of almost every other nation.... Notwithstanding military establishments in the several kingdoms of Europe..., the governments are afraid to trust the people with arms." If the people were armed, "the throne of every tyranny in Europe would be speedily overturned in spite of the legions which surround it."

Madison drafted what became the federal Bill of Rights, including the Second Amendment, which says that "the right of the people to keep and bear Arms, shall not be infringed." Madison endorsed the widely published, contemporaneous, and uncontradicted explanation by federalist leader Tench Coxe. He stated that "civil rulers, not having their duty to the people duly before them, may attempt to tyrannize," and "the military forces which must be occasionally raised to defend our country, might pervert their power to the injury of their fellow-citizens." Therefore "the people are confirmed...in their right to keep and bear their private arms."

Madison's philosophy and the Second Amendment are vindicated by 20th-century European experiences. In particular, the clearest example of a society where firearms were limited to the police and military was Nazi

Germany. A survey of Nazi statutes and decrees analyzed by the Library of Congress in a 1968 study concluded:

"This sampling of German statutes, decrees, and other documents concerning firearms indicated two points: First, the profound importance the German invaders attached to the possession of firearms. Second, the importance of these proclamations and decrees as a technique used by the Germans to obtain and limit weapons in the possession of the nationals of the invaded country. These proclamations were of course accompanied with searches and severe penalties.

"A totalitarian society, and particularly a totalitarian society occupying a country against its will, simply cannot permit the private possession of weapons to any great extent, except by those who have proven their loyalty.... These directives concerning firearms were consistently issued with varying degrees of penalties. For example during the occupation of Luxembourg, the unlawful possession of arms was punishable by fine, imprisonment, hard labor, or even death. If we take the regulations applicable to Poles and Jews in the Incorporated Eastern Territories of Poland, imprisonment or the death penalty applied not only to those actually possessing unlawful firearms, but also to those who had knowledge that certain people possessed those weapons and failed to inform the authorities."

In 1941, Congress understood the difference between a republic and a police state. It passed a law declaring that property requisitioned for war use would not "authorize the requisitioning or require the registration of any firearms possessed by any individual for his personal protection or sport." No law, Congress said, should be construed "to impair or infringe in any manner the right of any individual to keep and bear arms."

Congressman Edwin Arthur Hall explained at the time: "Before the advent of Hitler or Stalin, who took power from the German and Russian people, measures were thrust upon the free legislatures of these countries to deprive the people of the possession and use of firearms, so that they could not resist the encroachments of such diabolical and vitriolic state police organizations as the Gestapo, the OGPU, and the Cheka."

Even as late as 1986, in the preamble to the Firearms Owners' Protection Act, Congress reasserted "the rights of citizens to keep and bear arms under the Second Amendment" and "to security against illegal and unreasonable searches and seizures under the fourth amendment." Passage of the Protection Act was prompted by the lawless behavior of the Bureau of Alcohol, Tobacco, and Firearms against law-abiding gunowners. The abuses sparked Congressman John Dingell (D-MI.) in 1983 to call the BATF "a jack-booted group of fascists who are perhaps as large a danger to American society as I could pick today."

Madison introduced the Second Amendment and the rest of the Bill of Rights to Congress on June 8, 1789. Yet today, at the bicentennial of this great event in the history of human rights, proposals are racing toward passage that will ban firearms and destroy privacy rights. These proposals are more characteristic of a police state than a republic. And the media frenzy generated by the Purdy incident and the drug crusade only serves to mask that fact. It is unclear how long the Bill of Rights will endure this unconstitutional assault on 70 million American citizens.

4

THE GOVERNMENT MESS

Back to First Principles

Joseph Sobran

W hen Ronald Reagan was elected to the presidency in 1980, many conservatives (myself among them) were euphoric. They expected a wholesale reform in American government; there was even talk of a "Reagan Revolution." It seemed likely that there would be an early campaign to repeal the Great Society programs Reagan had always opposed, and, once that was accomplished, a repeal of the New Deal itself.

Liberals, meanwhile, nervously insisted that Reagan had "no mandate" for any such sweeping changes. Some of them predicted, with more hope than confidence, that "reality" would force Reagan to subordinate "ideology" to "pragmatism."

159

When Reagan left office eight years later, it looked as if the liberals had been right. Not much had changed. The system remained what it had been in 1980; Reagan hadn't even abolished the federal government's commitment to "affirmative action," which Lyndon Johnson had established by executive order, and which Reagan could have done away with by the same simple means—a stroke of the pen, requiring no legislative or judicial support.

Federal spending had doubled across the board. The federal government was committed to a budget of over a trillion dollars per year, or about $4,000 per U.S. citizen. Though nobody took a poll, it seems safe to say that few citizens felt they were getting $4,000 worth of government "services."

For all that, Reagan left the stage bowing to wild applause, as if his two terms had been an era of heroic achievements. Both he and his Democratic opponents had a vested interest in the idea that he had made radical changes—he because he wanted credit, they because they needed a bogeyman.

No doubt Reagan had made a difference in the *tone* of American politics. He had made conservative and free-market rhetoric fashionable, and helped put liberalism in disrepute. Reagan's presidency had also coincided with the collapse of socialism around the world, and may well have helped supply the impetus for it, though of course the ultimate cause of socialism's collapse was socialism itself.

It isn't easy to assign causes to historical processes. A great many things happen in any eight-year period, and Reagan was surely more symptom than motor of the decline of collectivism. It was part of his political and theatrical genius to personalize the process, modestly assuming the lion's share of the credit for what was happening anyway.

He did give dozens of worthwhile initiatives more support and encouragement than they would have had under almost any other president. Conservatives in Washington are now keenly aware that they enjoy much less access to President Bush than they did to President Reagan, under whom they encountered frustration enough, and there seems to be a concerted effort to remove "Reaganites" from the bureaucracies.

The result is that the conservatives now feel bereft by Reagan's absence. They regard his presidency as a lost opportunity, but at least while it lasted, it seemed an opportunity; now there is barely even the illusion of hope for real reform. George Bush is pretty clearly a status-quo man who wants more than anything to avoid conflict with Congress. He doesn't even daydream of radical change. In fact his rhetoric often implies that he is offering relief from the highly-charged ideological confrontations of the Reagan years.

In his own way, Bush supports the myth that the Reagan years were years of a drastic unsettling of the American political system. His special angle is the suggestion that Reagan's alleged achievements have been so fully realized that there is no need for him to disturb us further by adding anything significant to them.

Conservatives would be much happier, and better off, if they recognized frankly that Reagan was always primarily a politician and an insider, a loyal member of the establishment he seemed to challenge. He simply understood that the way to rise within the system was to make a special appeal to the voters who were dissatisfied with it from conservative motives—moral traditionalists and economic libertarians. He succeeded within that system by growling at it a little, enlisting popular discontent on his side. He was sincere enough. But he was also too prudent ever to enrage the establishment—including the pressure groups and tens of millions of voters who receive income and other special benefits from the federal government—by seriously threatening their interests. The main difference between Reagan and Bush is that Bush dropped his conservative campaign rhetoric almost as soon as he had won his election; Reagan kept speaking it while in office.

In short, Reagan posed as a right-wing outsider, while he was in fact not much more than the extreme right wing of the insiders. Maybe he couldn't have succeeded any other way; but it was his own success, not that of conservative causes, that was always his real concern. In that sense, Bush was his appropriate successor. Bush is merely less skillful at persuading conservatives that he has their interests at heart.

This is all to the good. Conservatives spent eight years waiting for Ronald Reagan to start acting like the messiah they were hoping for. "Let Reagan be Reagan," they said, unable to see that he *was* being Reagan by arousing their yearnings and enlisting their loyalties while letting them cool their heels. Now they may begin to understand that they are on their own.

During the Reagan years, conservative activists have developed a detailed agenda—securing government appointments for their own, implementing the Strategic

Defense Initiative, aiding various insurgent forces around the world—that may or may not be defensible in piecemeal terms but is less and less clearly related to broadly shared principles of government.

This agenda has something baroque about it: more and more, it resembles the familiar menus of liberal causes and programs. In fact, most of its items can co-exist with the liberal programs that have already been installed, which conservatives have quietly stopped trying to repeal. Jack Kemp, the conservative activists' favorite during the 1988 primaries, is the most conspicuous example of the conservative who has come to terms with the liberal programs that have been instituted since the New Deal; it's appropriate that he is now Secretary of Housing and Urban Development. The career of William Bennett—first as Education Secretary and then as drug czar—also illustrates how readily some conservatives drop their objections to federal power when it is exercised in the name of their "values."

Whatever may be said for fine-tuning liberal programs by adapting them to market incentives, this is not an approach that will make conservatism a powerful political force, because it does nothing to assert conservatism as an independent rival principle to collectivism. It merely tries to sell conservatism as a set of superior methods for achieving collectivist goals. This was also the weakness of supply-side economics: it offered to increase rather than cut federal revenues. It located itself in a marginal area of common interest between liberalism and conservatism.

Since Reagan, in other words, conservatives have lost their identity. Loyalty to Reagan himself has helped make them forget and abandon their traditional purpose of reducing the size of government, and, more fundamentally, of defining the role of government in strict and principled terms. If liberals have programs, conservatives now offer alternative programs. They seldom offer philosophical and constitutional objections to the *goals* of liberalism.

Among other things, this has relieved liberals of the necessity of having, or defending, a philosophy. As a practical matter, everyone seems to accept without discussion the crude assumption that government should solve whatever is presented as a political problem or redress whatever is asserted as a grievance. The result is an ever-growing accretion of State programs, enterprises, institutions, bureaucracies. These are usually failures or waste of money on their own terms, but since there are no firm criteria for success or failure except a literal-minded common sense that has no political purchase, it hardly matters; once established, they operate autonomously, their subsidization assured.

After all, Lyndon Johnson promised that the War on Poverty would attack the "root causes" of crime, as well as abolish poverty itself; he pledged that the programs would be dismantled if they didn't achieve these ends. Poverty (variously defined) is still with us, and the crime rate is higher than ever; but nobody in politics proposes to do away with the programs, least of all Secretary Kemp.

Conservatives now do little more than add to the confusion of the current scene. They have given up on the kind of thorough reform they thought was at hand in 1980; they have ceased posing a threat to the status quo of pragmatic interventionist liberalism. Something vital has gone out of the movement, something to which it owed all its original energy and appeal.

People have debated the meaning of conservatism for more than a century, but in the American political context, I think it should be defined fairly simply: it's an attachment to a classic Western understanding of the rule of law. It understands the role of the state to be that of umpire, custodian, and enforcer of some rather minimal rules of conduct, designed to allow citizens to pursue their own private purposes without coercion or violence or fraud.

In the *Politics*, Aristotle explains the character of law well. He recommends that there be as few laws as possible, and that they be altered as seldom as possible. The reason for this is that law should be an extension of our normal sense of right and wrong, so that people can observe it, for the most part, simply by living what they regard as morally upright lives. Law should seem to be impersonal, applying equally to all, rather than the expression of any special or partisan will or interest. The less frequently it changes and the more permanence it has, the more citizens will feel reverence for it.

When Jefferson says "that government is best which governs least," he is saying something similar. He means not that the ideal would be no government at all, but that the law should be so much in accordance with the spontaneous behavior of decent people, so harmonious with the community's moral consensus, that it requires a minimum of surveillance and enforcement. He would probably see the development of an entire "underground economy" as a sign that the state had grown far too powerful. A tax system in which cheating has become endemic among people who would never think of stealing from their neighbors is a sign of a state that takes far more from citizens than they instinctively feel to be fair.

The word "law" has become indiscriminately applied to two fundamentally different, incompatible, and even opposite sorts of things, which have in common only the fact that they may be imposed by the apparatus of the state. One is the genuine rule of conduct, usually negative ("Thou shalt not steal"), which limits rather than specifies behavior, and which requires people to behave as they might ideally behave anyway out of simple respect for their fellows. The other is the command, which is the imposition of the will of some upon others. ("And the King said, Bring me a sword.")

C. S. Lewis notes that the decline of the idea of natural law, an eternal order of right and wrong to which positive law should conform, gave rise in early modernity to the idea that the source of law is the will, whether the king's or the people's. By now we have come to take it for granted that this is not only natural but inevitable. The concept of a law that transcends will has been lost, though it lurks in our moral habits, and we act as if it were perfectly proper, in a democracy, for the majority to impose its will on the minority. There should be limits, of course: we somewhat incoherently reserve little pockets of "minority rights," without explaining to ourselves how these can fit in with the principle that the state is entitled to legislate as it pleases, and ought to be (in Lewis's phrase) "incessantly engaged in legislation."

Conservative and libertarian thinkers are converging on a common insight in this area. Both Michael

Oakeshott and F. A. Hayek have distinguished sharply between "nomocracy," or government according to impartial rules, and "teleocracy," or government intended to achieve some substantive purpose of the state itself. Both feel that nomocracy is the true Western tradition, and that this tradition of rule has been unfortunately confused by recent ideologies that can only understand governing as the pursuit of substantive goals, e.g., "social justice." Teleocracy, by its nature, demands that the individual subordinate his will and purposes to the state's. Under Communism, the individual may be directly conscripted into the state's enterprises. Modern democracies are less monolithic, combining a residue of nomocracy with various elements of teleocracy; taxation pays for both the services all receive (e.g., police protection) and for the appeasement of special interests through the redistribution of wealth.

Conservatives and libertarians have been widely dismissed by intellectuals as "reactionaries" defending what are essentially lost causes. On this view, history has passed them by. And those who felt that the Reagan era was their last chance are implicitly accepting this view. But if Oakeshott, Hayek, and Mises are right, the current despair of conservatives is groundless.

Reagan's election in itself was a symptom of enormous popular discontent with the present system. So are the underground economy and tax cheating; many other examples might be cited. Even the special interests that compete for our wealth have to use various moral and political subterfuges to justify what Frederic Bastiat calls "organized plunder": they don't dare to assert simply that their fellow citizens have a duty to support them, but are forced to claim "need" and "victimhood," implying that their demands are justified exceptions rather than direct rights to others' wealth. A moral stigma is still attached to the idea of "welfare" and to the very concept of "special interests." There is a widespread, probably ineradicable suspicion that special claims on the state's favor are subversive of genuine equality before the law, no matter how such claims are advanced in the name of equality.

The multiplication of special laws, lacking the character of genuine law, has done nothing to improve the lot of the average American citizen. The net effect, in fact, has somehow been to leave him more exposed to criminal violence than ever. Anyone who is not receiving subventions from the federal government is now likely to be deeply suspicious of all its works and pomps. It was this skepticism that Reagan so effectively exploited.

That skepticism deserves to be more seriously exploited. At bottom it is Western man's deep-seated resistance to teleocracy, to any state that pushes him around in the name of any cause, however high-sounding its pretensions.

Modern politics, in its corrupted versions, is a series of devices for obscuring lines of economic, moral, and even sexual responsibility. By directing its concern to alleged victims, while multiplying the categories of victimhood, it increases the number of its dependents and turns the productive into virtual defendants before the tax police. By depriving the earner of his reward, it destroys the ratio between act and consequence and renders constructive action futile and irrational. It systematically undermines not only property ownership but family relations. By pandering to man as victim of circumstance, it makes itself the enemy of man as responsible agent. And by the same token, its chief enemy is not the violent criminal, who after all poses no threat to the redistributive system, but the citizen who wants to keep his own money.

In the current political vocabulary, "need" means wanting to get someone else's money. "Greed," which used to mean what "need" now means, has come to mean wanting to keep your own. "Compassion" means the politician's willingness to arrange the transfer.

If they could leave off the specialized commitments they burdened themselves with during the Reagan years, conservatives could address the clashing principles at stake in every new statist initiative. They might find, to their surprise, that when the issues are properly defined, they belong not to a reactionary minority but to the abiding mainstream of the West. And millions of Americans who feel vaguely oppressed by their own political system, but are not burning with enthusiasm to aid the Nicaraguan contras or install an anti-missile system, might discover that their discontents, far from being idiosyncratic, stem from the irrepressible desire to live as free human beings.

Why Government Grows
Llewellyn H. Rockwell

In the 1980s, political rhetoric helped hide a government that—far from getting off our backs and out of our wallets—is more oppressive and expensive than ever. Republicans or Democrats, conservatives or liberals, there seems to be no end to federal taxing, spending, borrowing, inflating, and intruding. None of this is fore-ordained, of course, no matter how much the politicians might want us to think so; only in understanding the reasons for government growth, do we have a chance of reversing it.

1. *Interest groups*. There are two ways of earning a living: voluntarily through the market process and coercively through the political process. Special interests that prefer the latter method cluster around Washington like flies around a garbage can. These muggers in three-piece suits raid the Treasury and manipulate the government's regulatory apparatus to their own benefit. The politicians, with a very occasional exception, are happy to be their partners in return for power and money.

The most successful special interests have (1) a focused purpose and a coherent strategy; (2) a willingness to devote a lot of money to their efforts; (3) a heavy dependency on government intervention, where a slight change in regulations or subsidies can mean success or bankruptcy; (4) large and obvious benefits from the government, while the cost is hidden and spread throughout the economy; and (5) the ability to cover their depredations with a pretended concern for the general welfare.

Welfare spending, for example, doubled since 1980 in the name of helping the poor. But the cash flows to the interest groups that can bribe and lobby, not to the poor, who receive barely 8% of the total. The real money goes to poverty lawyers, consultants, public housing contractors, Medicaid doctors, hospitals, and other special interests, plus the bureaucrats themselves. The poor are intentionally turned into an enduring underclass, dependent on government, so that others may live well at the expense of the rest of us. Thanks to the welfare state, there is virtually no social mobility from the bottom. As Walter Williams notes, the bottom rungs of the ladder have been cut off—in the name of compassion.

2. *Permanency*. Thomas Jefferson wanted the entire government turned out of office at every election, to prevent individuals from entrenching themselves. Yet thanks to "civil service," most government officials have become permanent. And most politicians are permanent too, with 98% percent of House incumbents reelected every two years. Congressional staffs are also permanent, drawn from a pool of present and former Capitol Hill aides. As Jefferson feared, this has meant that these people get better and better at looting us.

3. *Bureaucracy*. Bureaucracy is necessarily inefficient because it doesn't operate on the basis of profit and loss. Without the pressure to economize resources, even well-intended bureaucrats typically overspend. And, of course, most bureaucrats are not well-intentioned. They are motivated only by increased power, income, and perks, which they get by increasing the number of bureaucrats under them on the all-important organization chart, and by spending every dime they're allotted. If they underspend, their budget can be cut. So the checking accounts are emptied in a spending frenzy at the end of every fiscal year, and then the agency—with the help of its affiliated special interest groups, on whom the budget is spent—appeals to the White House and Congress for more money. The president and Congress, who are also in hock to the special

interests themselves, then budget an increase for this important public service that was underfunded in the previous year.

4. *Crisis*. Government has grown fastest in this century during war and depression. A crisis is the perfect excuse for more power and money to "solve" the problem, while it paralyzes the opposition. One recent example is the stock market crash of 1987, which allowed the SEC to grab more power over the markets, and fueled the trend toward a European Central Bank and an eventual World Central Bank. Professor Robert Higgs, in his great book *Crisis and Leviathan*, shows that the public always loses, since it is saddled with a bigger government after the emergency is over.

5. *The Media*. We're taught that the big media are antagonistic to the government—a useful myth for both. In fact, they are allies on all bedrock issues. To take just one area, the media encourage government growth by parroting the government economic line. Whether it's the latest obfuscation from the Federal Reserve or White House claims about cutting the budget, the media are an echo chamber.

Government, as the dominant institution in our society, uses the media to define the proper bounds of opinion, bolstered by the special interests that control so much of the media's advertising. Nothing would be better for America, or worse for Washington, D.C., than the undermining and eventual abolition of the Federal Reserve and the income tax. But such Jeffersonian ideas are branded as extremist and therefore unworthy of consideration, thanks to the government-media-special interest combine.

6. *Interventionism.* The free-market economy is an intricate and carefully balanced network of prices and exchange relationships. When government intervenes to fix a real or alleged problem, it upsets this balance, causing even more problems, which in turn give an excuse for more intervention. Ludwig von Mises called this the "logic of interventionism"; it's why a mixed economy is so unstable. An interventionist system will always be moving in one direction or the other—towards socialism/fascism or towards liberty.

7. *Ideas.* A final reason for government growth is the lack of free-market understanding. Colleges and universities are dominated by leftists and other interventionists. Economics texts are improving, but they still preach that intervention is necessary. The public is often ignorant of the harm caused by government.

These are just some of the reasons government continues to grow. How do we counter it?

First, we should expose all government crimes, ripping away the cloak of lies hiding the real intentions of the special interests. Next time you hear someone call for more welfare spending, point out that welfare has destroyed the poor, while making the real welfare recipients—the special interests—rich at our expense through the gun of government. Real charity can only be private, as anyone who has ever dealt with church workers as versus government social workers knows.

Second, we should work for radical changes—for *abolishing* programs and bureaucracies, and not merely for ameliorating them (although we'll take that too). If our side starts out compromising, we have even less chance of marginal improvements, while tacitly agreeing to the whole system, and to its moral (or rather, immoral) underpinnings of theft and fraud.

Third, we should ourselves refuse to believe government propaganda and undermine it with others, supporting alternative sources of news and information.

Fourth, we should seek to place free-market professors and students in the institutions of higher learning, and try to mobilize the people through appeals to justice as well as economic efficiency. There is nothing like the realization that you are being ripped off as a goad to action.

Theft is immoral, whether private or public. In spreading the ideas of the free market and sound money, and denouncing and working against the criminals, we have our only chance to succeed. The obstacles are, of course, immense. But we have a world to win.

Our Tentative Economic Freedoms

Llewellyn H. Rockwell

Despite the vast U.S. government intervention into our economy, which Ludwig von Mises called "a method of bringing about socialism by successive measures," we are still relatively free. But this sort of system, as Mises also noted, is inherently unstable. It must always be moving either towards or away from omnipotent government. And the bipartisan ease with which U.S. government spending and regulating keep growing demonstrates where we're moving, and why our remaining freedoms have an uncertain future.

As the Founders of our country knew, freedom can only be securely grounded on inalienable rights. At the very least, a free economy means the right to liberty and property—not as contingent or subject to government-defined duties or responsibilities—but as absolute. But since these rights are no longer secure in America, our economic freedom is tentative, subject to revocation at government caprice.

The institution of private property has been most subverted, beginning with the income-tax amendment of 1913, which contains no legal barrier to the government's confiscating all American income. Only public opinion stands in the way.

The great libertarian Frank Chodorov called the income-tax amendment the "Revolution of 1913" that undid the "Revolution of 1789." Said Chodorov: "No measure in the history of our country has caused a comparable disregard of principle in public affairs." And indeed the amendment undermines our property rights, as does the power of local governments to seize homes, businesses, and farms for non-payment of property taxes.

Another culprit is the Federal Reserve System and its legal monopoly on counterfeiting. The Fed is empowered to inflate without limit, since the courts ignore the monetary clauses of the Constitution. When the Fed uses its inflationary power, it engages in mass thievery, which weakens private property and economic freedom. As Henry Hazlitt notes, "Inflation is an immoral act on the part of government."

Yet despite its immorality, the Fed enjoys prestige and economic legitimacy. Thanks to decades of disinformation, most people believe that central banking is a barrier to inflation. Of course, as Hazlitt says, despite government's attempt to portray inflation as "some evil visitation from without," it is "the result of deliberate government policy."

With the income tax and the Federal Reserve, the president and the Congress can seize enough of our money to finance socialized medicine, socialized day care, environmentalism, the drug war, or any other interventionist project.

So much for private property. But what about economic liberty?

In America, no private enterprise is free from bureaucratic coercion. To a shocking extent, our regulatory masters exercise unchecked and autonomous power. Under existing law, no industry is safe from nationalization by presidential edict. No piece of land is immune from the government's power of eminent domain. The drug war and RICO have institutionalized the government's power to seize any property it deems ill-gotten, not only before conviction in a court of law but even before an indictment. Our right to work is merely contingent, subject to revocation by the legislature and the courts.

Under this system, said Albert Jay Nock, "The individual has no rights that the State is bound to respect; no rights at all, in fact, except those which the State may choose to give him, subject to revocation at its own pleasure, with or without notice. There is no such thing as natural rights; the fundamental doctrine of the American Declaration of Independence, the doctrine underlying the Bill of Rights, is all moonshine."

Moreover, the government immunizes itself from responsibility for its failures. For example, the Great Society—and its counterparts in the Nixon, Carter, Reagan, and Kinder-Gentler administrations—have created and sustained an urban underclass. In the name of helping that underclass, the government has destroyed the core values, families, and communities of two generations. The result, after piles of money spent on government and its friends to "fight poverty," is a holocaust of no-go zones where drugs, child abuse, prostitution, and illegitimacy are the norm; government schools promote immorality; entrepreneurship is outlawed; and brute criminals run free.

But no one blames the bureaucrats. "Since the State creates all rights," said Nock, "and since the only valid and authoritative ethics are State ethics, then by obvious inference the State can do no wrong."

Despite the Constitution and the Declaration of Independence, let alone the traditions of Western civilization, the state does indeed view itself as the source of rights, only to be dribbled out if its subjects fulfill their alleged duties or responsibilities to society (by which is almost always meant the government). We have all been indoctrinated to accept this view, at least since Woodrow Wilson and the "Progressive" Era.

The correct view was stated by the great conservative libertarian Frank S. Meyer, co-founder of *National Review*: the rights of human beings "are not the gift of some Leviathan" and the duties of human beings are not "tribute owed to Leviathan."

Only when the absolute rights of liberty and property are again recognized will our economic freedom be secure.

That is why our energies must be focused not only on teaching economic truth, but also on fighting what Meyer called "the great enemy of our time, the Leviathan state."

The Great Society and 25 Years of Decline
William Murchison

F ailures of Soviet and Chinese communism are writ large in the eastern sky—and on the covers of the big news magazines. No serious political figure would today stand up for central planning. He would be hooted down.

All this being so, why can't Americans own up to the failures of their own in the public policy sphere? Why can't we even talk about these failures?

The 25th anniversary of Lyndon Johnson's Great Society comes round. The magnitude of the occasion seems not to have sunk in: still less the frustrations, vexation, overheated hopes, and downright dangerous trends set off by a presidential speech that should live in infamy.

Said Lyndon Johnson to the graduating class of the University of Michigan, Ann Arbor, May 22, 1964: "For you in your time we have the opportunity to move not only toward the rich society and the powerful society, but upward to the Great Society."

The Great Society raised democratic social engineering to its apogee. The New Deal, in which LBJ had participated as a young bureaucrat and, later, as a Democratic congressman, was a politically inspired scheme to redistribute wealth; the Great Society seemingly set out to change humanity. The intention bore fruit. The Great Society helped make Americans unhappier, less self-reliant, less moral, less connected to things permanent—even, in many cases, less prosperous, though this was the direct reverse of what the reformers had said they wanted.

Government was going to do everything. It would wipe out poverty; it would equalize opportunity; it would enrich the mind and the heart. Broadly speaking, government was going to make people satisfied, fulfilled, and happy. "The pursuit of happiness," a phrase from the Declaration of Independence, became under Johnson's prodigious prodding, an American entitlement.

It did not end as planned. The Great Society enjoyed two efflorescent years, 1964 and 1965, during which Congress passed the Economic Opportunity Act (War on Poverty), the Civil Rights Act, the Voting Rights Act, Medicare, Medicaid, the Appalachian Regional Development Act, the Elementary and Secondary Education Act, the Higher Education Act, and the legislation creating the National Foundation for the Arts and Humanities. What happened afterward to the Great Society is in some degree less interesting than what didn't happen to public perceptions of it. The Great Society fell flat. Education declined instead of advancing; racial tensions rose instead of falling. The welfare culture of the '60s created a whole new stratum of government dependents—the "underclass," unmotivated, uneducated, ridden with AIDS and cocaine. Intact black families, as Charles Murray's ground-breaking work has shown, sundered and shriveled, especially as moral forces. Yet the conventional wisdom still commends the Great Society for its idealism.

"Most of these things, most of these programs," says Sargent Shriver, who once generaled the War on Poverty, "are a part of our lives today." As are the 6,000 pages of federal rules and regulations governing welfare; as are 59 major poverty programs, with a 1985 cost of $132 billion, compared with $21 billion for all poverty programs in 1960. Poverty likewise still is with us.

What is the matter, that the Great Society's failures go widely unrecognized and unremarked, even while failed central planners in the communist bloc cringe from the spotlight?

The reason is the vested interest of the intelligentsia, special interests, and bureaucracy in seeing the Great Society perpetuated. The jobs it dispenses, the prerequisites it affords, are many and lucrative. Washington, until the coming of the New Deal, was a cozy Southern community which slumbered much of the year. The Great Society, by enlarging the bureaucracy and beefing up its functions, made Washington, D.C., yet more central to the nation's concerns. The first $100 billion budget, offered by Lyndon Johnson (with some creative arithmetic to hide its real dimensions), has increased more than twelvefold.

There is yet a second reason the Great Society does not take its fair share of lumps. It may be the most powerful; it is undeniably the saddest. We actually are not supposed to mention it in polite society, but I will take the chance anyway.

The Great Society achieves its real invulnerability from the perception that attacks upon it are racially motivated. Lyndon Johnson sought, so he said, to raise blacks from dependence and poverty to independence and affluence. The programs he persuaded Congress to pass could not have been better calculated to achieve the opposite. But a conspiracy of silence enshrouds this depressing datum. In effect we are invited not to judge programs by their consequences but by their intentions.

Charles Murray, in *Losing Ground*, writes that "social policy after the mid-1960s demanded an extraordinary range of transfers from the most capable poor to the least capable, from the most law-abiding to the least law-abiding, and from the most responsible to the least responsible." The consequence among the intended beneficiaries was a sharp rise in illegitimacy, drug use, and general dependence.

A fully credentialed liberal like Bill Moyers can occasionally mention these matters on television, provided he consents not to dwell on them at unseemly length. However, no such mention can occur in the context of an attack on the ideological foundations of the Great Society, because As Is Well Known (to self-styled spokesmen for minorities), people who advocate less government are indifferent to the poor and downtrodden.

It is chiseled in the minds of these "spokesmen" that government, not the free marketplace, can best address and solve the problem of submerged minorities, racial or otherwise. Whoever wants less government is no friend of the poor—and let's *don't*, contrary to Al Smith, look at the record, because that would overthrow the whole argument. It would establish that poor people prosper most where the market is free and choices open; and that the Great Society, far from increasing economic opportunities, has foreclosed them for many who would otherwise have enjoyed them.

What hope, then? Are we to go on noting the failure of collectivism abroad but ignoring its baneful effects at home? All we can do is keep talking. Ludwig von Mises knew "the fulsome praise of the stationary economy" to be "the last remaining argument" of the statists. Today, such fulsome praise embarrasses even communists.

Facts are impossible to disguise after a period of time, which is why Comrade Gorbachev, far from lying about his country's condition, openly laments it.

No fact bulks larger in American life than that the Great Society has not been built here; that the attempt to build it has sapped energies and incomes and impaired the well-being of almost the whole of society. We will persist in pointing to that fact. It should not be long before somebody notices.

Civil Rights and the Politics of Theft

Joseph Sobran

Proudhon's famous maxim, "Property is theft," seems to be the implicit credo of today's politicians, for whom taking others' property is always justifiable as a form of restitution. No specifiable act of theft has to be proved. It's enough that some are "haves" and others are "have-nots." That crude division places generic guilt, the presumption of tainted gain, on one side, and the presumption of both innocence and compelling need on the other. Let's have no prattle of production, earning, ownership: such terms are masks for privilege. The state's role is to shift possession from where it is to where it is not, with no apparent limit.

Consider the evolution—the dissolution, really—of the concept of "civil rights." Once it meant the rights of the citizen against the state. Now it means a confused bundle of things that hardly leaves room for the former signification. The current meaning is in fact a near reversal of the old.

When you hear the phrase now, you immediately intuit several things never quite acknowledged by the partisans who invoke it. You know it means favored treatment for blacks (or some other minority) at the expense of everyone else. You know it means an increase in the scope of state power. You know it likewise means a diminution of private freedom, especially in the use of one's own property. You know it's likely to entail a forcible redistribution of wealth.

The first laws passed in the name of civil rights, right after the War Between the States, simply made former slaves full citizens, requiring the states to recognize and protect, among other things, their property rights. This legislation simplified older law, removing an anomaly. It abolished a privileged status for some along with the oppression of others. All in all, it was a civilized and civilizing refinement of what had been a grossly imperfect feature of our way of life. Later civil rights measures forbade states to assign some citizens to an inferior status.

All these things appealed strongly to the Western sense of elementary fairness. But because their actual purpose was to benefit blacks, the term "civil rights" has been retained for rhetorical purposes by those seeking favored treatment for blacks, *and* by those whose goal is the expansion of state power. So the term "means" blacks now, not by rational definition but by concrete association.

The truth is that every "civil rights measure" advanced since about 1964 has meant an actual reduction in civil rights (including the civil rights of blacks) in the old sense of the term. Whites, who gain nothing and lose much by these measures, sense this more keenly than blacks, who stand to gain materially by the new measures. But it's hopeless to say so, because of the prevalence of usage and the confusion it has bred. Anyone who opposes the new state-sponsored privileges stands to be accused of being "against" civil rights.

Gone are the days when liberals spoke hopefully of a "color-blind society," to be ushered in by civil rights acts. The tendentious twisting of civil rights rhetoric has made us a color-*obsessed* society. The only rule of the game is that no claim made in the name of civil rights is to be denied. We've long since forgotten the assurances of liberals like Senator Hubert Humphrey that the new civil rights laws would equally forbid discrimination against whites. Anti-white discrimination is what "civil rights" has come to signify. "Racial justice" means group claims, never mind what these do to more basic considerations of individual justice.

Consider "affirmative action," which in practice amounts to compulsory discrimination in the name of civil rights. (Liberalism has only banned *voluntary* discrimination.) The argument for it is that it's an attempt to right a historical wrong. We aren't given a clue as to when the wrong will finally be righted, any more than we are told when the redistribution of wealth will finally achieve "fairness." All we know is that the state has crudely awarded all blacks, as such, "accredited victim status" (we owe this fine formula to John Murray Cuddihy). In any contest of claims, the black enjoys automatic preference over the white. The burden of proof in discrimination cases has shifted from the prosecutor to the defendant, who has to establish his own good motives.

Categories of accredited victimhood have also expanded to embrace other racial minorities, all women, handicapped people, and in some cases homosexuals. This is the short list, but it's enough to suggest that an organized lobby helps in acquiring accreditation among the officially oppressed. You have to have a lot of clout to be a victim.

When an act is wrong, the normal legislative response is to outlaw it, not to redirect its evil. We prohibit murder; we don't stipulate that the descendants of murder victims may correct some abstract balance by killing the descendants of murderers, or those of the same general gene pool as murderers. Advocates of affirmative action imply by their position that they have no strong objection to racial discrimination as such. Their goal, is not justice but tribal revenge. Their campaign goes beyond ex post facto law, since it imposes penalties for actions, legal in their own time, on people who didn't commit them, and hadn't even been born when they were committed.

Liberals in Congress have recently acted to prevent the U.S. Civil Rights Commission from investigating police violence against anti-abortion protesters. This intervention shows that civil rights activists and their political patrons don't even want their own laws applied impartially. Those laws are intended to serve as the proprietary weapons of a certain lobby, and the use of those weapons to protect others the law would seem to apply to is to be blocked.

The case also shows that politicians don't see themselves as serving the general public, but a narrow clientele of special interests. But it wouldn't do to put it so baldly, so the clients who seek privileged status can only do so by claiming a victim status that makes the bid for power appear as a mere plea for equality.

Such client groups are likely to be far better informed about a congressman's doings than his own constituency, and they may provide him with generous support from outside his district, support which, combined with all the advantages of incumbency, many give him overwhelming strength at election time against any challenger, who would have a hard enough time winning if the race were conducted entirely within the district itself.

Politics is big business now, and a smart politician quickly learns which "victims" are worth cultivating. In the House of Representatives, incumbents are re-elected at a rate of about 98%. The pursuit of liberal causes also gives a Congressman moral immunity from hostile scrutiny by the press and electronic media, which see nothing amiss in special favors for accredited victimhood.

The politics of victimhood is only a new guise for the perennial politics of favoritism, with which it meshes conveniently. A number of liberal Congressman have turned up among those who were abetting the use of funds from the Department of Housing and Urban Development to feather some posh private nests. The two leading Democrats in the House, liberals both, have been forced to resign because of their unseemly closeness to Wall Street and the savings and loan industry.

Even the cynical observer of Congress may be surprised at how easily the sweeping powers of the humanitarian state may be diverted to the rescue of the needy banker. But compassion knows no bounds, not when it's funded with other people's money and armed with a mandate to spot-weld all the ills of society.

The power to tax and spend has no limit. All it needs is a respectable cover. This is what humanitarian rhetoric provides. "Civil rights" has created a bloc of interests that can be augmented indefinitely. By helping destroy constitutional and other principled limits on government action, it serves as an opening wedge for the formless, limitless power we know too well. Politics, you might say, is theft.

Triumph of Liberty? Not in the U.S.
Robert Higgs

I f you have been spending your time in certain circles—among libertarians, classical liberals, or other pro-market people—you may well believe that the tide of history has turned in the United States decisively in favor of the free market and the social and political institutions that sustain such an economic order.

Many pro-market observers have exulted over the so-called Reagan Revolution. During the past decade, they believe, deregulation has swept away many of the governmental controls built up over the previous century. In their enthusiasm for the removal of regulatory fetters, supporters of the free market have tended to exaggerate what has actually been accomplished, and they have failed to notice that the political momentum for further deregulation evaporated years ago.

During the past decade, deregulation has been significant but far from revolutionary. Important deregulatory changes have occurred in only a few sectors, mainly transportation, communication, energy, and certain financial services. At the same time—and receiving far less notice—increased regulation or governmental manipulation of markets has occurred in other areas, including agriculture, international trade and finance, health care, the environment, safety, defense, and aerospace.

Moreover, one must take account of the enormous taxpayer-financed bailouts of the failing farm credit system and the bankrupt savings and loan institutions—bailouts that many eventually cost hundreds of billions. William Niskanen, a member of the Council of Economic Advisers in the early 1980s, recently concluded that "the net amount of regulations and trade restraints has increased" since 1980.

Paul Weaver has observed that the most one could say for Reagan is that "he kept the nation from reverting to liberalism." I disagree. He could not keep the country from reverting to liberalism because in fact it had never departed from the liberalism that has characterized the political economy of the United States since the New Deal.

As a check, one can secure an organization chart of the federal government for, say, 1979 and a corresponding chart for 1989. Comparing the two, can one see any evidence that the government's scope has been diminished? The Civil Aeronautics Board has disappeared, but the Department of Veterans Affairs has appeared. Bad test? Too simple? Then peruse the *Federal Register* for recent years to see whether the government has taken itself off someone's back.

But surely the vaunted tax cuts signify a blow against big government? No. There has been no tax cut, properly speaking. The best simple measure of the nation's tax rate is the proportion of the national product commanded by government spending. Total government expenditures for final goods and services (transfer payments are *not* included in this total) relative to gross national product averaged 29.9% for 1970-79 and 31.8% for 1980-88; the federal spending portion alone rose from 20.5 to 23.2% of GNP. No shrinking government here. Nor will any shrinkage be found when one examines the mushrooming totals from federal direct loan obligation or guaranteed loan commitments.

But even if the so-called Reagan Revolution stands revealed as almost entirely bogus, has there not been a dramatic shift of public opinion in favor of the market and against governmental intervention? James Buchanan recently observed that "the collectivist urge has surely lost some of its motive force." I agree with Buchanan that "the grounds of debate in the academy and even in journalistic circles have shifted," but again one must be careful not to exaggerate the changes that have taken place, even within the intelligentsia.

Liberals continue to dominate the establishments of journalism, academia, civic institutions, and politics. The *New York Times* recently reported that President Bush "faces growing Congressional and public pressure to revitalize the Federal regulatory machinery," and many members of Congress "are now poised to push for new controls." Almost simultaneously, the *Wall Street Journal* discerned the "government's role may soon grow again" because of renewed pressures for intervention in financial markets and the airline and trucking industries as well as for more vigorous antitrust measures and restraints on international trade. The Bush administration seems to have little interest in pushing strongly for additional deregulation and in some areas, such as the environment, favors even greater regulation.

Whatever may be the prevailing opinion among elites, there is little doubt that the general public continues to give strong support to a plethora of statist policies. In 1985, on the heels of President Reagan's reelection landslide, for example, 46% of those polled in a national survey either favored or expressed indifference toward "control of wages by legislation"; similarly, 59% for "control of prices by legislation"; similarly, 85% for "government financing of projects to create new jobs"; similarly, 90% for "support for industry to develop new products and technology"; similarly, 75% for "support for declining industries to protect jobs."

Proportions ranging from 36% to 65% agreed that government should either own or control the prices and profits of the following industries: electric power, local mass transportation, steel, banking and insurance, and automobiles. At least 95% agreed that government has either some important, or essential responsibility for "looking after old people," "seeing to it that everyone who wants a job can have one," "providing good medical care," and "providing adequate housing." At least 73% wished to see government spend more or at least the same amount now being spent on the environment, health, education, retirement benefits, and unemployment benefits; 54% wanted the same or greater government spending for culture and arts; 72% of those polled agreed that taxes on business and industry are either about right or too low. (All data from *Public Opinion Quarterly*, Fall 1987).

We may all devoutly hope that these data are inaccurate measures of true public opinion, but they are consistent with the data obtained by many other such surveys. If these are the opinions of a nation that has turned away from collectivism, then I am undoubtedly the King of Albania.

In sum? We now live, as we have lived for over 50 years, in a nation deeply committed, in practice and in preference, to statist institutions.

Increasingly, during the past couple of decades, supporters of individual liberty and a free economy have emerged from the obscurity and intellectual contempt that had shadowed them for most of the 20th century, especially during the modern Dark Age from the early 1930s into the 1970s.

But let us not live in a fool's paradise. In promoting the ideals and practices of a free society, the bulk of our work remains still to be done.

The Federal Agriculture Swamp

James Bovard

A merican agricultural policy offers many instructive lessons on how to cripple a major sector of the economy. For 60 years, the U.S. government has waged a war against the market. And for 60 years, American taxpayers and consumers have been the biggest losers.

Farm subsidies—roughly $20 billion a year in federal handouts and $10 billion more in higher food prices—are the equivalent of giving every full-time farmer two new Mercedes each year. Annual subsidies for each dairy cow in the United States exceed the per capita income of half the population of the world. With the $260 billion that government and consumers have spent on farm subsidies since 1980, the government could have bought every farm, barn, and tractor in 33 states. The average American head of household worked almost one week a year in 1986 and 1987 simply to pay for welfare for fewer than a million farmers.

The fundamental tool of agricultural policy is the price support. The government sets a price per bushel or pound it will pay for a commodity. Since the government guarantees to buy unlimited quantities of a crop at the price support level, farmers will not sell the crop on the market at a price lower than they can sell to the government, and the support price thereby becomes the minimum price for any sales of the crop in the United States.

These programs lead the government to pay farmers more than market value for their crops. Farmers respond by producing surpluses, which Congress then creates other programs to dump, distribute, or repress. This is American agricultural policy in a nutshell.

Federal farm policy is a maze of contradictions. By late 1985, the U.S. wheat surplus was large enough to provide 27 loaves of bread to every person in the world. Yet, in the 1985 five-year farm bill, Congress encouraged farmers to produce even larger wheat surpluses by promising farmers crop subsidies far higher than market prices. At the same time the U.S. Department of Agriculture

(USDA) paid farmers in 1986-87 to kill almost two million cows to reduce milk supplies, Congress lavishly rewarded other farmers for producing more surplus milk. The result: no decrease in milk production and continued government purchases of over five billion pounds of surplus milk a year.

"Prosperity through organized scarcity" is the core of American farm policy. In 1933, USDA began a temporary emergency program of paying farmers to slash production in order to balance production. In 33 of the last 35 years, the government has paid farmers not to work. In 1988, USDA rewarded farmers for not planting on 78 million acres of farmland—equivalent to the entire states of Indiana, Ohio, and much of Illinois. Government shut down some of the best American farmland in an effort to drive up world wheat and corn prices. Set-asides—programs to pay farmers not to work by "setting aside" or idling their cropland—are the opium of American farm policymakers, the annual tribute to the bureaucratic and political delusion that America somehow controls world grain markets.

Supply controls are introduced only after politicians and bureaucrats have mismanaged price controls. Government first artificially raises the price and then artificially restricts production. The higher Congress drives up the price, the greater the need for government controls on the amount produced.

USDA marketing orders annually force farmers to abandon or squander roughly 50 million lemons, one billion oranges, 100 million pounds of raisins, 70 million pounds of almonds, 7 million pounds of filberts, millions of plums and nectarines, etc. USDA announces each season how much of certain fruits and nuts will be allowed to be sold and how much must be held off the market in order to boost prices. USDA endows cooperatives with the power to effectively outlaw competition and to force farmers to let much of their crop rot or be fed to animals. To preserve federal control of the lemon business, USDA effectively bans new technology that would boost fruit sales and benefit both growers and consumers.

Congress responded to the agricultural recession of the early 1980s with a flood of subsidized capital. In 1985 alone, the government loaned almost a billion dollars to farmers who were already technically bankrupt. The injection of capital into agriculture has aggravated the problem of surplus production and driven up rental costs and land values in many areas. When the government announced a major debt forgiveness program in 1988, there was a fierce backlash from unsubsidized farmers.

Robert A. Dreyep, a farmer in Fenton, Iowa, complained that the government was "rewarding the poor managers who are also very inefficient farmers." Jerome Berg, another Iowa farmer, complained, "Many of those with debt write-downs are again buying more land and expensive equipment, cars, trucks, and living it up while the rest of us who paid our bills and lived within our means are now expected to help bail them out." The General Accounting Office reported in late 1988 that the Farmers' Home Administration, the agricultural credit agency, has lost $33 billion.

The federal government attempts to hide some of the damage with lavish export subsidies. In 1986, it paid four times the world price to dump sugar and rice on the world market, and three times the world price to dump butter. In 1987, the U.S. paid export subsidies equal to 150% of the cow's value in order to dump American dairy cows on world markets. It would have been cheaper simply to shove the cows off the Brooklyn Bridge. The government paid farmers $4.35 a bushel for wheat in 1986 that was sold to the Soviets for less than $2 a bushel. In 1988, the U.S. provided almost a billion dollars in credit to Iraq, thereby making American taxpayers underwrite the Iraqi war machine.

Farm program costs routinely far exceed the farmers' entire profits. For 1986 the wheat program and wheat export subsidies cost $4 billion; wheat producers' total net cash income was only $2 billion. In 1986, the rice program cost taxpayers $2.7 billion while rice producers received only $236 million in income; the cotton program cost $2.1 billion while cotton producers net cash income was only $1.3 billion. The wool program cost taxpayers $99 million while sheep producers realized only $13 million in profits from their operations.

The clearest effect of the USDA in the 1980s is to decrease the productivity of American agriculture. USDA does not reward farmers for improving their efficiency but for playing by the government's rules. Every farm bailout has discouraged farmers from maximizing their productivity and efficiency. Costs of production always tend to rise to the government guaranteed price, thereby making American agriculture appear less competitive internationally than it otherwise would be. And politicians respond with more subsidies and protective barriers.

The history of modern agricultural policy, both in the United States and elsewhere, is largely the history of a political struggle against changes in relative prices. Wheat, corn, oat, and cotton prices have been gradually declining in real terms for over 200 years, and have nosedived in comparison to units of labor required to purchase them. Prices have declined largely because of the invention of tractors, new seed varieties, powerful fertilizers, etc. Yet politicians perennially proclaim that because wheat prices are lower now than they were 10, 20, or 30 years ago, this proves that society is treating farmers unfairly and that farmers deserve recompense. Each decade, as prices trend downwards, politicians and farm lobbyists have warned that farm production is no longer profitable and that society will soon have a severe food shortage unless immediate action is taken to raise prices. Yet, in every decade farmers have produced more.

The key to understanding American agricultural policy is to realize that the vast majority of the 400 farm products produced in America receive no federal handouts. There is no fundamental difference between subsidized and unsubsidized crops—only a difference in campaign contributions to congressmen by different farm lobbies. (Not that congressmen are the only problem. President Reagan went from preaching about the "miracle of the marketplace" in 1981 to bragging in 1986 that his administration had given more handouts to farmers than any in history.)

The only solution to the "farm problem" is to abolish federal farm programs. It is a crime for government to provide any handout to any businessmen, and for politicians to molest the economy for their own personal profit.

Government Garbage

Llewellyn H. Rockwell

I n the loony leftist town where I live, we're ordered to separate our trash into seven neatly packaged piles: newspapers, tin cans (flattened with labels removed), aluminum cans (flattened), glass bottles (with labels removed), plastic soda pop bottles, lawn sweepings, and regular rubbish. And to pay high taxes to have it all taken away.

Because of my aversion to government orders, my distrust of government justifications, and my dislike of ecomania, I have always mixed all my trash together. If recycling made economic sense—and this is an economic question, not a dogma of the mythical earth goddess Gaia—we would be paid to do it.

For the same reason, I love to use plastic fast-food containers and non-returnable bottles. The whole recycling commotion, like the broader environmental movement, has always smelled of buncombe. So I have never felt guilty—just the opposite—nor have I yet been arrested by the garbage gendarmes. But I was glad to get some scientific support for my position in the December 1989 issue of *The Atlantic Monthly*.

Professor William L. Rathje, an urban archaeologist at the University of Arizona and head of its Garbage Project, has been studying rubbish for almost 20 years, and what he's discovered contradicts almost everything we're told.

When seen in perspective, our garbage problems are no worse than they have always been. The only difference is that today we have safe methods to deal with them, if the environmentalists will let us.

The environmentalists warn of a country covered by garbage because the average American generates eight pounds a day. In fact, we create less than three pounds each, which is a good deal less than people in the Third World today or Americans 100 years ago. Gone, for example, are the 1,200 lbs. of coal ash each American home used to generate, and our modern packaged foods mean less rubbish, not more.

But most landfills will be full in ten years or less, we're told, and that's true. But most landfills are designed to last ten years. The problem is not that they are filling up, but that we're not allowed to create new ones, thanks to the environmental movement. Texas, for example, handed out 250 landfill permits a year in the mid-1970s, but fewer than 50 in 1988.

The environmentalists claim that disposable diapers and fast-food containers are the worst problems. To me, this has always revealed the anti-family and pro-elite biases common in any left-wing movement. But the left, as usual, has the facts wrong as well.

In two years of digging in seven landfills all across America, in which they sorted and weighed every item in 16,000 pounds of garbage, Rathje discovered that fast-food containers take up less than *1/10th of one percent* of the space; less than 1% was disposable diapers. All plastics totalled less than 5%. The real culprit is paper—especially telephone books and newspapers. And there is little biodegradation. He found 1952 newspapers still fresh and readable.

Rather than biodegrade, most garbage mummifies. And this may be a blessing. If newspapers, for example, degraded rapidly, tons of ink would leach into the groundwater. And we should be glad that plastic doesn't biodegrade. Being inert, it doesn't introduce toxic chemicals into the environment.

We're told we have a moral obligation to recycle, and most of us *say* we do so, but empirical studies show it isn't so. In surveys, 78% of the respondents say they separate their garbage, but only 26% said they thought their neighbors separated theirs. To test that, for seven years the Garbage Project examined 9,000 loads of refuse in Tucson, Arizona, from a variety of neighborhoods. The results: most people do what they say their neighbors do: they don't separate. No matter how high or low the income, or how liberal the neighborhood, or how much the respondents said they cared about the environment, only 26% actually separated their trash.

The only reliable predictor of when people separate and when they don't is exactly the one an economist would predict: the price paid for the trash. When the prices of old newspaper rose, people carefully separated their newspapers. When the price of newspapers fell, people threw them out with the other garbage.

We're all told to save our newspapers for recycling, and the idea seems to make sense. Old newspapers can be made into boxes, wallboard, and insulation, but the market is flooded with newsprint thanks to government programs. In New Jersey, for example, the price of used newspapers has plummeted from $40 a ton to *minus* $25 a ton. Trash entrepreneurs used to buy old newspaper. Now you have to pay someone to take it away.

If it is economically efficient to recycle—and we can't know that so long as government is involved—trash will have a market price. It is only through a free price system, as Ludwig von Mises demonstrated 70 years ago, that we can know the value of goods and services.

Environmentalists don't seem to understand this. They ask their adherents to ignore price signals and cut their consumption of everything from gasoline to paper towels. This one plank in the environmental platform I agree with, since it will make these goods cheaper for the rest of us. I'm happy to have my standard of living raised by voluntary poverty from what Ronald Reagan once called "the tree huggers."

Some liberal economists claim prices can't solve the garbage problem because of "external diseconomies." Since greedy capitalists are out to make a fast buck, the theory goes, they produce goods that impose costs external to their businesses, i.e., trash. But all businesses have spill-over effects, good and bad, and in a free market, this creates opportunities for other entrepreneurs. The donut industry may help make people fat (an external diseconomy). Should it be forced to sponsor Weight Watchers? Or, more to the point, should the public be taxed for a new federal Department of Corpulent Affairs?

The cave men had garbage problems, and so will our progeny, probably for as long as human civilization exists. But government is no answer. A socialized garbage system works no better than the Bulgarian economy. Only the free market will solve the garbage problem, and that means abolishing not only socialism, but the somewhat more efficient municipal fascist systems where one politically favored contractor gets the job.

The answer is to privatize and deregulate everything, from trash pickup to landfills. That way, everyone pays an appropriate part of the costs. Some types of trash we would have to pay to be taken away, others would be picked up free, and still others might command a price. Recycling would be based on economic calculation, not bureaucratic fiat.

The choice is always the same, from Eastern Europe to my town: put consumers in charge through private property and a free price system, or create a fiasco through government. Under the right kind of system, even I might start separating my trash.

Artistic "Entitlements"

Doug Bandow

The summer of 1989 was not the first time that public funds have been used to underwrite sacrilegious and pornographic art, but the outcry has been significantly louder than before. Nevertheless, the House rejected an attempt by California Rep. Dana Rohrabacher to kill the National Endowment for the Arts (NEA) and Texas Rep. Dick Armey's attempt to reduce the NEA's budget by 10%. Instead, the House agreed to cut $45,000, the amount granted to two exhibits that inflated public anger against the NEA.

The first exhibit is a photograph, entitled "Piss Christ," of a crucifix in a jar of urine, part of an Andres Serrano exhibit paid for by a $15,000 grant of which one-third came from the NEA. Had Serrano chosen to photograph a toy soldier submerged in urine one could still ask what Serrano had done to justify a $15,000 check, which comes to three-fourths of the average American's income. But his decision to show contempt for the religious views of millions of Americans raises an even more important issue: why should people be forced to pay for "art" that is intended to insult them? The NEA has been deluged with letters from congressmen as well as angry voters; the sponsor of the exhibition in which the Serrano picture appeared, the Equitable Life Assurance Society, has also been inundated with mail.

Serrano's photo, though blatantly offensive, at least can be shown in polite company. Gay photographer Robert Mapplethorpe's work, however, does not even meet this test.

The NEA gave Philadelphia's Institute of Contemporary Art $30,000 to organize a traveling exhibit of Mapplethorpe's photos, called "The Perfect Moment." Newspapers delicately described his work as "homoerotic" and "sadomasochistic," but that hardly conveys the full impact of some of Mapplethorpe's photos. There are, for instance, pictures of Mapplethorpe with a whip handle stuck in his anus, two women engaging in lesbian acts, a man in a suit with his penis exposed, and a man urinating into the mouth of his bound lover.

Concern over political consequences caused the Corcoran Gallery of Art to cancel a scheduled showing, but the Washington Project for the Arts, which has received NEA grants in the past, subsequently announced that it would play host. "It's a really beautiful exhibition, and the way the work is presented is done very sensitively," explained WPA Director Jock Reynolds. Indeed.

Despite Congress' timidity, it's time to rethink public funding of the arts and other cultural activities. In 1989, the U.S. government provided $169 million to the NEA to fund what one official calls the "expression of America's culture"—symphonies, dance companies, painters, and sculptors. Another $153 million goes to the National Endowment for the Humanities (NEH), which focuses on cultural research "to increase understanding and appreciation of the humanities," explains the agency. Together these Washington bureaucracies constitute America's de facto ministry of culture.

The United States survived for nearly two centuries without a federal cultural presence but the Johnson New Deal meant more than welfare for the poor. It also plowed new ground by providing handouts to the intelligentsia. In 1965 Congress created the NEH and gave it $2.5 million. During an era when there were no perceived spending constraints, cultural outlays increased rapidly: by 1980 the NEA's budget was $152 million and the NEH's expenditures were $157 million.

For a time Ronald Reagan's appearance in Washington seemed to threaten the survival of the ministry of culture. Though the administration did not attempt to eliminate the two endowments, it did propose to cut both agencies' budgets by roughly one-third in future years, arguing that "funding for artistic and cultural pursuits is a relatively low priority budget item." But the administration never pushed its proposals very hard and the beneficiaries of the more than $300 million in largesse—artists, researchers, museums, universities, et al.—rallied to protect their grants. Congress enacted only minor reductions, and later raised spending for both endowments. Uncle Sam, having seized control of virtually every other form of human endeavor, was not interested in giving up his hold over the nation's culture.

Ironically, many conservatives, while echoing Reagan's criticism of big government, seemed more interested in controlling than in demolishing the NEH. Indeed, early in the administration, conservative activists bitterly battled over the endowment chairmanship, with neoconservative William Bennett beating out paleoconservative M.E. Bradford. Bennett and his successors then used the agency in part to fund neoconservative intellectuals and endeavors, and to push their agenda within the Reagan administration.

The NEA, in contrast, was largely ignored by the right, and the chairmanship went to a nonideological campaign aide, Frank Hodsoll. (The conservatives' lack of interest would seem to be myopic. Though the NEA's work is less overtly political than that of the NEH, the former remains an important banker for many activists who would dismantle our essentially individualist bourgeois culture.) However, in the Bush administration, where symbolism is so much more important than philosophy, it has been the fight for control of the NEA that turned into a royal slugfest. For the sort of ideological eunuchs attracted to the Bush administration the NEA chairmanship was a plum position, with the availability of millions of taxpayer funds automatically making the NEA head a BMOC in the art world.

What justification is there for a ministry of culture? There's no public demand for the two endowments—a recent *Newsweek* poll found that 47% of the public oppose federal support for the arts, compared to only 35% in favor of subsidies. Instead, the federal programs reflect the influence of America's cultural elite, both directly, through their ability to sway political leaders, and indirectly, through many people's perception that the arts are a critical pillar of our civilization requiring government backing.

Indeed, no longer does America's cultural industry have to justify its position at the federal trough. Politicians may argue over the size of the artists' dole, but they don't question its existence. This "ask no questions" dynamic extends to many states and cities. New York, for instance, is in the midst of a bitter political battle over proposals to cut subsidies. But no one is suggesting that culture should develop without tax dollars; the only issue is how large the checks should be. In short, artists' subsidies have become just another entitlement, such as welfare, Social Security, and student loans. The social "safety net" has grown to underwrite farmers, businessmen, students, and old people irrespective of economic circumstance, so why not artists?

Now, however, there may be an opportunity to debate the fundamental issue again, for America's ministry of culture has run afoul of public opinion by funding exhibitions designed to outrage the people paying for them. Not that the NEA has not previously funded curious projects, such as pornographic poetry. (The NEH's grants have been largely noncontroversial, though the agency did spend $615,000 to underwrite the blatantly anti-Western, pro-statist *The Africans* TV special.) However, with the NEA up for reauthorization and no one yet appointed chairman to replace Hodsoll, that agency is unusually vulnerable. Even congressional allies of the arts industry, such as Illinois Rep. Sidney Yates are on the defensive. Says Livingston Biddle, chairman of the NEA during the Carter administration, "A confluence of factors has made this the worst firestorm for the endowment in the 25 years of its existence."

Though the wave of protests against public funding of sacrilegious and pornographic exhibitions should have come as no surprise, the art world reacted as if the Gestapo had shot the artists and closed the organizations involved. "The question here is one of censorship," said Harvey Lichtenstein, president of the Brooklyn Academy of Music. Serrano is just a pawn "to censor, to restrict cultural free expression," wailed Ted Potter, executive director of the Southeastern Center for Contemporary Art. And so on, ad infinitum.

Now, whether Serrano's and Mapplethorpe's work can satisfy the dictionary definition of art—the realm of what is "beautiful, or of more than ordinary significance"—is debatable, but no one has suggested that they be suppressed. Even a vote-minded politico such as New York's Sen. Alphonse D'Amato stated of Serrano's photo that "I don't care if this guy wants to produce a thousand of these things—just don't do it with taxpayers' money." His argument is not only simple, but compelling: if you want to do something disgusting, vulgar, and offensive, don't expect your neighbors to pay for it.

Yet virtually no political figures—Rohrabacher excepted—have suggested dismantling either of the endowments. Rep. Richard Armey, a free-market Texas Republican, initially only pushed for greater accountability to the public; only later did he propose a 10% budget cut. However, with the public against public funding, it's time to ask the more fundamental question: why a ministry of culture at all?

Years ago the NEA and NEH became part of the bipartisan boondoggle that fills Washington. Liberals and conservatives, Democrats and Republicans, all support the continuation of federal support for the arts industry. But there's no justification for taxing lower-income Americans to support glitzy art shows and theater productions frequented primarily by the wealthy. And there's certainly no justification for funding artists who are dedicated to smearing the values held by those picking up the tab.

Government cannot be trusted to pick and choose acceptable art, and that's merely one more reason to junk the two endowments. It's time Congress and the administration promoted unlimited free expression by abolishing federal handouts to those doing the expressing.

What To Do About Traffic Congestion
Walter Block

Traffic congestion has to be one of the most annoying occurrences known to mankind. It limits vehicles capable of 150 miles per hour under specialized conditions, and 65 miles per hour under normal conditions, to crawling along, bumper-to-bumper, at five miles per hour.

Congestion is also a danger. Apart from psychological buffeting, frayed tempers undoubtedly create traffic accidents. The vehicles, too, deteriorate at a faster rate than they otherwise would, and overheated engines, etc., are the cause of even more highway injury.

The economic costs are monumental. Millions of productive workers are forced to sit idle for long periods in the morning, and another long period in the evening, while their vehicles use costly fuel.

In many large cities, almost anything out of the ordinary can trigger congestion, from the end of a ball-game to people returning from the beach. In New York and other major cities, the problem is reaching crisis proportions.

A crisis calls for urgent solutions, but almost no one is addressing the fundamental problem: the fact that the roads are owned and run by the government, therefore prohibiting the price system from solving congestion.

Traffic congestion is not unique. On the free market, people are continually choosing between lower-priced but more crowded conditions, and higher-priced but less congested alternatives. Should they patronize a crowded fast-food chain or a quiet, expensive restaurant? A discount department store or a full-price boutique? But with our roads, there is no market where consumers can make their preferences known; there are no congested but cheaper highways competing with more expensive but emptier ones.

There are plenty of "non-pricing" solutions to this problem. But because none rely on consumers expressing their wishes in a free market, all will fail.

A perennial government favorite is staggered work hours. The government need do nothing: instead the employer, and his recalcitrant employees, can be made scapegoats for congestion.

But restaurants are busiest during breakfast, lunch, and dinner time. Thus they too suffer from congested traffic. But were a restaurant owner to propose that customers stagger their meal times, he would be laughed out of business. Instead, he accommodates himself to the customers.

Many bowling alleys are open 24 hours a day, but "suffer" peak-load congestion in the late afternoon and early evening. They solve this cutting prices during the less busy hours. Customers are satisfied because they can coordinate their plans with the prices they choose to pay. But the exhortation to "stagger" travel times displays a typically callous government disregard for consumers.

Another strategy is the conversion of two-way streets into one-way ones, to align the direction of traffic in accord with the majority of motorists (outbound in the evening, inbound in the morning) and prohibit turns on and off these main thoroughfares, to keep traffic moving as quickly as possible.

This may sound like a panacea. But none of the cities implementing this plan have succeeded in ending rush hour congestion. There is simply too much traffic for the streets to handle. This policy also restricts motorists' travel. Every time a two-way street is converted into a one-way, the driver must cover a greater amount of territory to get where he is going. For if the one-way streets follow an every-other-street-in-a-different-direction pattern, the motorist will have to go around the block in half the cases. And the greater the number of prohibited turns, the greater the difficulty in maneuvering. Many motorists will have to go several blocks out of their way to turn, which only adds to the congestion.

Other solutions involve the metering of entrances to highways with lights. But these schemes do not eliminate highway congestion. They merely transform it into a situation where cars travel at medium speeds and wait in long lines to get on. What's worse: slow speeds and no lines, or long lines with medium speeds?

Some people in the "transportation community" say congestion cannot be solved by itself; instead we should have more public transportation and government planning: more buses, restrictive land-use controls, expensive subways, car pooling, "high-occupancy vehicles" lanes, etc. Since government control hasn't worked, we therefore need more of it.

Governments have poured billions into public transit schemes, and the results have been disappointing to disastrous: taxes continually increased to pay for an unworkable and inconvenient systems, which are eventually taken over by society's most destructive elements. These comprehensive plans are always based on bureaucratic estimates of "social"—as opposed to individual—costs and benefits; they treat consumers as if they were a homogeneous unit, whose individual needs do not matter.

The individual motorist vastly prefers his private mode of transportation to most conceivable mass transit alternatives. For planners, this is the ultimate frustration. So some planners have suggested the ultimate solution, therefore, is to ban cars.

All these "solutions" are bad substitutes for the price system. If congestion occurs on the free-market transportation network, where all roads are private, the response will resemble what accompanies "excess demand" for any other good or service: the businessman does not rest day or night till he provides the extra services the market is clamoring for.

The fast-food restaurant with long lines hires additional workers as soon as possible; the movie theater which must turn people away soon expands its facilities. That's because in the private economy, "congestion" is a golden opportunity for expansion of output, sales, and profits. It is only when the government takes over that customers clamoring for additional services are denounced and thwarted.

As long as government owns the roads, we will see no real solution to traffic congestion. Only when we privatize our nation's roads will we see the benefits of the price system inherent in the free market, and an end to the traffic jam as a daily feature of American life.

Time for An American *Perestroika*
Robert Higgs

The astonishing developments in the Soviet Union and Eastern Europe suggest that after more than 40 years, the Cold War may be about to end or at least to enter a less menacing phase. But not everyone is rejoicing at the turn of events. Many people have a strong vested interest in the continuation of a high level of military spending. The prospect of a more reliable peace scares them to death.

The reaction is described as "panic" as headlines proclaim "Arms Companies Fear Guns Will Turn to Butter." Said one investment strategist, "we were all joyous at the scenes of people climbing on the Wall, but the problem is, how do you make money on this?" Is it gauche to suggest that superfluous military firms try to make money by producing goods consumers are willing to buy?

Of course, one should not expect to collect the peace dividend. The widely discussed "cuts" of $180 billion in military spending, which Defense Secretary Dick Cheney asked the armed services to consider, are not actually cuts from the present level of spending but cuts in the Pentagon's desired spending increases over the next five years.

At present military spending is about $300 billion per year. So the U.S. military economy is roughly the same size as the entire economy of East Germany. And like that economy, it is centrally planned. Long ago Ludwig von Mises showed that the authorities in a planned economy cannot calculate to achieve an economically rational allocations of resources. Without prices ratified by consumer demands and without asset values established in open capital markets, a planned system must necessarily misallocate resources. By now everyone, including communists from Gorbachev on down, acknowledges that the planned economies of the Soviet bloc have been failures. The U.S. military economy also has been a failure, for the same reasons.

But if the military economy has been an economic failure, squandering resources right and left, it has been a political success—at least for those who command its heights or feed at its troughs.

Defense, of course, is often taken to be the classic "public good," and it is true that virtually all Americans want the government to do whatever is necessary to deter attacks from abroad. But no one knows with any certainty what the relation is between military spending and national security. Obviously, vast sums can be, and have been, spent for worthless weapons. Other weapons work well enough but trigger offsetting reactions by adversaries, leaving the nation no more secure or even less secure, but assuredly poorer.

Further, no one knows how much of the military effort goes toward protecting the lives and property of U.S. citizens and how much goes toward advancing the interests of the U.S. government, which are by no means synonymous with the interest of the general public. But however problematical true national security may be, military spending undoubtedly generates private benefits in the form of jobs, incomes, votes, and power. For these prizes, there has been no shortage of seekers.

The military-industrial-congressional complex (hereafter the MICC) includes all those who have found a way to turn a bad public situation, the Cold War, into a good personal deal. Members of Congress, especially those who belong to the key military committees, milk the system to gain reelection. Arms contracting firms, many of which lack the ability to compete successfully in commercial markets, rake in large profits, often with little or no risk. The military services, with their bloated officer corps and labyrinthine bureaucracies, gain positions, pay, and perquisites, not to mention one of the cushiest retirement plans in the land. On the periphery of the MICC thrives congeries of military-oriented lobbyists, consultants, research institutions, academicians, and labor unions.

The companies that supply the Pentagon talk a good private-enterprise game, but in practice they are at best mutant and twisted actors in the market. They are subject to no genuine market discipline; the government is the sole buyer of the arms they produce. But the government purchasers are using other people's money and have no bottom line of their own.

Small wonder if the big military companies all form political action committees to channel millions into the campaign coffers and personal accounts of many members of Congress. Hardly surprising if the firms hire thousands of retired military officers, former congressmen, and congressional staffers to help them acquire additional arms contracts. Big arms companies in trouble can confidently apply for a government bailout.

The whole business reeks of corruption, some of it illegal but much of it, like the blatant bribes ("honoraria") paid to members of Congress, perfectly legal. The FBI, eavesdropping on a telephone conversation between two men engaged in a Pentagon procurement fraud, recorded one of them saying, "If the farmers in Indiana knew what you sons of bitches were doing with their money, they would come up there and kill you with their pitchforks."

But despite the scandals that flare up every few years, the public either doesn't know or feels powerless to do anything about the conduct of the MICC. Like the East Germans who toiled in poverty while their masters lived in luxury, the average citizen surrenders the funds to feed the gargantuan military economy year after year.

As William J. Stern recently wrote, the political insiders who flourish when the government maintains a vast military economy are "our version of the East bloc's Nomenklatura and they have absolutely no wish to see anything change." For a perfect example, read the history of Wedtech—it doesn't get any sleazier.

Over the years, numerous real or pretended efforts to reform the system have been made. Three major studies by presidential blue-ribbon commissions, the latest being the Packard Commission of 1986; many acts passed by Congress; various in-house efforts at the Pentagon; scores of investigations by the General Accounting Office; countless proposals by scholars and private groups—all have come to naught.

Secretary Cheney took office pledging to carry out effective fundamental changes. But his actual plan, announced late in 1989, was correctly described as leaving "intact the structure and authority of the entrenched Pentagon procurement bureaucracy." Cheney sought to avoid alienating the top civilian and military leadership of the armed services. The result: no substantive change.

Now, as the public sees less and less justification for the maintenance of an enormous military establishment, especially one designed for another world war in central Europe, the MICC will surely come under attack. But its political resources are enormous. Even if military spending is cut, it is unlikely to be cut very much very fast. Regardless of events in Eastern Europe and the Soviet Union, those whose positions and incomes derive from high levels of military spending will continue to resist the spending cuts.

They may also be tempted to stir up fears of new threats or to revive the Cold War—after all, the past 40 years are littered with weapons "gaps" and other forms of scare-mongering. The public would be well advised to anticipate such tactics.

As the welfare state has matured, people have come to appreciate better that groups seeking to redistribute income to themselves always present their plans wrapped in a claim to promote the public interest. Those who seek to feather their nests in the warfare state use the same tactic even more effectively.

Perhaps, if the Cold War really does end, the basis for this far-reaching redistributive activity will erode. Then *perestroika* may become possible in the United States, too.

Immigration and Private Property

Llewellyn H. Rockwell

L ast year, 50,000 Haitian immigrants gathered in the streets of New York, angry at an FDA hint that they consider not giving blood. With the appalling AIDS rate among Haitians, and the ease with which some infected blood can pass the screening tests, it seemed an unobjectionable idea. But not in Manhattan, 1990.

You may think there's no right to poison the American blood supply, but you'd be wrong. State-licensed victims have special rights, and for violating them, the FDA has done penance.

At the Haitian hate-o-rama, one speaker said that since AIDS was a white plot to wipe out blacks, Haitians should "turn it back on white folks," presumably by further polluting the blood supply. Since Haitians take great pride in a revolution whose central act was the massacre of all the white men, women, and children in the country, perhaps the speaker was simply upholding his national tradition.

Such things make it difficult to be a libertarian on immigration these days. Until one realizes that many natives behave even worse, and that Haitians aren't typical. There are also the north Asians, whose decent communities, strong families, rooted culture, and economic triumph seem to vindicate, all by themselves, the open borders that were the American tradition until 1921. Of course, most other immigrants fall somewhere between these two extremes.

A free market means free movement of goods, capital, and people. From an economic point of view, the borders of the U.S. ought to have no more significance than those of Illinois. But economics doesn't tell us everything.

In the 19th century, our unregulated and therefore booming economy easily absorbed everyone who wanted to work. There was no welfare state, no ideology of victimhood, and no inferiority complex about our values. Far from being ashamed of "centuries of white, Western oppression," our fathers knew that the Republic represented something uniquely good in history. It was—after all—why immigrants flocked here, and willingly conformed to a the norms of a self-confident culture.

Everyone became an American; everyone *wanted* to become an American. This didn't, as it should not have, prevent German immigrants, for example, from wanting to preserve their language and culture in parochial schools, but there was no nonsense about bilingual public education to prevent assimilation. Nor were voo-doo cultures exalted at tax-payer expense over the West. And it would never have crossed anyone's mind that English wasn't the official language of the United States.

Progressivism perverted all this, of course. And now we have immigrants who use the welfare system, and the politics of ethnic victimology, to gain privileges at the expense of the rest of us.

But willing hands and minds are a valuable resource. Despite the bad apples, most immigrants come here to work. They do the work no one else wants to do, from running shops in black ghettos to punching cows in Wyoming. They supply the low-cost labor we need, but which our welfare system has exterminated, to the detriment even of the drones.

Immigration of all sorts is actually low: about 650,000 people a year, .25% of the total population. Illegal immigration is less than a third of that, and declining, which is too bad. Illegals are willing to work hard for low pay, and they shun government offices, including welfare. In the illegal market, with people anxious to work cheaply as seamstresses, maids, and yard boys, we get a glimpse of what immigration in an unregulated economy would be like, and how we would all benefit.

Should immigration be opposed because there are too many people? For 15 years, our fertility rates have been below replacement level. Do all immigrants go on welfare? Since they are a younger population than the natives, they tend to use less Social Security and Medicare wel-fare. And this is true for all "social services." Do immi-grants "take jobs" from Americans? The question is economically ignorant. It not only posits a static view of the economy, with X jobs to be divided, it is also an argument against college education and on-the-job training, both of which allow people to "take" jobs they would otherwise not have been able to get. In fact, most immigrants—because they are economically produc-tive—help create jobs for others.

But the fear, in these interventionist days, of immi-grants gaining privileges through political pressure is a legitimate one. To assuage it, and for reasons of simple justice, all immigrants should be in effect guest workers. There is no right to vote nor to go on the dole; both ought to be denied permanently to immigrants. (And while we're at it, no American on welfare should be able to vote either.)

Under today's egalitarian system, most immigrants come from culturally inharmonious places like Haiti and Iran instead of from Europe. That's why we should eliminate the quotas on free businessmen to hire (and fire) without egalimania interfering. At present, busi-nessmen can be fined for not hiring and for hiring Hispanics, by various federal civil rights and immigration enforcers.

Businessmen should also be free once again to do as they did in the 19th century: interview and hire contract workers in other countries. Labor unions lobbied to outlaw this practice, which insured that these immi-grants—who came here as employees—would not be-come public charges.

But our ultimate goal should be to make our country a network of private neighborhoods. There is no right of public access on private property. If commercial districts were like malls, and communities had access restricted to the people the residents wanted—as some do today— we would not have to worry about bums and felons infesting our streets, nor about unwanted immigrants.

Then, if a community didn't want 50,000 Haitian AIDSophiliacs on their streets, they wouldn't be allowed there. *That* is the kind of society we ought to work for.

5

THREATS AND OUTRAGES

End the War on Drugs

Joseph Sobran

Though the prestige of literal war has plummeted, we find ourselves embroiled in various metaphorical wars: on poverty, on terrorism, and, most urgently, on drugs. Describing a grandiose political drive as a "war" (especially when it's too nebulous to be plausibly called a "plan") seems to be an appealing way for politicians to express inspiring resolve and to imply that total victory is feasible: problem X, we are encouraged to infer, will soon be banished forever. All it takes is concerted will, which is what "war" stands for.

But wars against abstract enemies, as opposed to determinate human enemies organized in polities, have a way of bogging down. The war on poverty has left us with two intractabilities, poverty itself and a huge anti-poverty apparatus. We can end neither poverty nor the war against it. No light is visible at the ends of *these* tunnels. And no wonder, since poverty really means, in America, *relative* poverty, which exists whenever people are free to make money at their own rates. If the natural disparities of wealth are regarded as a public scandal, the government can award itself an open-ended mandate to attempt the impossible. The goal of victory will of course trump all concerns about budgetary constraints or property rights. "Victory" need not ever be defined, except as the hypothetical absence of a condition that is all too visibly present. (Or even *in*visibly present: the late Michael Harrington set the fashion of speaking of "invisible poverty," which, like the Emperor's Clothes, may only be discerned by those whose consciousness has been raised.)

As for the war on terrorism, nobody even knows how to commence it, unless by declaring Iran the embodiment of terrorism and dropping a few bombs.

Drugs are an even more elusive adversary. Most recreational drugs derive from plants that may be grown in endless remote expanses outside American jurisdiction and imported at countless points by various ingenious means. There is no single headquarters, hence no target for warfare. Only comprehensive control will do.

Or will it? Illicit drugs have proved uncontrollable even in our most intensely controlled domains: prisons. Which has provoked the observation that if America were turned into a totalitarian system, where the powers of the state were absolutely unlimited, the black market in drugs would still flourish.

Police work always limps after energies that bound over laws. It takes several policemen to catch a single criminal, unless he operates from a stationary address. This ratio means that law and order always depend primarily on voluntary compliance by the overwhelming majority of the populace. When a critical mass of citizens disregards the law, law enforcement is futile. And the drug-selling and -consuming sectors of America are as fluid as they are enormous.

Like all soldiers, our drug warriors will naturally feel that they aren't getting enough support when they aren't winning. From their point of view, this is perfectly rational. Their unconditional assignment is to win, period. That's what war means. But the "war" isn't serious. It's rhetorical, a gesture of determination we don't really feel, though we feel we *ought* to feel it. The men who actually do the fighting, at great risk, are frustrated by the gulf between our professions of hatred for the enemy and our unwillingness to provide anything approaching the means needed for victory.

And at the drug Pentagon, the senior strategists will call, like generals, for more funding, more troops, more national *will*. Our drug czar, William Bennett, keeps proposing increasingly drastic measures, and it's predictable that he and his successors will continue egging us on with periodic reports of both the encouraging "headway" we are making on this or that front (casual drug use is down this year, for example) and horrifying iterations of the total dimensions of the problem.

Ah, the problem. In America every evil is a "problem," therefore soluble. But as James Burnham used to say, "When there's no solution, there's no problem." To be sure, *individuals* have drug problems. It's meaningless to speak of a *national* drug problem. What we have is a national complex of drug-related evils we're confusedly treating as a single entity.

The most salient of these evils is the violent crime associated with distributing drugs and paying for personal drug habits. The gang violence of Prohibition was comparatively sporadic; and today, though legal alcohol consumption generates more violence than legal drug use ever will (narcotics *retard* violent impulses), whiskey is distributed without incident. But the *craving* for drugs and drug profits, a double craving perversely sustained by law, results in millions of crimes against persons and property—daily killings in large cities, four million burglaries per year, for instance. This, at least, is a genuine problem, in the sense that it's susceptible of amelioration. Llewellyn Rockwell estimates that decriminalizing drugs would cut street crime 75%. If so, the debate should stop right there.

All this is not meant as an advertisement for drug use itself. Americans have legitimate worries about what decriminalizing drugs would mean. More drug consumption? Yes. Present laws do deter some people, a fraction of whom would acquire drug problems if the law stopped deterring them from use. Many others would sample drugs without becoming addicted or disabled. It's hardly conceivable, though, that drug abuse would produce anything approaching the hundreds of thousands of deaths now caused by alcoholism and tobacco use. Moreover, legalized drugs would certainly be less lethal than black market drugs, for the same reason that Jim

Beam is safer than moonshine, as Mark Thornton of Auburn University has pointed out.

What about kids? Wouldn't decriminalizing drugs mean more young people with drug problems? Maybe not. The opposite might be true. If drugs were legal for adults but forbidden to minors (with tough penalties for selling or giving them to the underaged), the price of drugs would be too low to make the risk of breaking the law worthwhile. Age-stratified legalization might well segregate the very young from drug consumers, in a way that the present black market does not.

Probably the deepest reservation most Americans feel against decriminalizing drugs stems from the identification of the moral with the legal. We feel that what is immoral ought to be illegal, and that what is legal must be morally approved. But, after all, we managed to repeal Prohibition without making drunkenness an inalienable right. Drunk drivers go to jail; alcohol abuse can be grounds for dismissal and divorce. There lurks in each of us the irrational fantasy of America turning into a nation of stupefied addicts. Few are old enough to remember when today's controlled substances were uncontrolled, and nobody spoke of a national drug problem. Opium, cocaine, and other drugs, readily available, were sometimes abused, but were never associated, in the public mind, with violence. (It took the law to create that connection.)

Informal social sanctions, as always, did most of the work of governing society. They will do the same when Americans are forced again to take responsibility for their own behavior, without federal agencies to keep watch on their voluptuary habits. Most of us would go on living as we have, without the drugs that are currently banned; most of the rest would come to terms with drug use, avoiding serious abuse.

It's an accident of circumstance that when most of us think of illegal drugs, we picture villainous purveyors: pock-faced dictators, ghetto toughs. This association makes talk of war on drugs emotionally powerful. But nobody today thinks of Al Capone and gin together. The end of Prohibition broke the link between alcohol and organized crime. Decriminalizing drugs will break up similar fatal clusters. Continuing the bogus war will only saddle us with both a criminal drug subculture and a consumptive drug bureaucracy, equally and symbiotically permanent.

Mr. Bennett is receptive to the idea of decapitating drug dealers. That gruesome and worse-than-useless suggestion perfectly expresses the logic of the war on drugs. We'd do well to recall Hydra, whose severed heads grew back doubled. The Hydra of drug crime has many times more heads now than when we started. We can't kill it. Maybe we can domesticate it.

Drugs and Adultery

Llewellyn H. Rockwell

Europeans accuse Americans of being childocentric, and I guess I'd have to plead guilty. My nine-year-old adopted daughter, Alexandra, is the apple of my eye, and of my heart.

I fought for the right (i.e., for the Right) before she came into my life. But now I fight even harder, because

I worry about the country she will inherit. I want her, and other children, to live in a society that is moral and free, and that looks as much as possible like the old American Republic, unsubverted by the welfare-warfare state and its cultural and religious apostasy.

As a paleolibertarian, I don't see the federal government as useful in achieving this, except in the negative sense of preventing crime, invasion, etc.

That does not mean I approve, as too many libertarians do, of everything I wouldn't outlaw. I see the traditional family as the essential building block of society, for example, so I wish Elizabeth Taylor hadn't married nine times. But I wouldn't put her in jail for it.

I worry about drugs and children, but I'm convinced that when kids don't become addicts—and the vast majority do not—it has everything to do with parents and religion, and little to do with accessibility. Even in my quiet town, drugs are available to any young person who wants them, despite the police and the federal War on Drugs.

The choice is *not* between a society that is drug-free or drug-ridden. We have the latter already, despite billions in spending, thousands of agents, and hundreds of restrictions on our personal and financial liberties. (In fact, I would argue that just as Prohibition increased drunkenness, so the drug war has increased drug abuse.) Instead the choice is between a society where these problems are exacerbated by government, and one where they are not.

If I could wave a magic wand and make illegal drugs disappear, I would gladly do so. But I do not have that wand, and neither does the government. The government does have a gun, however. But—just as during Prohibition—it is not capable of using it to suppress the traffic in things enough people want, whether for good or ill.

The government cannot suppress adultery, for example, even though breaking the marriage covenant, with its consequent divorce, damaged children, and other shattered moral values, does even more harm than drugs.

Let's suppose that, knowing this, Jimmy Carter had launched a War on Infidelity.

The Federal Marital Enforcement Administration—in cooperation with vice squads at state and local levels—would institute national spying, and impose long prison sentences on those caught. Motels would be under surveillance, and couples would have to provide proof of marriage to check in. Mail would be opened and phones would be tapped. There would be 800-number informer lines. Even parties would be watched. Who knows what could go on?

Next would come a massive federal education program, with grants from the National Institute of Marriage to favored intellectuals and activists. Roseann Carter would ask us to "Just Say No" to illicit liaisons, and the IRS would use them as an excuse to restrict financial privacy, since cash could be used to fund adultery without leaving a paper trail.

Would any of us think that family values could be protected, let alone enhanced, by such a system? Federal tyranny undermines *all* our values, no matter what the excuse. Yet many Americans support fighting drugs in this manner, with exactly the same success that a federal marital crusade would have. Or rather, with even less success, since the war on drugs also reaps a harvest of violent crime.

When it comes to drug use, people tend to fall into four categories: (1) those who would not use drugs even if they were free as well as legal; (2) those who might experiment in some limited way, but would never become addicts; (3) those who can become abusers, but can also be helped by moral and educational counselling; and (4) "natural" addicts.

Categories one and two are not societal problems. Category three should be the target of our anti-drug efforts, and medical and moral healing. Category four probably cannot be helped by any human means.

As the last nine years have shown, the government cannot make these pathetic individuals abstain. But it can make sure that they visit their misery on the innocent.

Even a massive, and massively funded, drug war, complete with shootouts in American streets and invasions of other countries, hasn't prevented these people from getting what they want, nor other undesirables from getting rich providing it.

After nine years of crackdown, we have more than *double* the amount of drugs available, by the government's own statistics, and they are more potent. Just as Prohibition gave bootleggers the incentive to produce high-profit, high-proof alcohol rather than less profitable (but milder) beer or wine, the drug war has led to the U.S. producing, for example, the most potent marijuana in the world. Not Jamaica. Not West Africa. But Northern California.

Even though the government cannot suppress these substances, it *is* capable of raising the price, thus making sure that drug dealers get rich while the innocent are mugged, burglarized, and murdered.

Street crime is at horrific levels in our major cities. It warps the lives of decent people, with the poor and elderly living in permanent terror.

If decriminalizing drugs meant nothing more than drastically cutting street crime—and it would—we should support it. We can't prevent addicts from using drugs, but we can make sure that they harm only themselves, while freeing the police to concentrate on crimes against innocent persons and their property.

There are many vices which ought not to be crimes. Enforcing the moral law against these vices is the job of families and churches, not politicians. To put the Cranstons and Quayles of the world in charge is to abdicate our individual responsibilities, to fail abjectly, and to move closer to authoritarianism.

It's no coincidence that recent anti-drug laws have eliminated the remnants of domestic bank privacy, restricted the honest use of cash, allowed unreasonable (and unconstitutional) searches and seizures of private property, constructed computer dossiers on every American, and expanded the powers and size of the IRS. And now the State Department is pushing a United Nations drug treaty that would establish an international police force and tax agency.

In 1912, when all now-banned substances were legal, there was no "national drug problem," but only individual abuse. Widely sold medications, alleged to be "good for any ailment of man or beast," consisted of opium and alcohol, yet our cities were safe.

Then America had no welfare state, no globaloney, no Federal Reserve, no income tax, no urban terror, and no drug laws. It had strong families, strong churches, a strong culture, and a strong social order. It was no utopia—we still suffered from the effects of Northern imperialism, for example—but it looks mighty good from today's standpoint. And it looks all of a piece.

Would Legalization Increase Drug Use?

Lawrence W. Reed

I f drugs were legalized, says drug czar William Bennett, drug use "would skyrocket." George Will echoes him. They offer no evidence for this claim, of course. Judging from America's last experience with Prohibition, they are probably wrong. If we ended the War on Drugs, drug use might even decline.

In his 1963 book *How Dry We Were: Prohibition Revisited*, Henry Lee gives us a fascinating and instructive account of what happened when alcohol was prohibited from 1919 to 1933.

When Prohibition was enacted, everyone predicted the dawn of a New Moral Era. Dr. Billy Sunday said: "The slums will soon be only a memory. We will turn our prisons into factories and our jails into storehouses and corncribs. Men will walk upright now, women will smile and the children will laugh. Hell will be forever for rent."

And George Will agrees: "The fact is that Prohibition worked. Alcohol consumption during the twenties declined." The reality is otherwise.

Lee's facts and figures show, as we might expect, that prohibiting alcohol simply drove its production and consumption "underground" and even had the perverse effect of increasing both. Many people drank more than ever, or for the very first time, just because the stuff was illegal. "Men were drinking defiantly," writes Lee, "with a sense of high purpose, a kind of dedicated drinking that you don't see much of today."

One place where they drank was the "speakeasy." In Rochester, NY, for instance, 500 licensed saloons in the days before Prohibition gave way to twice as many speakeasies when booze was outlawed. On Eagle Street in Albany, there were 18 speakeasies; before Prohibition there were only three saloons.

Public drunkenness was illegal both before and during Prohibition, but in Detroit, drunkenness arrests increased steadily from 6,590 in 1920 to 28,804 in 1928. Drinking even increased among members of Congress during the Prohibition!

During daylight, "Prohibition did cut down the amount of drinking," says Lee. "Probably because it was illegal, people preferred to do their imbibing at night, more than making up for their daytime abstinence."

Another indication of all the booze sloshing around in the 1920s was "the most spectacular agricultural event" of the decade—the 470% increase in corn sugar production. The stills were operating at full tilt; neither the revenuers nor Elliott Ness's "Untouchables" put much of a dent in their growth. In 1929, one state alone confiscated more stills than the nationwide total in 1913, while the grand total of all state and federal seizures was a dozen times higher.

America's total national "drunk tab" during Prohibition was in the neighborhood of $2.9 billion (in 1929 dollars), putting the bootleg liquor business "right up in the category of steel, autos, and gasoline." Millions of first-time drinkers were brought into the underground.

Lee is backed up by the most respected analyst in the field, economist Clark Warburton, whose data in his *The Economic Results of Prohibition* (1932) come from law enforcement officials, consumers, and producers. He shows that alcohol use increased dramatically during Prohibition: liquor, from .3 gallons per capita to 1.86 (520%); wine from .44 to .87 gallons per capita (97%); and beer from 1.26 to 6.9 gallons per capita (447%). During Prohibition, America went on a drinking binge, and, says Warburton, the data for spirits may be underestimated.

Prohibition also made the liquor much more potent (as with drugs today) and alcoholism much more common. After 11 years of Prohibition, wrote British author G.K. Chesterton, "Alcoholism has never threatened disaster as it is threatening America today. It isn't normal that girls at 16 should go to dances and drink raw alcohol." Alcohol-induced deaths appeared and increased. Of the 480,000 gallons of liquor confiscated in New York state during one Prohibition year, 98% contained poisons.

Bennett and Will are wrong. Prohibition didn't work, and meanwhile, taxpayers were picking up the bill for the massive enforcement effort. And though decent people might have used alcohol, they didn't manufacture or distribute the illegal stuff, leaving those lines of work to some of the sleaziest and most violent crooks in our history. Crime rates soared in the "Roaring '20s," most of it Prohibition related.

My guess is that if we outlawed soda pop, we could produce a similar effect. Bootleg cola-from-a-still would flow like water; people would pay a high price for illegal root beer; criminal gangs would supply it; and the feds would spend billions fighting the soda-pop cartel.

Making drugs illegal only increases their lure, and with the profits available in the drug trade, there is more incentive to advertise and get others hooked.

Experience strongly suggests that drug abuse, like alcohol abuse, is a demand problem. Attacking it from the supply side is inherently futile and even counterproductive.

Lower prices, which legalization would bring, always increases the quantity demanded. But probably just about everybody who wants to use drugs is using them now. People can get them easily, even in federal prisons. There simply is no pent-up demand among those who are not currently drug-users. And legalization would end the "forbidden-fruit phenomenon," in which some young people are attracted to drugs precisely because they are illegal.

Bush and Bennett want people to stop abusing drugs. I couldn't agree more. What they haven't explained, however, is just exactly why this latest stepped-up attempt at Prohibition will work any better than the last time we tried it.

Mickey Leland: Humanitarian?

Llewellyn H. Rockwell

I f the ancient Roman maxim—"Of the dead, say nothing but good"—has any application, it is to private citizens. Not to politicians, and certainly not to politicians who whitewash tyranny. Yet we are being subjected to the virtual beatification of Congressman Mickey Leland.

Despite his sad death while on a junket in Ethiopia, Leland was no hero. An open Communist sympathizer, he was known as "V.I. Leland" to at least one of his colleagues. Another told me: "I wouldn't be surprised if he had been an actual Communist Party member."

Leland, whom Fidel Castro called "my close friend," made a dozen trips to Havana, where he praised the "achievements" of the Cuban government and the "intellect" of its leader.

Another of Leland's friends was Mengistu Haile Mariam, the military dictator of Ethiopia. As Michael Johns of the Heritage Foundation points out, Menguistu is responsible for "a state-sponsored holocaust: the death of more than a million people. He is in the same category as Cambodia's Pol Pot."

Leland made five taxpayer-funded excursions to Ethiopia "in a noble cause—trying to feed the hungry," said President Bush. And indeed Leland helped persuade Congress and the Reagan and Bush administrations to send more than $800 million in food and other aid to Ethiopia for famine relief. Leland also campaigned for closer relations with the Ethiopian government. But was this really noble, and was it really relief?

Washington columnist Chris Matthews, former aide to Tip O'Neill, says Leland was a great humanitarian because he "could sit with a dictator like Ethiopia's Mengistu and try to find common ground." As a "good diplomat," at lunch with Mengistu—instead of complaining about the food—he would "dig right in." Matthews says he had the "courage" to "do the right thing, to fight the right causes."

Excuse me, but even in Washington this ought to be seen as rubbish. Mengistu—who modeled his regime on North Korea's—deliberately starves people to death. As even the *Washington Post* once admitted, the Ethiopian famine was caused by the "Mengistu government's farm collectivization and resettlement policy," and not by the weather. But we would never have known it from Leland.

Just as apologists for socialism used to blame 70 years of bad weather for the Soviet food shortages, Leland said lack of rain was Ethiopia's problem—that and lack of U.S. taxpayers' money.

The West just doesn't understand Col. Mengistu, Leland used to say. But in truth we understand him all too well. Like Stalin in the Ukraine, the Ethiopian Communist Party uses control of food during a government terror famine to ensure its power.

The abolition of private agriculture did part of the work. Then families who opposed the government, or who belonged to tribes that are traditional opponents of the ruling ethnic coalition, are "resettled" by force in desert areas and left to die without food or water.

How could Leland not know this? And knowing it, how could he have averted his eyes? He denounced the oppression of black people in South Africa, yet supported virtual genocide in Ethiopia.

Leland knew that the Ethiopian Communists use U.S. aid—plus millions more from rock concerts and other loony-left fundraising events—to feed party enforcers and to punish the government's enemies. He knew that such aid only fastened a totalitarian government more tightly on the back of the Ethiopian people.

To advocate U.S. aid to the government of Ethiopia— as Leland so single-mindedly did—is to be an accessory to mass murder. For the people of Ethiopia aren't threatened by "hunger" as an abstract, but by government-*caused* hunger, and Mickey Leland endorsed its perpetrators.

Even in Washington, where all standards are laughably low, giving other people's money to Stalinist killers shouldn't count as humanitarianism.

Some real humanitarians include: Mother Theresa helping those in need, Ludwig von Mises spending his life showing only freedom can prevent starvation and other disasters, and Thomas Jefferson leading a revolution against government oppression. Dining with mass murderers isn't included.

Like so many congressmen, Leland put a foreign government ahead of American taxpayers—in his case, a particularly monstrous government. We can mourn his death, but we can also mourn his misbegotten ideology.

Leland was a counterfeit humanitarian who supported what Isabel Patterson called the "humanitarian with the guillotine." It does the cause of justice no good to pretend otherwise.

Choice in Schooling

Sheldon L. Richman

The choice-in-education movement has been building momentum in recent years. But it is now in
danger of being co-opted and eventually destroyed by the
Bush administration. If the education bureaucrats in the
federal government succeed, this will be a setback for
quality education and for parents and children everywhere.

The *Washington Post* summed up the problem even
before George Bush took office: "The Reagan administration came into office talking a lot about 'parental
choice' in education; what the phrase meant was tuition
tax credits, voucher plans or, toward the end, magnet
schools. Now President-elect Bush and others who talk
about 'choice,' as they strive not to fumble the ball of a
still-accelerating reform movement, mean something different and less ideologically blood-soaked. The kind of
'choice' gaining attention...is a more limited type of plan...."

While this editorial gave the Reagan administration
more credit than it deserved (see below), the main point
was correct. Two months after his inauguration, Mr.
Bush, the "education president," abandoned the cause
of real choice in education, as well as a campaign promise
and the GOP platform, and endorsed a plan for ersatz
choice. In rejecting tuition tax credits, he used that
catch-all excuse for not reducing taxes: the federal budget deficit won't allow it. Bush here was using the pernicious doctrine of "tax expenditures," by which money left
in the hands of the taxpayers is regarded as government
spending. The government cannot afford to let parents

keep their own money to spend on the education of their choice, Bush was saying.

His alternative? "I think everybody should support the public school system." But what about parents who dislike the quality of the government's schools and want something better for their children? The "education president" told a group of students, "If, on top of that [the public schools], your parents want to shell out in addition to the tax money, tuition money, that's their right, and that should be respected. But I don't think they should get a break for that."

A "break"? Here President Bush takes the "tax expenditure" doctrine to insulting limits. Parents permitted to keep their own money to spend as they see fit on their children's education would be getting a break, a subsidy, a privilege.

As this shows, the failure to think in principles leads so-called pragmatic politicians ultimately to surrender what they claim are cherished values.

When the government lets parents keep their own money, it is neither a subsidy nor a government expenditure. It can only be construed that way if the government, not the producers, is the legitimate owner of all income. But, at least according to the founding principles of the United States, we are not supposed to believe that. The doctrine of tax expenditures is an especially un-American idea.

Moreover, it is sad to see the notion of choice in education twisted so out of shape. It did not begin with Bush. As with so many other things, the Reagan administration's reputation in this area is clearly undeserved. Although Ronald Reagan claimed to be a champion of the choice-in-education movement, he betrayed it by failing to halt—and indeed by furthering—the centralization of education in the United States.

After campaigning on a promise in 1980 to abolish the Department of Education, which Jimmy Carter had set up as a favor to the National Education Association in payment for its endorsement, he of course did not abolish it. On the contrary, his first secretary of education was the establishmentarian Terell Bell and the department's budget grew.

His second secretary was neoconservative William J. Bennett (now drug czar), who, while talking about choice in education, proposed a national curriculum. The conservative's lack of outcry against this idea was deafening. Other "innovations" by the Reagan Department of Education included an annual national report card on school performance and a national board for teacher certification. Nationalization is hardly the direction in which we should be going.

President Bush, unlike Reagan, won't even pay lip-service to freedom in education. His abandonment of tax credits for tuition was immediately recognized as a blow to the choice-in-education movement. Predictably, the vice president of the Los Angeles teachers union was enthralled. "That's outstanding news," said Frances Haywood. "It's a great departure from the stance of the Republican Party." The spokesman for the Los Angeles Archdiocese was understandably crestfallen: "I'm disappointed. This president has called himself the education president, and he's ignoring a sizable segment of the American population in not recognizing the needs of parochial school students."

The most pernicious part of all this is how choice in education is being distorted into something very different. What the Bush administration means by choice and competition is the following: parents should be allowed to send their children to any government school in their school district. In some cases, state and other funds would follow the students to their chosen school. The rationale is that this would make the schools competitive. Poor schools that lost students would lose money. Good schools that gained students would gain money.

The problem with the idea is similar to the problem with market-socialism schemes: it is an attempt to play competition. School administrators would not be risking their own capital, and they would have every reason to believe that the government authorities would not let a poor school go bankrupt. Imagine what will happen when inner-city schools see most of their students leave. Will all the money really go with them?

Any "solution" that merely tinkers with the government schools, without making private schools a real option for parents, is phony. And the only way to make private schools a real option, and to create true competition, is to let parents get a refund of their tax money when they pay tuition. Whether this is done through tax credits or vouchers is less important than other considerations, for instance, that the government *not* impose a curriculum on the private schools or certification requirements on teachers.

This is the only way to get innovation in education. It is also the only way to have real local control of education. Local control in a political context is a chimera, as we've seen over the years. Elected school boards are always captives of education bureaucrats, who are in turn part of a national education establishment tied to the federal bureaucrats. The tendency will always be toward nationalization of education, even if it is nominally local.

In a system in which parents can use private schools without paying twice, there is real local, parental control. The mechanism of control is obvious. It's called consumer sovereignty: parents can withdraw their support, and children, from a school at any time and shift them to competitors.

To make this system complete, compulsory-education laws—a form of conscription—would be abolished, recognizing that there are countless ways to get an education. Nothing that the education bureaucrats dream up could compare with a truly competitive system, which is why they are trying to divert our attention with their ersatz schemes.

This also disposes of the hot debate about whether values and religion should be taught in the schools. Parents would be free to pick the school that reflects their own ethical and religious outlook. Since no tax money would be involved, no one could claim that values were being imposed on anyone's children.

Finally, there is the old canard that the reason we have government schools in the first place is that the market was unable to do the job right. This story has been shown by many scholars to be bogus. Privately provided education was abundant, inexpensive, and good beginning in the colonial period of America. The same was true in Great Britain. Education entrepreneurs were responsive to consumers and they educated many people. Literacy was high.

One education historian, Robert Seybolt, writes, "It is a significant fact in American education that the curriculum developed most rapidly in the private schools" and that "curricular response to popular educational demands was initiated by private, rather than public enterprise." "In the hands of private schoolmasters the curriculum expanded rapidly," he says. "Their schools were commercial ventures, and, consequently, competition was keen." This "element of competition," forced the private schools "to add new courses of instruction," and "constantly to improve their methods and technique of instruction."

Contrary to the education establishment's version, government schools were not set up because schooling was scarce. The were set up because only government schools could fulfill the social-engineers' agenda. The agenda included the homogenizing of American culture, which was said to be threatened by immigrants and Catholics. The motive was not educational, but jingoistic.

It is hard to ignore this history when viewing current events. The Bush administration's commitment to government schooling can't be explained by a desire to better educate students: too many decades of failure have gone by to think that government could do that. It is better explained by a desire to more efficiently crank out homogeneous, servile, taxpaying citizens. The choice-in-education movement will have to continue without any help from Washington.

The High Court Stems the Tupperware Threat

Sheldon L. Richman

A merica is the land of free speech and press. The principle is enshrined in the First Amendment to the Constitution: Congress shall make no law abridging freedom of speech and of the press. Any school kid knows this—well, there was a time when any school kid knew it.

Okay, the government has made exceptions. If the expression is deemed obscene it is not protected. And Congress has outlawed the destruction of American flags, such as the kind you can buy in the five-and-dime. But speech and press are substantially free, right?

How about so-called commercial speech?

Commercial speech has for decades been treated differently from regular speech. For example, cigarette ads on television and radio have been banned by Congress. And the government has rules regarding the kinds of claims advertisers can make, even when they aren't fraudulent. Billboards are frequently banned from public highways. And as Michael Gartner, president of ABC News, pointed out, "if you say 'Buy Finnegan's Ice Cream,' that has less protection than if you say 'Ice cream is good for you.'" The Supreme Court wrote in 1978 that commercial speech enjoys "a limited measure of protection, commensurate with its *subordinate position in the scale of First Amendment values*" and is subject to "modes of regulation that might be impermissible in the realm of noncommercial expression." (Emphasis added.)

Maybe I've missed something, but the First Amendment seems not to have a scale of values. It says simply "Congress shall make no law...." There is something palpably anticapitalistic in the law's view that speech leading to a commercial transaction is inferior to other kinds of speech. During the Industrial Revolution the old aristocracies regarded commerce as base. This attitude lives on at the U.S. Supreme Court.

In 1980 the court affirmed the distinction between commercial and noncommercial speech, and it set out standards for regulation of the former. Essentially, the government could regulate, the court said, to advance a substantial government interest so long as the regulation was the *least restrictive* possible.

This was bad enough, but it didn't take long for the court to erode its own standard in favor of a much more permissive one. In 1986 the court upheld a prohibition in Puerto Rico against casino advertising aimed at local residents. It seemed unconcerned with whether the prohibition was the least restrictive method.

Then just last June the court openly abandoned the "least-restrictive" test for the ambiguous "reasonableness" test. The State University of New York (SUNY) prohibits businesses from operating on SUNY campuses, except for those providing food, books, etc. Nevertheless, a student held a Tupperware-style party in a dormitory. Present was a saleswoman with a housewares company, American Future Systems, Inc. The campus police asked her to leave and when she refused, she was charged with trespassing and soliciting without a permit. Some students sued SUNY for violating their freedom of speech.

The students won in the lower courts, but then the case landed in the Supreme Court. In an opinion written by Justice Antonin Scalia, the court upheld the law. Scalia wrote that the court's past decisions only require—quoting the Puerto Rico case—a "'fit' between the legislature's ends and the means chosen to accomplish those ends," a fit "that is not necessarily perfect, but reasonable."

While even the "least-restrictive" test allowed regulations out of spirit with the First Amendment, the new test of "reasonableness" is even worse. One at least can show that a regulation is not the least restrictive by coming up with something less restrictive. But how can one rebut the government's assertion that a regulation is reasonably related to its objective? Scalia has moved this area of the law from the (relatively) firm to the hopelessly soft.

Free commercial speech advocates are nervously watching another case now before the court. It involves a lawyer accused of violating an Illinois law forbidding lawyers from advertising themselves as "certified" or as "specialists." The lawyer, Gary E. Peel, noted on his letterhead that he is certified by a trial-lawyers' group. And interest groups in the United States are agitating to have Congress ban alcohol and cigarette advertising altogether, and the House has held hearings on a bill to prohibit tobacco ads that could be seen or heard by anyone under 18 years old.

Thanks to the Supreme Court, the future does not look good for free capitalistic speech. It is worth remembering that this is the one they call the Reagan Court.

Welcoming the Vietnamese

Murray N. Rothbard

From its inception America was largely the land of the free, but there were a few exceptions. One was the blatant subsidies to the politically powerful maritime industry, trying to protect what has long been a chronically inefficient industry from international competition. One of the initial actions of the first American Congress in 1789 was to pass the Jones Act, which protected both maritime owners and top employees. The Jones Act provided that vessels of five or more tons in American waters had to be owned by U.S. citizens, and that only citizens could serve as masters or pilots of such vessels.

Times have passed, and whatever national security considerations that might have required a fleet of private boats ready to assist the U.S. Navy have long since disappeared. The Jones Act had long become a dead letter. But let a law remain on the books, and it can always be trotted out to be used as a club for protectionism. And that is what has happened with the Jones Act.

Unfortunately, the latest victims of the Jones Act are Vietnamese immigrants who were welcomed as refugees from Communism, and who have proved to be thrifty, hard-working, and productive residents of the United States, working toward their citizenship. Unfortunately, too productive as fishermen for some of their inefficient Anglo competitors. In the early 1980s, Texas shrimpers attempted, by use of violence, to put Vietnamese-American competitors out of business.

The latest outrage against Vietnamese-American fishermen has occurred in California, mainly in San

Francisco, where Vietnamese-Americans, legal residents of the United States, have pooled their resources to purchase boats, and have been engaged in successful fishing of kingfish and hagfish for the past decade. In recent months, in response to complaints by Anglo competitors, the Coast Guard has been cracking down on the Vietnamese, citing the long-forgotten and long unenforced provisions of the Jones Act. While the Vietnamese-Americans have been willing to pay the $500 fine per citation to keep earning their livelihood, the Coast Guard now threatens to confiscate their boat-registration documents and thereby put them out of business. The fact that these are peaceful, legal, permanent residents makes all the more ridiculous the U.S. government's contention that they "present a clear and present threat to the national security."

Dennis W. Hayashi of the Asian Law Caucus, who is an attorney for the Vietnamese fishermen, notes that all of them "are working toward citizenship. They were welcomed as political refugees. It is noxious to me that because they have not yet sworn allegiance to America there is an implication that they are untrustworthy."

In the best tradition of Marie Antoinette's "let them eat cake," the government replies that the Vietnamese are free to work on boats under five tons which would be fishing closer to shore. The problem is that the Vietnamese concentrate on fish that cater to Asian restaurants and fish shops, and that such kingfish and hagfish have to be caught in gill nets. So why not use gill nets in small boats closer to shore? Because here, in a classic governmental Catch-22 situation, our old friends the environmentalists have already been at work. Seven years ago the environmentalists persuaded California to outlaw the use of gill netting in less than 60 feet of water. Why? Because these nets were, willy-nilly, ensnaring migratory birds and marine mammals in their meshes. So, once again, the environmentalists, speaking for the interests of all conceivable species as *against* man, have won out against their proclaimed enemies, human beings.

And so, seeking freedom and freedom of enterprise as victims of collectivism, the Vietnamese have been trapped by the U.S. government as pawns of inefficient competitors on the one hand and anti-human environmentalists on the other. The Vietnamese-Americans are seeking justice in American courts, however, and perhaps they will obtain it.

The Double Danger of AIDS

Richard Hite

A IDS is bad enough, but the government is making it worse. The feds are using this horrible disease as an excuse to expand at our expense. Already, they have used it to justify legislative and judicial interventions in employment, insurance, research, and education. And there is worse to come.

Consider the case of the Florida company that—concerned for the safety of its other employees—dismissed an AIDS-carrier. The AIDS-infected employee sued, won $190,000, and forced his employer to rehire him. The court claimed AIDS is a handicap that cannot serve as a reason for discrimination.

Why? Because Title VI of the Civil Rights Act of 1964 and Section 504 of the Rehabilitation Act of 1973 allegedly prohibit it. Section 504 states that firms receiving federal funds, very broadly defined, cannot discriminate against an individual with a physical handicap, and the courts have classified AIDS as a handicap—the only communicable disease so defined.

There are at least two things wrong with this. First, it restricts the right of employers to choose their employees freely, which leads to an array of bad economic consequences. Second, people with AIDS are given privileges that are withheld from other diseased persons, such as those with cancer or heart problems.

Today, an employer properly has the right to discriminate against cigarette smokers. He may refuse to hire smokers for any number of reasons, including to appease nonsmokers who don't like smoke, or who fear its possible health effects. Similarly, an employer should have the right to discriminate against AIDS carriers, whether to calm other workers or to reduce the marginal chance of contracting AIDS.

There are other legitimate reasons employers might not want to hire AIDS carriers. For example, they may fear drastic increases in health insurance premiums. By not being allowed to discriminate, employers may have to cut back on insurance to others, or eliminate it entirely. When employers spend time training new employees, they are investing scarce resources now in expectation of a return later. Why should they invest resources in training AIDS-infected persons who unfortunately offer little potential for a long-run return?

Nor will laws against AIDS discrimination stop employers from discriminating. These laws will only lead to different sorts of discrimination. In order to screen out potential AIDS carriers, employers will tend not to employ members of groups perceived to be at high risk. That is, they will be less likely to hire single, male, black, poor applicants, and those they think might be homosexual.

By shifting their discrimination toward those who they *think* may be in a high-risk group, employers will tend to favor applicants who are married, female, white, non-poor, and apparently heterosexual. That's why it makes sense for employers to have the freedom to require that all job applicants take an AIDS test.

The government-AIDS mania has also infected insurance. In 1986 the District of Columbia forbade insurance companies to discriminate against those who are "AIDS infected, perceived to be infected with AIDS, or perceived to be at high risk to AIDS infection." That is, non-AIDS carriers have to subsidize AIDs carriers through higher insurance premiums.

To fulfill their very important economic function, insurance companies must operate on the principle of calculated risk. It doesn't take much calculation to assess the possibility of paying out large sums to AIDS-infected persons. The total could reach $50 billion in the next five years.

If the practice of forcing insurance firms to cover AIDS grows, premiums will become so high that most people could not afford them. It's all too likely that government will then step in to "help" the victims of "uncaring" profit-minded businesses with more programs and regulations.

AIDS has been especially hard on the U.S. taxpayer, with the government shelling out more than $1 billion per year for alleged research and education. Recent bipartisan bills before Congress would increase the amount to $3 billion per year by 1990.

Research accounts for $600 million of this total and education about $450 million. And there is no shortage of organized groups anxious to be added to the public payroll. Medical researchers are one, and the American Medical Association is currently lobbying hard for more AIDS funding.

Between 1981 and 1987, 67,000 cases of AIDS were reported and 30,000 people died of AIDS. Yet 65,000 people die of heart disease every month. Surgeon General Everett Koop estimates that 270,000 cases of AIDS will occur by 1991. Yet by 1991, there will be *one million* new cases of cancer. Even if I accepted a federal role in health, and I do not, I still have to wonder why huge sums of taxpayer money should be spent on a disease which affects such a small portion of the population, and which is preventable by behavior changes.

Practitioners of "unsafe sex" and intravenous drug users should be allowed to make choices like everyone else. But they, and not the taxpayers, should assume the risks for the consequences of their actions. If the government spends billions to find cures and provide insurance for AIDS-infected persons, maybe it should do the same for high-wire walkers and human cannonballs.

As economics would predict, government has misallocated the money it spends on AIDS. Most has gone to notoriously inefficient and bureaucratized government labs or government-run labs, while the FDA harasses private vaccine development. But the key is that there is a lot of money to be made by the government-medical-industrial complex. And the same goes for the $450 million that Washington wastes annually on AIDS "education." A recent survey of D.C. residents found that 86% knew that AIDs is primarily spread through intimate sexual contact. However, 33% did not know that a blood transfusion can transmit AIDS, 39% did not know that sharing needles transmits AIDS, 16% thought toilet seats can transmit AIDS, and 28% thought drinking glasses can carry AIDS. The half billion is, as usual, largely going for salaries in the bureaucracies and grants to Beltway-bandit consultants who lobby for the funding to begin with. AIDS education would be much more effective if carried out by profit-motivated advertising.

If the government would simply get out of the way, the private sector would have a chance to provide preventative and curative measures. In the meantime, AIDS will continue to endanger us, not only medically, but with the violations of liberty perpetrated in its name.

The Megaeconomic Threat
Llewellyn H. Rockwell

The government spends billions of our dollars to tell us how wonderful it is. Too bad the truth-in-advertising laws don't apply, for this is one of the great frauds in American history.

Washington has inflicted appalling taxes, spending, regulation, and inflation on us for more than 75 years. The excuse has been economic stability and social welfare.

But the result has been an erratic economy and a poorer people. (Of course, government as an institution is more stable and prosperous, and so are the private interests that live off it, but that is another story.)

The disinterested observer might think it was time to junk federal planning and give the free market a try. But Washington has a better idea. It wants to help run a World State.

In the 1930s, John Maynard Keynes urged the creation of global institutions to bring the benefits of Keynesianism to the entire planet. The International Monetary Fund and the World Bank were two of his offspring, intended to redistribute wealth worldwide through foreign aid and central banking. Keynes didn't achieve his dream, thanks in large part to an American public opinion distrustful of internationalism. But the Keynesians never gave up, and in recent years they've been making unsettling progress.

Under the aegis of the Bank for International Settlements—the self-styled "central bankers' bank"—is now regulated on a global basis. And the Bush administration is pushing for world regulation of the stock, bond, and futures markets. The administration is also promoting—with the other G-7 industrialized nations—international cash controls, international financial police, [international fiscal controls] international tax collusion, and a UN treaty to make confidential banking a crime. With Washington's backing, Europe is moving towards One Big Government by 1992, with a European central bank to manipulate the world monetary system run the world monetarily in conjunction with the Federal Reserve and the Bank of Japan.

The liberal *New Republic* calls this "unipolarism," although it notes that proponents of world government "now avoid the eerie idea of 'world federalism' and espouse instead more subtle sources of order." The magazine touts the influential World Policy Institute (WPI)—once more honestly called the Institute for World Order—and its advocacy of global central banking, world inflation, and internationally managed trade.

Especially influential, notes *The New Republic*, is David Rockefeller's Trilateral Commission, which advocates a different version of unipolarism: what *The National Review* calls "a dominant condominium of capitalist powers ruling the world." The Trilateralists put more emphasis on military power than the liberal WPI, but both agree that national sovereignty should, in every meaningful sense, be eliminated.

"Megaeconomics," a term coined by WPI economist Walter Russell Mead, is Keynesian "macroeconomics" raised to a world level, and emphasizing the "community of nations" instead of the "narrow self-interest of individual nations."

Economically, of course, this is crazed. The "megaeconomics of unipolarism" will fail even more catastrophically than the macroeconomics of multipolarism. The Federal Reserve creates domestic inflation and business cycles; global central banking will give us worldwide monetary depreciation and depressions. World regulation will build global cartels just as domestic regulation does at home. And coordinated fiscal expansion will mean more efficient looting of private resources for world politicians, bureaucrats, and special interests to spend on themselves.

When the federal government unconstitutionally seized policy making from the states, we lost much of our economic freedoms. If world bodies pick up where the federal government leaves off, our future will be grim indeed.

Once these global institutions are erected, to whom will they be accountable? How will we influence the "world community"? A grass-roots letter-writing campaign to the G-7 or the World Bank?

We all know how hard it is to make our voices heard at city hall, let alone in the state capital or Washington. A world government would be immune to influence from middle-class taxpayers, which is part of its appeal.

Writing in *Omnipotent Government* in 1944, Ludwig von Mises worried about "the substitution of cooperative intervention of all or many governments for the independent interventionism of every national government." He pointed out that domestic intervention creates "a class of bounty receivers and a more numerous class of bounty payers."

"The domestic conflicts engendered by such policies are very serious indeed," he says. "But in the sphere of international relations they are incomparably more disastrous." Mises concludes: "It would be difficult to imagine any program whose realization would contribute more to engendering future conflict and wars."

We in the United States can stop world government. But to do so, we must educate ourselves about the moves now taking place, educate our fellow citizens, and seek to stop the growth of our own big government—and then roll it back.

Controlling the World Economy

Graeme B. Littler and *Jeffrey A. Tucker*

International trade and investment are growing—and that's great news for consumers, investors, and companies. But there's a dark side: politicians and bureaucrats are internationalizing their controls.

Some pundits believe that the global marketplace has permanently outrun the ability of governments to control: "It is no longer possible or desirable to control borders, manage trade, manipulate currencies, or otherwise interfere with global commerce," says supply-sider George Gilder. "The fabric of relationships among American, Asian, and European businesses is woven too tight."

Certainly government interference with global commerce is undesirable. But to claim that it is "no longer possible" is naive. Governments never relinquish power unless forced to; wherever the economy leads, governments are sure to follow.

Now that so much of the economy is international, governments have found new ways to interfere. Here are just some of them:

Cash

To intervene, governments need complete and accurate information about sources and directions of cash flows. The U.S. government has largely met this requirement domestically by building a huge network of computerized financial dossiers on American citizens. The misnamed Bank Secrecy Act, for example, requires bank customers to reveal information about themselves (name, age, SSN, amount, etc.) on a Currency Transaction Report (CTR) if they withdraw or deposit more than $10,000 in cash. (The de facto ceiling is much lower.) These forms are then sent to government agents for careful analysis.

The CTR enables the government to monitor *both* cash and non-cash transactions. Banks already must keep photographic records of all checks. Combined with the CTR, this creates a permanent paper trail that the government can access at any time. Real criminals can escape because they know these requirements inside and out. But they are not the intended targets. The real victims are law-abiding citizens who want their rightful privacy.

Now that cash is flowing over the borders and into the world economy, the government wants to put a tail on it. It is currently negotiating several international agreements that would extend the state's power to keep track of global financial affairs. They include:

1. *A Global CTR*. A U.S.-sponsored treaty being negotiated in the UN right now would require a global CTR. The provision is buried deep within the treaty, which is supposedly directed against drugs.

2. *A Global Currency Control Agency*. President Reagan signed a bill in November allegedly to fight the drug war, which calls for the "Treasury to negotiate with finance ministers of foreign countries to establish an international currency control agency." With no public notice or debate, the Federal Reserve and the Office of the Comptroller of the Currency recently made a deal with the International Criminal Police Organization (Interpol) to swap information on cash flows. The target

is supposedly "international financial crimes," but under exchange controls, that would include an honest American wanting international diversification and privacy.

3. *The War on Offshore Banks.* The U. S. government is seeking to eliminate private overseas banking. Investigators from Congress's Permanent Subcommittee on Investigations (PSI) have been junketing around the globe for three years, interrogating businessmen and warning banks to obey. The PSI recommends in a recent report, for example, the ratification of a United States-sponsored UN treaty to force all banks worldwide to disclose information on clients automatically and simultaneously. Says the report: the United States should impose "sanctions against those havens who [sic] express no interest in treaty negotiations" including limiting "direct airline flights to and from the havens."

4. *A Global Tax Treaty.* If the U. S. Senate passes a treaty that was drafted and passed by the Organization for Economic Cooperation and Development (OECD) at the behest of the U. S. State and Treasury departments, it will take a giant step towards a world IRS. The "Administrative Convention on Tax Matters" will establish a global tax-collection agency, responsible for collecting and keeping track of everything from income taxes to local property tax. All major industrial countries are members of the OECD.

Capital

For months after the October 1987 stock-market crash, we heard calls for more securities regulation. In the past, this might have meant new restrictions on American stock markets. But with international capital markets, and around the clock trading, regulators know that investors can easily move abroad to freer markets. So the regulators have decided to pursue global controls.

In November 1988, SEC Commissioner David Ruder outlined what London's *Financial Times* described as "the first authoritative blueprint for the creation and regulation of a truly global market system." The plan was announced at the annual conference of the International Organization of Securities Commissions (IOSC).

The increasingly powerful IOSC is working with other international bodies—such as the Bank for International Settlements and the OECD—to standardize controls over banking, accounting, and securities. Although moves toward standardization can reflect greater competition in the free market, *these* particular changes are not the result of market competition. Standardized regulations will only increase the power of regulators to interfere with the international flow of investment capital.

The SEC is also working to exchange information on securities transactions. The SEC's principal tool is the "Memorandum of Understanding" (MOU) which establishes formal mechanisms for swapping information and requires regulators to conduct investigations on behalf of foreign regulators. The SEC has already reached MOUs with Canada, Britain, Japan, and Brazil. It has information-swapping treaties with Switzerland, Netherlands, and Italy. And the recently passed Insider Trading Act gives the SEC authority to conduct investigations on behalf of foreign governments *even if the activity in question doesn't violate U.S. law.*

The Committee on Government Operations, which oversees the SEC, agrees with the SEC that it needs authority to deny "uncooperative countries" (i.e., those with bank secrecy laws) access to U. S. securities markets. The Committee also recommended that the SEC—in conjunction with the State, Justice, and Treasury departments—develop "a system of linking trade and other benefits to foreign government cooperation with the SEC and other U. S. agencies."

On another front, the SEC is banning electronic trading links between foreign and U. S. stock exchanges unless is can swap information and conduct surveillance with foreign regulators.

Money and Banking

In the heyday of the gold standard, politics and money were largely separate. Not so with today's fiat money and central banking.

In Reagan's first term, the administration largely followed a policy of "benign neglect," which allowed the dollar to rise and fall according to the dictates of the world-money markets. In Reagan's second term, the president abandoned this policy and replaced it with government-managed "reference ranges" for currencies. Governments and central bankers agreed to buy and sell one another's currencies to keep them trading with a specified range. As a result of these agreements, central bankers spent $120 billion to support the dollar during 1987.

The upshot will be the re-fixing of exchange rates within a world of fiat paper money. Fixed-exchange rates were harmful even under the Bretton Woods system (1945-1971), and they will be even worse if implemented today. Under Bretton Woods, world currencies were at least indirectly tied to gold. Today, the only limit to money and credit expansion is the central bankers' fear it will cause their respective currencies to depreciate relative to others. If the Fed expands dollars too quickly, traders can dump dollars and move into yen or marks. The prospect acts as a brake on inflation.

Fixed-exchange rates remove that restraint by forcing global currencies into a pre-set trading relationships. Then inflation is spread uniformly throughout the world economy while the culprits avoid detection.

Current trends in Europe toward monetary and banking integration foreshadow what could eventually happen worldwide. Twelve European currencies have been packaged into a single unit called the European Currency Unit, or ECU. The ECU has already become the world's fourth largest trading currency; ultimately, it could replace all of Europe's national currencies. European financiers and governments are lobbying to make the ECU the single currency and to create a European central bank. This will permit Europe-wide inflation. Eventually, the same steps could be taken to unite the yen, ECU, and dollar into a single world-wide currency.

Thinking Globally

Economic integration is a desirable goal. But political integration will only mean more powerful government under even less citizen control. Political borders have limited governments' jurisdiction to fixed geographic regions. When governments seek to extend their control over borders, liberty is threatened. What is true domestically is also true internationally: free markets work best when they are unhampered by government control.

The Dangers of "National Service"

Sheldon L. Richman

One of the most talked about pieces of legislation these days is a bill, sponsored by Sen. Sam Nunn (D-GA), that would set up a so-called national service program. The Nunn bill would induce young people into military or civilian service by promising vouchers worth $10,000-$12,000 for every year of service. The vouchers could be used for college tuition or a down payment on a house.

As currently planned, the program would be voluntary. No one would have to participate. But Nunn would also end existing student-aid programs (in itself a good idea), making national service more of a necessity for poor people than for the affluent.

There is a grave danger that this program will be seen as uncontroversial, will quietly get through the Congress, and will be signed by President Bush. The media have been setting the public up for complacency. For example, on a recent MacNeil-Lehrer News Hour (on PBS), Nunn defended his program against three "critics." The word is in quotation marks because each began his remarks by lauding the underlying principle of national service, before taking issue with some minor details of the plan. Could the show's staff not find one *real* critic?

What are some of the faults with Nunn's program? The problem is deciding where to begin. The premise of the program is that young people owe something to their country. This debt, so the argument would go, cannot be discharged except by having them be at the service of the government for a year or two. The first thing to note is that a voluntary program is a weak reflection of the premise. And this is why the program would not remain voluntary for long. After some time, proponents of national service will notice that the program is filled mostly with poorer people who have no other way to get money for college or a house. The more affluent can avoid the service because the inducement doesn't work for them. This will be denounced as unfair and out of spirit with the intent of the program. Amendments to make it universal and compulsory will be proposed.

That a voluntary program is just the first step to a compulsory one is reason enough to reject the Nunn plan. But it is not all, for even if it could never become compulsory, there are reasons to reject it.

First, what of the government's promotion of "civic duty"? It directly contradicts the moral foundation of free society. In such a society the government may not promote a moral code beyond the minimum of respect for individual rights. Anything more infringes freedom of conscience. Yet under the Nunn plan the government will spend $5 billion a year (not including the cost of the vouchers) to promote the idea that young people owe a duty to the state or society.

A good case could be made that the notion of service owed to the state or society is characteristic of 1930s European despotism, but in this context it is enough to say that the government should have nothing to say about it. If people want to perform service for their communities or country, there are countless private organizations in which they can do it. But it is well beyond the scope of limited government for it to tax people in order to induce others to perform service. Any taxpayer who objects to the idea that one has unchosen obligations to others would thereby have his conscience violated. (Needless to say, a compulsory program would be an even more egregious usurpation, because the government would be claiming an ownership right to a portion of the time of its citizens. This would be temporary slavery.)

The discussion so far has given too much away to the national-service advocates, for they imply that one does not create social benefits through private market activity. That of course is absurd since to be successful in the marketplace, one must be sensitive to the needs of others. Even if one's only motivation is personal profit, one cannot help but benefit others while pursuing it. That surely should discharge any obligation to the satisfaction of the national-service advocates. The reason it doesn't is that service to society is not the same as service to the government. As we will see, the national service proposal, because of its political nature, would have little to do with one's fellows and much to do with serving special political interests.

There are specific economic problems with the Nunn plan as well. How will the government decide where to allocate the labor services it will have at its disposal? In the free market, entrepreneurs observe prices for inputs and outputs to discover worthwhile investments. They then bid for the labor needed to execute their plans. If the wages they must pay are within the constraints set by final consumer valuation of the product, the enterprise is viable. If the wages are outside those constraints, this is a signal that others are willing to bid more for the services. The wage market, in other words, provides

THE ECONOMICS OF LIBERTY

indispensable signals for the rational allocation of labor and resources.

This system of signals would be of no interest to the administrators of the national-service program. The program would not face a profit-loss test and it couldn't go out of business, because the people who finance it—the taxpayers—could not withhold their revenue if they were displeased. So its standards for allocating labor would be different from those of entrepreneurs. What standards would it use? More than likely it would use the usual bureaucratic standards that we observe in other government programs. Blind to the signals that indicate the consumers' preference for resources, the bureaucrats assigning personnel would favor projects that can further their careers and prestige. For example, we could expect to see an inclination to favor organizations in the districts of congressmen who sit on the committee that approves the budget of the national-service program. Not every choice would be that obvious, but the principle underlying the program's decisions would be the same.

While the government program would be assigning people to jobs without regard to market signals, those people would be unavailable to entrepreneurs trying to satisfy consumers. The smaller labor pool would lead to higher wages, which in turn would make some enterprises uneconomical. Consumers would thus face fewer choices and higher prices.

Proponents of national service will surely object that the people in the program would perform needed services. But before we can say that a service is needed, we must see what the market says about it. There are many ways to provide a given service; the only way to know how to provide it is to let the price system work. A national-service program would circumvent the price system.

On the program's own terms, there are nagging questions. Why are young people the target? If people owe service because of the benefits they have gotten from society, it would seem that older people, who have collected more benefits than the young, have a greater obligation. Yet the program ignores this. Moreover, time off for national service would seem to be a greater hardship on young people, who are eager to set out on their own and begin their careers, than people already established in their work. Could it be that despite their rhetoric about the opportunity to serve, this is just another way for adults to control "kids"?

Perhaps a more serious indictment of such a program is that it would shift responsibility for many social problems away from their source, the government. The people who promote national service say that the poor would be helped by it. But this country has a permanent underclass because of countless regulations and restrictions—licensing, the minimum wage, rent control, to name a few—put in place by the same government that now is said to be able to help the poor by instilling the dogma of national service in America's young people.

The Mandated-Benefits Scheme
Sheldon L. Richman

If there is a salutary side to the mammoth federal budget deficits of the Reagan years, it is that they have somewhat inhibited those who would otherwise be proposing big new spending programs. When the government is already $250 billion in the red, it's harder to make a case for spending billions more for some pork-barrel project or another.

In the old, pre-Big Deficit days, interventionists would think nothing of proposing that the government provide a variety of goodies to the allegedly suffering masses: health care, food stamps, and the like. But with the budget in such disarray, what's a social engineer to do? Never fear: those who lust after your paycheck are not so easily beaten. They have come up with a formula that must seem to them as potent as any witch doctor's magic chant: mandated benefits.

If we can't have the government pay for things outright, the reasoning goes, let's have it mandate that others—employers—provide them. Budget outlay: zero. Ingenious!

The first of these mandated benefits has already been enacted. With the blessing of then President-elect George Bush, Congress ordered that businesses give 60-days' notice to unions before closing a plant or executing a big layoff. The next mandated benefit will likely be health insurance. A bill sponsored by Senator Edward Kennedy would require employers to provide health coverage to all employees working 17 1/2 hours or more a week. This idea has been adopted in Massachusetts and was part of Michael Dukakis's late presidential campaign. Other mandatory benefits being talked about include parental leave.

Of course, just because a program doesn't cost the federal government anything does not mean it is free. Medical insurance is not found superabundant in nature; someone has to pay for it. The only question is who.

The simplistic answer is that employers will pay. Let's trace this out: Assume that employers must pay $200 a month per employee to provide health insurance. Where does that money come from? Obviously it will come out of the worker's pay. Any expenses associated with a worker—Social Security, workman's compensation, unemployment insurance, medical benefits—are part of that worker's compensation package. Providing insurance on top of the workers' current pay would be to give them a raise. But if a raise were economically justified for all workers, the competitive labor market would already have bid wages up to the amount of the health-insurance premium.

Many people have trouble understanding this, but there is nowhere else for the money to come from. As the great economist W. H. Hutt wrote in *The Strike-Threat System*, worker benefits are "amenities which are purchased, so to speak, *for* the worker out of his earnings, by a decision which he is unable *individually* to influence.... The partition of labor's remuneration between pecuniary and nonpecuniary forms is obviously independent of the factors which determine labor costs.... Fringe rights and benefits are an alternative to cash receipts...."

Employers could try to raise prices to recoup the added cost from consumers. But that is not a promising move. Presuming that consumers have no more money than before the law was passed, they won't be able pay more for all that they buy. So they will cut their demand for products. That will cause firms to lay off employees or even go out of business. These workers will not only be without health insurance, they will also be without wages. Mandated benefits become mandated pauperism.

Perhaps the interventionists think employers should pay for the benefits out of their profits. But what is the justification for the forced transfer of property from employers to employees? Moreover, when profits drop, so do investment, business expansion, and opportunities. Mandated benefits would channel investment from labor-intensive to capital-intensive industries and to countries that are more hospitable to business. All of this would hurt workers here.

So the ingenious plan goes awry somewhere, and the interventionist mind can't understand why. A radio commentator who favors mandated benefits, after being confronted with these arguments, said in exasperation, "Why can't employers just treat it as a cost of doing business?" That's precisely what employers will do. To the interventionist, a cost of doing business is a mere bookkeeping phenomenon without consequences. The interventionists thinks wages, and all prices, are arbitrary inventions of businessmen. If businessmen don't want to provide these benefits, it's because they're stingy.

But wages are not arbitrary; they are set by the market. Along with the prices of all factors of production, wages are reflections of how badly consumers want the product or service in question versus all other products and services in the market. A firm cannot pay workers more than their contribution if it is to stay in business. If the law requires it, some workers will be paid more only at the expense of others who will be paid not at all. The law will have distributed wealth not from business to labor, but from one set of workers to another. This is presumably not what the idealistic proponents of mandated benefits had in mind.

As we've seen, mandated benefits violate the freedom of choice of workers by dictating the form their compensation must take. If the law requires health insurance to be provided, the benefit will displace money income that the employees otherwise would have gotten. Some employees, however, prefer cash to insurance—for instance, young, healthy workers and those who already have coverage through parents or spouses. These people will be worse off, thanks to this "humanitarian" legislation. Mandating benefits is wrongheaded when you consider that workers already have the freedom to convert some of their wages into benefits. Ordinarily, employers would have no objection; on the contrary, they might prefer that workers spend their money on things aimed at keeping them healthy. The legislation removes the workers' choice.

Similarly, a mandated 60-days' notice for plant closings is an expense that will be made up one way or another: lower cash salaries, fewer jobs, fewer plants, etc.

In a competitive labor market, some firms may choose to bear a portion of the extra burden in the hope of keeping their workers from being bid away. In this case, mandated benefits will reduce competition because the relative burden is greater for smaller firms than for big ones. Union pressure has already led many big firms to provide mandated benefits. It may be in their interest to have the government force smaller firms to bear similar costs to reduce the threat of competition.

Mandated benefits are a fraud perpetrated on the workers of America. The proponents never say outright that they believe workers are not good judges of how to spend their incomes and should have less choice in the matter. But that is what is implied by their proposals. As Hutt wrote, "When the magnitude and form of the non-cash part of labor's remuneration are a matter of governmental decision, the danger of the politically weak being sacrificed is very real."

Animal Crackers

Llewellyn H. Rockwell

Ancient pagans at least worshipped a golden calf; their modern counterparts in the animal-rights movement cherish crustaceans.

Recently PETA—People for the Ethical Treatment of Animals—bought six lobsters from a Chinese restaurant in Maryland to prevent their being "killed, dismembered, and eaten." PETA then flew the "liberated lobsters" to the Maine coast, where they were released into the Atlantic. (And where, we can hope, they made a nice meal for sea bass and other natural predators.)

That sort of harmless if loony activity affects only donors to PETA's $6 million budget. But the animal liberationists have a more ambitious agenda: they want to outlaw any use of animals in food, research, or clothing. And they don't hesitate to use violence to bring this about.

After all, says Ingrid Newkirk, director of PETA: "A rat is a pig is a dog is a boy." Adds Alex Pacheco, PETA's chairman, "We feel that animals have the same rights as a retarded human child."

Such a view, especially in the 20th century, has consequences. Animal Abu Nidals have bombed medical research labs, torched fried-chicken restaurants, burned down fur stores, burglarized turkey farms, stolen medical records, assaulted zoo employees, and vandalized butcher shops.

To animal rightists, it's a matter of simple justice. All are "acceptable crimes" if they save the lives of animals, says PETA's Pacheco. Vicki Miller, head of the Canadian Animal Rights Network, even looks forward to the prospect of "a vivisector shot in the street."

As long as the rotten RICO law is on the books, why doesn't the Justice Department stop persecuting innocent stockbrokers and indict the organized crimes of these bloodthirsty vegetarians? If they want to eat bean sprouts and wear plastic shoes, fine, but they should leave the rest of us alone.

The animal rights philosophy holds that bug or bird, manatee or man, we are all equally valuable to Mother Nature's ecosphere. But this is paganism. The Judeo-Christian tradition teaches us that God created the earth and all its creatures for mankind. They are ours to eat, wear, use, and enjoy.

What I want to know is why, if animals have the right to life, animal activists aren't out making citizens arrests of natural predators? Why aren't they interposing themselves between, say, a Kodiak bear and a salmon?

For some reason, intra-animal eating doesn't bother them. Only we aren't allowed to eat fish or meat. If these pantheists get their way, prepare to carve a 20 lb. roast tofu next Thanksgiving.

The Humane Society, which used to be relatively moderate, now says bacon and eggs are the "Breakfast of Cruelty." PETA calls McDonald's "McDeath" for serving cheeseburgers, and activists scrawl that epithet on restaurant walls.

Along with outlawing the use of cows for their meat and leather, or even raising them for milk and cheese, animal rightists want to ban the eating of fish, chicken, and even snails. Eating "our fellow creatures is cannibalism," one told me. They also want to forbid the sale of goosedown pillows, wool suits, and silk blouses, for geese are plucked, sheep are sometimes nicked when sheared, and the occasional silkworm is "boiled to death."

Silkworms are not the only insects favored by the crusaders against "speciesism," the "vicious belief that humans are the master race," an activist told me. A bug-free kitchen is also out. Cockroaches too "have a right to live," and serve the environment by being "efficient little garbage collectors."

Next on the agenda: microbe rights. A Canadian activist told the *Toronto Globe and Mail* that "viruses such as smallpox should be reintroduced as part of the earth's natural ecosystem."

Naturally, the animal ideologues such as PETA oppose the use of rabbits to test cosmetics, even if it means skin problems or eye disease for women. And, says Pacheco, animal tests must be banned in medicine too. Human welfare should take a back seat to the lab rat, as modern research against cancer, Alzheimer's, strokes, and heart disease is forbidden. "It is not a large price to pay," a PETA employee told me.

At this time of the year, the greatest ire is reserved for fur. Steve Siegal, director of Trans-Species Unlimited, even advocates spraypainting any woman with a fur coat in imitation of Swedish anti-furrists. Others use razor blades to slice up fur coats on display. And PETA also advocates chanting "fur is dead" at women in fur coats, who presumably think otherwise.

Minks, foxes, and other fur-bearing creatures are raised in "animal Auschwitzes," a PETA aide told me. These animals are "maltreated while alive, killed cruelly, and worn in savagery." Morally, this is no different from Ilse Koch, "the Buchenwald commandant who made a lampshade out of human skin."

Aside from the nature of this rhetoric, which offers an interesting glimpse into the animal-rightist soul, this is disinformation. Fur ranchers must treat their animals well. If they don't, they will have sick animals, and as any pet owner knows, that means unattractive fur.

Even though most fur coats are made from commercially grown animals, trapping is also used. This is necessary for animal husbandry, but it also serves other purposes. Bears destroy bee hives; coyotes kill livestock; beavers flood farmland and roads; and foxes, minks, and weasels attack poultry.

Thanks to violence and propaganda, fur sales have been in a recession in the United States for three years. In northern Europe, fur sales also fell, but they have since bounced back. May the same happen here, especially as the glorious pelts from the arctic areas of the Soviet Union become more available under *perestroika*.

For Christmas, PETA urges us to sing carols to zoo animals "to draw attention to their imprisonment." I have a better idea. To aid a beleaguered industry, we should give fur this Christmas. We can make another human happy and at the same time outrage the animal idolaters.

What a warming thought as we sit down to slice our nice rare Christmas roast beef.

Christian Economics

Carl C. Curtis, III

A merican evangelicals are approximately 20 million strong, and, despite their current bad press, still claim to be a powerful force in American politics. But there is another force among the evangelicals that has not received as much publicity as the religious Right, but which has proved its potency among publishers, editors, and pastors. This is the evangelical Left.

Listen to one of their leading lights, Ron Sider, in a *Christianity Today* article entitled "Mischief by Statute: How We Oppress the Poor." The capitalist West, because of its private property and markets, is "dooming more people to agony and death than slavery did" and keeping a "stranglehold...on the economic growth of the Third-World." In case Christendom missed his point, he later expanded his argument to a book, *Rich Christians in an Age of Hunger*.

And Sider is not alone. He is joined by an interna-tional cadre of professors and pastors determined to spread the Good News of socialism. Andrew Kirk of the London Institute for Contemporary Christianity and au-thor of *The Good News: The Kingdom's Coming* dreams of the future socialist state. In that golden age, the government will establish not only a minimum wage, but a maximum one as well. Unemployment benefits will match the minimum wage—a happy prospect for those who prefer not to work—and all money earned above the maximum will go to charity via "steeply progressive" taxes. Leaving aside the fact that this dream system is practically in effect in our country, Kirk apparently thinks every man, woman, and child will be healthy, wealthy, and wise under his inspired scheme. Whether or not he also believes, as Sourier did, that the sky will periodically rain lemonade, he does not say.

According to Kirk, justice and hope are not to be found in the capitalist formula, but in Marxism, "the only place where man finds his own real humanity by discovering that of his neighbor."

Much of what Kirk says was echoed by Jose Miguez Bonino, whose book *Christians and Marxism* has also influenced Left evangelicals. He too finds free markets to be fundamentally opposed to biblical teaching. "The basic ethos of capitalism is definitely anti-Christian: it is the maximizing of economic gain, the raising of man's grasping impulse, the idolizing of the strong, the subordination of man to the economic production.... In terms of their basic ethos, Christians must criticize capitalism radically, in its fundamental intentions."

Bonino has often spoken of his infatuation with Marxist theory. And not the "ideal" variety we hear so much about (but never see), the kind that eschews the abuses of Lenin, Mao, and Castro. In fact, he says he is impressed by these three totalitarians and "their deep compassion for human suffering and their fierce hatred of oppression and exploitation."

The French theologian Jacques Ellul opines in his book *Money and Power* that money is evil because it "creates a buying-selling relationship" necessarily subordinating men to itself. He further observes that "in every case (i.e., every transaction) one person is trying to establish superiority over another." Evidently, Ellul has never heard about the Austrian concept of mutually beneficial exchange. To him, sellers act only from the basest of motives. "The idea that selling can be a service is false; in truth the only thing expressed by the transaction is the will to power, a wish to subordinate life to money." Those unfortunate enough to buy Ellul's book must draw their own conclusions about his "will to power" in performing such a base act.

Though it is true that the writers and intellectuals cited here are largely in Europe and Latin America, their influence in America is as powerful as it is noxious. American evangelicals have been imbibed the brew concocted by their foreign mentors.

We might have reason to despair were it not for an equally active and infinitely more reasonable group of writers providing a rear-guard action against these socialists. In this group, one of the clearest writers and most consistent proponents of Austrian economics is Dr. Ronald H. Nash, professor of philosophy and religion at Western Kentucky University. His recent book *Poverty and Wealth: The Christian Debate Over Capitalism* successfully challenges the evangelical Left and makes the Christian case for free markets.

Nash recognizes a constant theme running through the books of the evangelical Left: the "zero-sum game." This is the contention, common to socialists everywhere, that free exchange is a type of exploitation. Nash shows how this thinking violates reason and common experience, and Nash demonstrates how free exchange—which depends on the cooperative judgment of individual subjective value—promotes mutual happiness and peace within society. This may seem obvious to readers familiar with Ludwig von Mises or Henry Hazlitt, but it is something many evangelicals deny.

Nash is also quick to pick up the evangelical Left's adulation of the state. Is this, Nash asks, Christian? Are we to put our faith in the coercive power of the government? Are we to think that a handful of men can decide questions of market pricing, proper preferences, the production and distribution of all goods and services, in offices in Washington, London, or Moscow? Such men would have to possess the knowledge of God or at least of Angels. And that is of course precisely what men do not have and what Christians throughout the ages have been admonished to remember they can never have.

A brief acquaintance with the writings of Kirk, Sider, Ellul, Bonino, and the others might tempt one to think them errant on the subject of economics, but otherwise well-intentioned Christians. A closer examination must lead to another conclusion. These men are not simply misguided. They are socialists: materialistic, dishonest, and totalitarian to the core. Theirs is not the love of God, but the love of the state, and it is imperative that they be exposed for what they are.

Breaking Up the Opinion Cartel

Llewellyn H. Rockwell

Where have all the ideological battles gone? When I first became politically active as a young conservative in the middle 1950s, everyone on our side—including those in Washington—knew that freedom was our goal and big government our enemy. Every student argument, every political battle, was couched in those terms. Today, that sentiment seems almost to have disappeared.

Too many agree with George Bush when he condemns the "divisiveness" of politics and praises the "new breeze" that will make the "old bipartisanship...new again." And, indeed, since January, hot air from the executive and legislative branches has blown serious discussion of ideas out the window. In Washington, it is hard to find more than a marginal difference of opinion on any issue.

Fred Barnes in the *New Republic* calls this is a "new era in American politics and government..., an era of consensus, conciliation, and compromise." "Serious ideological disputes are a thing of the past," he said. "Republicans and Democrats have narrowed their differences on big issues. Their fights are now over small and often barely relevant issues, or over personalities."

Barnes says the latest *anti*-consensus era lasted from 1965 (when Lyndon Johnson broke his campaign promise and escalated the Vietnam war) to 1987 (when the Iran-Contra scandal petered out without doing any damage to Ronald Reagan).

One can quarrel with his dates, but not with Barnes's analysis. Since Bush and the new bipartisanship arrived, we've gotten agreement on the S&L bailout, the Brady Plan bank bailout, a higher minimum wage, a massive increase in environmental regulation, gun control, and budget prevarication that's unusual even for Washington.

Running through all these policies, and making a thousand points of light in our pocketbooks, is the triumph of interests over values. If there is value in a free market, individual liberty, private property, and truth, then we have to oppose the Brady plan, gun control, budget fraud, and all the rest. But, since interests rule ever more openly in Washington, the S&L bailout and the rest of these bipartisan plans sail through, reminding us that bipartisan means they have both their hands in our wallets.

Fred Barnes is wrong when he describes the origins of the new bipartisanship as part of an inevitable cycle. In fact, it is a result of what Walter Lipmann once approvingly described as the government's "manufacture of consent."

Our country has a wonderful lack of official restraints on freedom of speech and press. But we combine that with a narrow range of respectable opinion, which is no coincidence. The officials, academics, media owners, and pundits who define that narrow range constitute a deliberate opinion cartel.

All governments, and the elites that live off them, want to control public opinion. Most do it through open censorship and official propaganda. Ours uses subtler and therefore more effective techniques to insure that we do not oppose the host of programs that take money from producers and hand it out to non-producers—government and its friends.

Professor Noam Chomsky, a famed linguist, explains it this way: "Where obedience is guaranteed by violence..., it is enough that people obey; what they think does not matter too much. Where the state lacks adequate means of coercion, it is important to control what people think as well."

"In wartime," said Winston Churchill, "truth is so precious that she should be attended by a bodyguard of lies." Maybe that's to be expected, but Washington follows this rule in peacetime as well. And how wonderful that it does, says Professor Everett Ladd, a specialist in public opinion: this is "the essence of statecraft." The government "must...engineer democratic consent."

Despite the myth of government-press antagonism, the national media are all too useful in this effort. Typically, the media simply recycle government handouts, from Keynesian economic projections to phony statistics on the size of the federal deficit.

Here are just a few of the issues on which consent is engineered by the opinion cartel, but which desperately need a public hearing if we are to secure human liberty:

Income tax. The income tax distorts production, reduces prosperity, violates property rights, and trespasses on financial privacy. It provides 40% of a federal budget now more than twice the size of Jimmy Carter's, but no one questions it.

Central banking. The Federal Reserve debauches the purchasing power of the dollar, distorts interest rates, creates the business cycle, and privileges big banks. It does more harm to savers and investors than any other agency, but it too is unquestioned.

Deficit. The economically destabilizing federal deficit used to be defined as the annual increase in the national debt. For the purpose of disinformation, it now means only the official deficit, while the real red ink is almost twice as large. For the S&L bailout, the Bush administration wanted the borrowing "off-budget." The Democrats wanted it "on budget," but not to count against the already leaky Gramm-Rudman ceiling. No one in Washington says the budgetary emperor is naked.

Minimum wage. The unions have waged a two-year campaign to raise the minimum wage, which will throw marginal employees out of work and strengthen the competitive position of overpaid union crews. One expects Teddy Kennedy to support this nasty business, but so does the Bush administration. The only argument is: how high? No one opposes any increase, let alone the repeal of this malodorous law.

Federal spending. The government spends more than $1.1 trillion a year. Where does all that cash end up? Very little provides the "services" we're allegedly taxed for. The poor, for example, receive a tiny portion of the welfare budget, with the vast majority going to special interests. It is the same in every area of the government.

Bureaucracy. Washington, D. C., is crawling with the most overpaid and underworked people in the world. Almost all the bureaucrats at the departments of Education, Labor, Commerce, Health and Human Services, etc. do virtually nothing. And the few who do work usually gum up the economy for the rest of us. But no one talks about eliminating these unconstitutional departments.

Environmentalism. We are all supposed to prefer tax-payer-financed wilderness to human economic development. But why should the majority pay to support the aesthetic preferences of the few? The environmental movement openly seeks bigger government and poorer people. Should the "rights" of plants and animals really take precedence over the rights of people?

These and other issues are vital to America's future, yet they are never discussed. The opinion cartel bars them from the public forum.

Yet it is not our job to convert the cartel, which is probably impossible. It is to work around it, in the academic world, in public policy, in the media, and with the general public. Here, unlike in Washington, we're making progress.

The average American is convinced of a sort of popular public choice: that most politicians are corrupt, and that they seek their own interest over the common good. It is not a giant step to convincing the people that these same crooks and clowns should not be running our economy and our lives. The popular opposition to the Congressional pay raise shows what can be achieved.

Not that it will be easy. We have been losing this battle for too long, and the thought police are ever on guard, not only to fool us, but to keep the American people passive and apathetic.

But I don't believe that a consensus in Washington on ripping us off is permanent. Nor do I agree with Fred Barnes that "Americans, it turns out, like big government." They have only been fooled and cowed into it. Breaking up the opinion cartel is therefore the first step toward mobilizing a people that still longs for liberty.

Lyndon Baines Bush?

Llewellyn H. Rockwell

George Bush may deride ideology as the "vision thing," but he has one too, and it's statist.

Ronald Reagan presented himself as the people's representative to the government. George Bush, a long-time federal functionary who identifies with the government, sees himself as representing it to the people.

Standing before Congress and the nation in January 1990, the president promised to talk, not about the "state of the government," but about the "state of the union." Unfortunately, he doesn't see any difference.

For here was a Republican president, to the cheers of Republican Congressmen, promising a fatter welfare state. No wonder Tom Foley was pleased; George Bush sounded more like LBJ than Ronald Reagan.

The government's "challenge," said the president, is "a job for everyone who wants one" (and welfare for those who don't), government child care for working mothers (yet another slap at the traditional family), a "roof over the head" of every homeless person, schools where no one fails, cheaper medical care, and zero drug use among young people. He didn't promise us longer lives and stronger teeth, or maybe I missed that part of the speech.

A Republican president, from a party that used to oppose federal aid to local schools—let alone the Jimmy Carter-NEA Department of Education—now crows over "record-high" federal spending while "announcing America's education goals."

What is this, Bolivia? In America, we have many goals—individual, family, business, and community—

and none of them is set by Washington. We don't elect a president to tell parents in Alabama or North Dakota, how to educate their children. The very idea is authoritarian and un-American. Yet this Republican president proposes to establish a national curriculum and monitor all children "at the fourth, eighth, and twelfth grades" against these bureaucratic norms.

And to those who might cut the Social Security tax, or reform any part of that Ponzi scheme, the president says: don't "mess" with it. Which seems an appropriate verb for this New Deal welfare program. The Republicans cheered that line too.

The "environmental president" is also transfiguring the EPA into the Department of the Environment (but without any more "bureaucracy or red tape," he said with a straight face). He proposes to spend billions more on the non-growing environmental bureaucracy; on the "greenhouse-effect" eco-pork scam; and on "America the beautiful": planting one billion saplings, none of them members of Congress.

The president wants higher spending on HUD and its HOPE (Home Ownership for People Everywhere); the National Endowment for the Arts; the Department of Transportation's "magnetic levitation" trains; foreign aid; export subsidies for big business; the IRS; and much, much more.

"The anchor in our world today is freedom," said George Bush, even as he cut away at the anchor rope, since every dime taken to Washington diminishes the freedom of the people.

Jefferson and the other Founding Fathers believed that government which governs least, governs best. None of them can have envisioned the Rev. George Herbert Walker Bush telling us: Come unto me, all ye that are heavy laden, and I will give you jobs, homes, child care, education, and trees.

And not to worry about the cost: "the money is there." The money is really *here*, of course, but to make sure it gets there, the president is also adding 3,667 new IRS agents. Kinder and gentler ones, no doubt.

For someone whose attention span is greater than a politician's promise, this has uncomfortable echoes. Twenty-five years ago, another president from Texas gave his first state of the union address. He too was a "conservation president" and an "education president." He too was a *apparatchik* who gloried in "public service." He too had been schooled on Capitol Hill.

Lyndon Baines Johnson was a different sort of man, of course. He didn't inherit his wealth—he stole it. And he also stole elections. But in his 1965 state of the union speech, LBJ too was a preacher.

He told of a Great Society where government would "increase the beauty of America," cure environmental problems, end poverty, and provide free medical care to Social Security recipients.

That president promised a new Department of Transportation, to build "high-speed rail transportation," more federal aid to education, subsidies for "the achievements of art," and a new Department of Housing and Urban Development for cities where people can find "significance." In short, a government that would "enable our people to live the good life."

The Bush-Johnson analogy isn't exact, of course. After all, LBJ's budget 25 years ago was, in constant dollars, *less than half* of George Bush's budget, and the Johnson budget deficit was 3% of today's. And Johnson was fighting the Vietnam war, not facing a non-existent Warsaw Pact.

But both presidents displayed the messianic streak endemic to big government. Yet it is not up to government to help man find "significance," nor to make us virtuous. That is the job of philosophy and religion. Nor can government give everyone a job, a roof, an education, and security in old age. That is the job of the market. The attempt of government to do so is bankrupting us, morally and fiscally. Bureaucratic planning doesn't work any better here than in Eastern Europe.

It is no coincidence that since LBJ's first state of the union, the underclass has grown, the family has been undermined, morality has diminished, and the economy has been shackled by regulation. America is, in almost every sense, a *less* great society.

Yet even LBJ, crook that he was, might not have given more money to the federal agency that gave us Andres Serrano's "Piss Christ" and Robert Mapplethorpe's pornography. But George Bush did.

It's instructive to read the Constitution. Unlike today's federal documents, it's short, well-written, and easy to understand, and it describes a citizen president very different from the imperial figure who presides over us today.

The president's job is to protect the borders, and enforce constitutional laws. That's it. He is not national goal setter, nor commander-in-chief over the lives of the American people.

The Environmentalist Threat

Llewellyn H. Rockwell

The New Socialism

The last Stalinist, Alexander Cockburn, has gone from attacking Gorbachev (for selling out Communism) to defending Mother Earth. His new book, *The Fate of the Forests*, is both statist and pantheist.

Cockburn, a man who supposedly cares about peasants and workers, instead decries their cutting down the Brazilian rain forests to farm and ranch. People are supposed to live in indentured mildewtude so no tree is touched.

Cockburn is part of a trend. All over Europe and the U. S., Marxists are joining the environmental movement. And no wonder: environmentalism is also a coercive utopianism—one as impossible to achieve as socialism, and just as destructive in the attempt.

A century ago, socialism had won. Marx might be dead, and Lenin still a frustrated scribbler, but their doctrine was victorious, for it controlled something more important than governments: it held the moral high ground.

Socialism was, they said, the brotherhood of man in economic form. Thus was the way smoothed to the gulag.

Today we face an ideology every bit as pitiless and messianic as Marxism. And like socialism a hundred years ago, it holds the moral high ground. Not as the brotherhood of man, since we live in post-Christian times, but as the brotherhood of bugs.

Like socialism, environmentalism combines an atheistic religion with virulent statism. But it ups the ante. Marxism was at least professed a concern with human beings; environmentalism harks back to a godless and manless Garden of Eden.

If these people were merely wacky cultists, who bought up wilderness and lived on it as primitives, we would not be threatened. But they seek to use the state, and even a world state, to achieve their vision.

And like Marx and Lenin, they are heirs to Jean Jacques Rousseau. His paeans to statism, egalitarianism, and totalitarian democracy have shaped the Left for 200 years, and as a nature worshipper and exalter of the primitive, he was also the father of environmentalism.

During the Reign of Terror, Rousseauians were what Isabel Patterson called "humanitarians with the guillotine." We face something worse: plantatarians with the pistol.

The Old Religion

Feminist-theologian Merlin Stone, author of *When God Was a Woman*, exults: "the Goddess is back!" The "voice of Gaia is heard once again" through a revived "faith in Nature."

Gaia was an earth goddess worshipped by the ancient Greeks and James Lovelock, a British scientist, revived the name in the mid-1970s as appropriate for "the earth as a living organism" and self-regulating "biosphere."

There is no Bible or "set theology" for Gaia worship, says the Rev. Stone, now making a national tour of Unitarian churches. You can "know Her simply by taking a walk in the woods or wandering on the beach. All of

Nature forms Her scriptures." Industrial civilization is "acne on the face of Gaia," says Stone, and it's time to get out the Stridex.

Ancient pagans saw gods in the wilderness, animals, and the state. Modern environmentalism shares that belief, and adds—courtesy of a New Age-Hindu-California influence—a hatred of man and the Western religious tradition that places him at the center of creation.

Environmentalism also has roots in deism—the practical atheism of the Enlightenment—which denied the Incarnation, made obeisance to nature, and saw mankind as only one of many species.

Early environmentalist John Burroughs wrote: we use the word "Nature very much as our fathers used the word God..., a Nature" in whose lap "the universe is held and nourished."

The natural order is superior to mankind, wrote ecologist John Muir more than a century ago, because Nature is "unfallen and undepraved" and man always and everywhere is "a blighting touch." Therefore, said the human-hating Muir, alligators and other predators should be "blessed now and then with a mouthful of terror-stricken man by way of a dainty."

Christianity, adds ecologist Lynn White, Jr., "bears an immense burden of guilt" for violating nature. It brought evil into the world by giving birth to capitalism and the Industrial Revolution.

Since we must think of nature as God, says William McKibben, author of the bestselling *End of Nature*, every "man-made phenomenon" is evil. We must keep the earth as "Nature intended."

To punish man's desecration, ecologist Edward Abbey urged anti-human terrorism in his influential novel, *The Monkey-Wrench Gang*. And the fastest-growing group in the Gaia liberation movement, EarthFirst!, uses a monkey wrench for its symbol.

Founded by David Foreman, former head lobbyist for the Wilderness Society, EarthFirst! engages in "ecodefense," from spiking trees (which maims loggers) to sabotaging road-building machinery to wrecking rural airstrips. One of its goals is cutting the world's population by 90%, and it has even hailed AIDS as a help.

Foreman is in prison pending trial for trying to blow up electrical pylons in the desert (using, I'm sure, environmentally safe bombs), but his example lives on. One of the respected, mainstream environmentalists, David Brower—former head of the Sierra Club and founder of Friends of the Earth and the Earth Island Institute— urged that land developers be shot with tranquilizer guns. As McKibben says, human suffering is much less important than the "suffering of the planet."

We must be "humbler" towards nature, and use technology like "bicycle-powered pumps." McKibben—who lives on an expensive Adirondack farm—wants the rest of us "crammed into a few huge cities like so many ants" because "it's best for the planet." We shouldn't even have children, for "independent, eternal, ever-sweet Nature" must be disturbed as little as possible.

McKibben admits to one sin: he owns a 1981 Honda. But a man who lives a properly ascetic life is "Ponderosa Pine," as recently celebrated in the *San Francisco Examiner* (with no mention of the "tree corpses" needed to print the paper).

A life-long leftist, Pine—whose real name is Keith Lampe—was an apparatchik of the black-power Student Non-Violent Coordinating Committee (which didn't have many students or much non-violence) and a founder of the Yippie Party. He rioted at the 1968 Democratic Convention and has been arrested nine times for civil disobedience.

Converted by Allan Ginsberg to environmentalism (and, one hopes, to nothing else), Pine split with his wife and twin sons. She had complained about his "Tibetan vocal energy science"—a continuous, hour-long, top-of-the-lungs shout each morning as an act of "communion with Mother Earth."

With his civil disobedience campaign against logging, and environmental news service, newspaper columns, and newsletter (more dead "tree flesh"), Pine has been extremely influential, though there is some dissent about his demand that we go barefoot to be in "more intimate touch with the earth." And David Brower denounces the Pinian *nom de terre*; did he, Brower asks angrily, have "permission from the Ponderosa pines to use their name?"

But even Brower agrees with the knotty Pine's crusade to collectivize the United States, return us to a primitive standard of living, and use the Department of Defense to do it. "I want to change the military's whole focus to environmentalism," says Pine. "Greetings," Uncle Sap might say, "You will hereby report to the Big Green One."

Nature Without Illusions

Ron James, an English Green leader, says the proper level of economic development is that "between the fall of Rome and the rise of Charlemagne." The "only way to live in harmony with Nature is by living at a subsistence level," as the animals do.

The normal attitude for most of human history was expressed by the Pilgrims, who feared a "vast and desolate wilderness, full of savage beasts and men." Only a free society, which has tamed nature over many generations, enables us to have a different view.

"To us who live beneath a temperate sky and in the age of Henry Ford," wrote Aldous Huxley, "the worship of Nature comes almost naturally." But "an enemy with whom one is still at war, an unconquered, unconquerable, ceaselessly active enemy"—"one respects him, perhaps; one has a salutary fear of him; and one goes on fighting." Added Albert J. Nock, "I can see nature only as an enemy: a highly respected enemy, but an enemy."

Few of us could survive in the wilderness of, say, Yellowstone Park for any length of time (even though the environmentalists let it burn down because fire is natural). Nature is not friendly to man; it must be tempered.

Environmental Hysteria

Because they know that the vast majority of Americans would reject their real agenda, the environmentalists use lies, exaggerations, and pseudo-science to create public hysteria.

POOR   The environmental movement is cheering the criminal indictment of the Exxon Corporation for the Alaska oil spill, its possibility of more than $700 million in fines. The one shortcoming, say the Sierra Club and the Natural Resources Defense Council, is that Exxon executives won't be sent to prison.

Exxon cannot be allowed to get away with an "environmental crime" which despoiled the "pristine wilderness of Alaska," says Attorney General Richard Thornburgh. But the legal doctrine underlying this indictment is inconsistent with a free society, notes Murray N. Rothbard.

Under feudalism, the master was held responsible for all acts of his servants, intended or not. During the Renaissance with growing capitalism and freedom, the doctrine changed so there was no "vicarious liability." Employers were correctly seen as legally responsible only for those actions they directed their employees to take, not when their employees disobeyed them. But today, we are back in feudal times, plus deeper-pocket jurisprudence, as employers are held responsible for all acts of their employees, even when the employees break company rules and disobey specific orders—by getting drunk on duty, for example.

From all the hysteria, and the criminal indictment, one might think Exxon had deliberately spilled the oil, rather than being the victim of an accident that has already cost its stockholders $2 billion dollars. Who is supposedly the casualty in the Justice Department's "criminal" act? Oiled sand?

If I may use the environmentalists' own language: oil is natural, it's organic, and it's biodegradable. It will go away. (Although if it didn't, it wouldn't exactly be the end of the world.)

WETLANDS   One of the great engineering achievements of the ancient world was draining the Pontine Marshes, which enabled the city of Rome to expand. But no such project could be undertaken today; that vast swamp would be protected as wetlands.

When John Pozsgai—an emigrant from communist Hungary—tried to improve some property, he found this out. After buying the former junkyard and clearing away the thousands of tires that littered it, Pozsgai put clean topsoil on his lot in Morrisville, Pennsylvania. For this, the 57-year-old mechanic faces three years in prison and $200,000 in fines. For his property was classified as wetlands under the Clean Water Act.

After ordering a bureaucrat to "get the Hell off my property," Pozsgai was arrested, handcuffed, and jailed with $10,000 bail. Quickly tried and convicted, Pozsgai is appealing his brutal sentence, which the prosecutor said would "send a message to the private landowners, corporations, and developers of this country about President Bush's wetlands policy."

John Pozsgai has a different view: I thought this "was a free country," he told the *Washington Post*.

RUBBISH William L. Rathje of the University of Arizona says there have always been garbage disposal problems. The difference is that today we have safe and efficient methods to deal with them, if the environmentalists would let us. They warn of a country covered by garbage, but in fact Americans generate less than Mexico City today or America 100 years ago. And 62% less than the environmentalists claim.

Most landfills will be full in ten years or less, the environmentalists warn, and that's true. But most landfills are only designed to last ten years. The problem is not that they are filling up, but that businessmen are not allowed to create new ones, thanks to lobbying by the environmental movement.

The environmentalists complain most about disposable diapers and fast-food containers, revealing their anti-family and pro-elite biases. But Rathje discovered that fast-food containers and disposable diapers take up only 1.1%, with all plastics totalling less than 5%. The real culprit is paper—especially telephone books and newspapers.

We're ordered to save our newspapers for recycling, so the market is flooded with newsprint. In New Jersey, this drove the price of used newspapers from $40 a ton to minus $25. Collectors once bought old newspapers. Now people must pay someone to take it away.

Bureaucrats, acting at the behest of environmentalists, want us to recycle as a sacrament of the earth religion, not because it makes economic sense.

Yet it is only through a free price system, as Ludwig von Mises demonstrated 70 years ago, that we can know the value of goods and services. We must privatize the entire garbage system. Only then can we know if it is economically efficient to recycle.

ALAR   Just before the publication of a National Research Council study extolling fresh fruits and vegetables (why do government scientists get paid to repeat what our mothers told us?), and pooh-poohing the trivial pesticide residues on them, the environmentalists arranged an ambush.

A PR man for the Natural Resources Defense Council was featured on *60 Minutes*, points out syndicated columnist Warren Brookes, and Ed Bradley denounced Alar as the "most potent carcinogen in our food supply." This was disinformation, though Bradley hasn't been given the Rooney treatment (though we will undoubtedly see naturephobia and speciesism made Official Thought Crimes.)

Alar—used safely since 1963—helps ripen apples, keeps them crisper, and retards spoilage. Using an EPA-mandated dosage of 22,000, the maximum intake of even an apple-crazy human, one rat out of the thousands tested developed a tumor. This was the extent of the "scientific proof" used not only to harm the manufacturer, Uniroyal, which had to pull Alar off the market, but the entire U.S. apple industry.

A saner voice—Dr. Sanford Miller, dean of the medical school at the University of Texas at San Antonio—noted that "the risk of pesticide residues to consumers is effectively zero." But apple sales dropped, and apple growers lost more than $250 million, with many driven into bankruptcy.

Says Dr. Miller: 99.9% of the pesticide carcinogens now eaten by humans are natural. If the Alar standard were applied to all food, "we would starve to death, because we would have to ban" everything. As man-made pesticides and fungicides are banned, we are endangered. "Fungi produce the most potent carcinogens in nature."

BAKING?   Fifteen years ago, environmentalists warned that we faced a new ice age unless the government took immediate and massive action. Today, using much of the same data, they claim we are endangered by global warming. Increased levels of carbon dioxide in the atmosphere will melt the polar icecaps and coastal areas will flood. As temperatures increase, Dallas will become a desert and Baked Alaska more than a dessert.

The proposed solution to this "Greenhouse Effect" is, surprise!, more government spending and control, and lower human standards of living. President Bush's new budget has $375 million for greenhouse research.

Yet the "net rise in world surface temperature during the last century is about one degree Fahrenheit," nearly all of it before 1940, notes syndicated columnist Alton Chase. "And the northern oceans have actually been getting cooler. The much-vaunted 'global warming' figures are concocted by averaging equatorial warming with north temperate cooling."

There is, in fact, virtually no evidence of global warming, and even if it were to take place, many scientists say the effect would be good: it would lengthen growing seasons, make the earth more liveable, and forestall any future ice age.

OZONE A similar hysteria has been raised about the ozone layer. High in the upper atmosphere, it is supposedly "Mother Earth's sunblocker" keeping us from being fried. Yet the scientific evidence is far from convincing.

Even less convincing were the "holes" that opened up over the poles, justifying the proposed abolition of refrigeration, air conditioning, and spray cans as harmful to the ozone layer. The holes turned out to open and close naturally. But the ozone panic has yet to subside.

ACID RAIN S. Fred Singer calls the acid rain issue "a billion-dollar solution to a million-dollar problem," but is it even a million dollar problem?

The official story is that northeastern forests are being eaten away by acid rain caused by sulfur dioxide and nitrogen oxide emissions, and that we need a giant spending and regulatory spree to keep the earth from being dissolved. The Bush administration is proposing to spend up to $10 billion in this cause.

Aside from the assumption that nature has the right to rainwater of a certain pH, there are several problems: (1) no one knows what causes acid rain. A giant and expensive decrease in sulfur dioxide and nitrogen oxide emissions has not diminished the acidity of rainwater in the northeast; (2) rainwater can be normally acidic; and (3) no one knows if acid rain is really harmful. There is even some evidence that acid rain helps most species of trees!

As a general rule, we should oppose any proposed public works program to cure alleged environmental ills. It is probably a scam. And even if the problem is real, more government is hardly the solution. More government is, in fact, the most serious danger to the human environment.

We need a system that allows property owners, if their trees are damaged by acid rain—and again, this is unproven—to bring suit. We do not need more bureaucrats spending more of our money on the special interests.

The environmentalists are adept at choosing language—acid rain is a perfect example—that implies we are all going to die unless some expensive government program is undertaken now.

A slight and perhaps routine increase in acidity does not mean that sulfuric acid is dropping from the sky, only that the litmus paper turns a different color.

Animal Lovers and People Haters

One of the fastest growing and most radical parts of the environmental movement is the animal rightists. They too worship nature, but make a cult out of animals whom they equate to human beings, and in fact place above us.

BABY SEALS About ten years ago, we were subjected to a barrage of photos and news stories about big-eyed seal pups hunted for their fur. Greenpeace stirred a worldwide propaganda campaign, and the European Community and others banned the import of the pelts.

This not only wiped out the livelihood of the natives who hunted the seals, but it harmed the fishing industry. With no hunting to keep the seal population under control, the animals are devouring increasingly scarce fish and damaging nets.

Some bureaucrats are proposing a government seal hunt (no private hunters, of course), but the environmentalists have prevented it. Meanwhile, stocks of cod and other fish continue to drop. Do the environmentalists care? We "shouldn't eat anything with a face," one told me.

FLIPPED The environmentalists' Victim of the Month is now the dolphin. Some of the animals are caught inadvertently by tuna fishermen, but *Flipper* reruns on TV must have convinced millions of Americans that dolphins are more intelligent than their Uncle Fred, so the environmentalists have been able to persuade them to spear the tuna industry.

Santa Barbara, California, has declared a Dolphin Awareness Day; school children all across America are engaging in letter-writing campaigns (those who still can, despite the government schools); and San Francisco kids are denounced if they bring tuna sandwiches to school.

The Audubon Society, the Humane Society, the Society for the Prevention of Cruelty to Animals, Greenpeace, People for the Ethical Treatment of Animals (PETA), and a host of similar organizations want an end, in effect, to the organized tuna industry, and they may get it.

The Marine Mammal Protection Act, passed by Congress and signed by President Reagan in 1981, imposed convoluted regulations on the industry in the name of saving dolphins. But that's not good enough, says Congresswoman Barbara Boxer (D-CA): dolphins "have creative centers larger than humans." Or at least larger than members of Congress. So new federal restrictions are needed.

The livelihood of tuna fishermen, with the life savings of whole families invested in expensive boats and equipment, are irrelevant. The environmentalists admit that they also cherish the tuna, and want it protected from fishermen, but it will have to wait. *Charlie* hasn't had his own TV show yet.

EXTINCTION   From the snail darter to the furbish lousewort, every existing animal and plant species must be kept in existence by the government—claim the environmentalists—even if human rights are violated. But why?

Most of the species that have existed since the creation, from trilobites to dinosaurs, are now extinct through normal processes. Why not allow this to continue?

If, for scientific or entertainment purposes, some people want to preserve this species or that on their own land and at their own expense, great. Zoos and universities do this already. But the rest of us should not be taxed and regulated, and have our property rights wiped out, to save every weed and bug. The only environmental impact that counts is that on humans.

FUR   In Aspen, Colorado, voters defeated a proposed ban on fur sales, but in most places it is the furaphobes who make themselves felt, especially since they are willing to use almost any tactic.

They spray paint women in fur coats, slash coats with razors, and burn down fur stores. Last year, they put incendiary bombs in the fur-selling areas of department stores all over the San Francisco Bay area. Police suspect the Animal Liberation Front (ALF), which has been charged with using identical devices elsewhere. But such is the environmentalist influence in the media that there was little publicity.

ALF, which the California attorney general calls a terrorist organization, admits it seeks "to inflict economic damage on animal torturers," from fur sellers to medical researchers.

MEDICAL RESEARCH   A physician researching Sudden Infant Death Syndrome, Dr. John Orem, "conducted groundbreaking—and painless—research on cats," notes Katie McCabe in *The Washingtonian*, "until his lab was trashed by the Animal Liberation Front." Children may die as a result, but ALF says: so what? Anything is justified to stop the use of animals.

Congress listens respectfully to animal-rights lobbyists, and has passed legislation making medical research more expensive. One amendment from then-Sen. John Melcher (D-MT) requires researchers to protect the "psychological well-being" of monkeys (whom Congressmen must feel close to) at an estimated cost of $1 billion.

This plays, however, directly into the hands of people-killers. Who knows how many cures will go undiscovered because of these restrictions? Thousands of babies have been saved because we know about the Rh factor, which was discovered through the use of rhesus monkeys. But animal rights advocates say it is better that babies die than that monkeys be used to save them.

Even Rep. Bob Dornan (R-CA) has pushed animal-rights legislation that would add billions to medical research costs. Not that he goes all the way with these people. Although named "Legislator of the Year" by the radical PETA, Dornan still "wears leather shoes." Until PETA outlaws them, that is, for the animal rightists see cow leather as no different than human skin.

Fred Barnes reports in the *New Republic*—itself pro-animal rights—that the Bush administration has buckled under animal rights pressure (Barbara is rumored to be a supporter) and "strongly opposed" legislation empowering the FBI to investigate terrorist attacks on medical research facilities.

In a cover story on the subject, *New Republic* senior editor Robert Wright says he was converted by the "stubborn logic" of the animal-rights movement, although he—like Dornan—doesn't go all the way. He still believes in "the use of primates in AIDS research."

ANTS AND SWANS
The animal rights lobby wants them to outlaw any use of animals in medical research, food, or clothing. There is "no rational basis for saying that a human being has special rights," says Ingrid Newkirk, director of PETA. "The smallest form of life, even an ant or a clam, is equal to a human being."

The "murder of animals," says Alex Pacheco, chairman of PETA, is equivalent to the "murder of men." Eating oysters on the halfshell makes you Charles Manson.

Recently there was an uproar in southern Connecticut. The state's wildlife division had proposed, in the face of an out-of-control swan population, to "shake eggs." The swans—large, heavy, aggressive birds with no natural predators in the area—were attacking children. The swans couldn't, of course, be hunted, so rangers were deputized to rattle fertilized eggs to prevent hatching. But thousands of residents protested this violation of the swans' rights.

Let's get serious, says Newkirk: "Six million Jews died in concentration camps, but six billion broiler chickens will die this year in slaughter houses."

The Politics of Environmentalism

From FDR to the present, the Democrats have been bad on environmentalism. It played an important part in the New Deal and the Great Society (Lyndon Johnson called himself "the Conservation President"), and any day I expect to see the Democrats name trees as what Joe Sobran calls an Officially Accredited Minority, with a certain number of seats (plastic, of course) in their national convention.

But environmentalism got its political start under the original liberal Republican: Teddy Roosevelt. As no one who knows Washington will be surprised to learn, there were special interests at work.

When the federal government established the national park system, and locked up millions of acres, it made other land—held especially by the timber and railroad interests associated with J. P. Morgan, Roosevelt's mentor—much more valuable. Some of these interests were the funders of the original conservation lobbying organization.

Unfortunately, Richard Nixon continued this tradition when he established—by executive order—the Environmental Protection Agency. Not surprisingly, the EPA's budget has been dominated by sewage-treatment and other construction contracts for well-connected big businessmen. But small and medium businesses, and the American consumer, have suffered from its endless regulations.

And now the EPA is to be elevated by President Bush—the "Environment President"—into a cabinet department. Typical of what we can expect is just one provision of the president's new Clean Air bill, which gives the EPA dictatorial power over any American business whose products might be harmful if burned. "This is a grant of centralized economic control," says Tony Snow in the *Washington Times*, "since just about any product can harm human health when burned."

Just as "the failures of centralized economic control" become obvious in other parts of the world, "we are about to embrace it" through environmentalism. "Forget about hammers and sickles," says Snow. If "collectivism takes root in the United States," we can thank "George Bush-types, bearing sincere faces and saplings."

President Bush has also proposed a New Deal-style $2 billion program to plant a billion saplings, none of them members of Congress.

Are we short of trees? No, but the president is "genuinely fond of trees," says a White House aide. And although no one thinks it will "cure the Greenhouse Effect," it's "symbolic of his commitment to the environment." America's foresters, farmers, landowners, and homeowners don't know the proper number of trees, but Washington, D.C., does.

The president has also endorsed a host of anti-gasoline provisions in the Clean Air bill, and higher CAFE standards (fleet-wide economy regulations) that will have the effect of mandating lighter and therefore more dangerous automobiles.

All other things being equal, the heavier the car, the safer it is in a crash. Present CAFE regulations have caused an estimated 50,000 deaths in the kiddie cars Washington has designed for us. There can be no moral or economic justification for raising the CAFE regulations (especially when they ought to be abolished), except to appease the environmentalists who would just as soon outlaw cars as individualist fripperies and make us all ride in mass transportation—until machines are abolished.

World Government and the Environment

Some problems, like alleged global warming, are so enormous, say the environmentalists, that only world government can solve them. And the one-world-types who infest the national Democrats and the resurgent Rockefeller wing of the Republican Party are glad to comply.

Establishmentarian Elliot L. Richardson, writing in the *New York Times*, says that "nothing will be done" environmentally "without an institutional mechanism to develop, institute, and enforce regulations across national boundaries."

To build "a global Environmental Protection Agency," perhaps run like "the United Nations General Assembly," that could levy taxes and impose controls to make sure there is "equitable burden sharing," the U.S. government must lead the way in the "interest of the entire world community."

Ever since Woodrow Wilson, liberals have been infected with the idea of world government. With the melding of the European Community and the coming establishment of its tax authority and central bank, the Trilateralist ideal has come closer.

Patriotic Americans must reject this globaloney, and not only on grounds of national sovereignty. We know how difficult it is to deal with city hall, let alone the state or federal government. A world bureaucracy would be a taxing, meddling nightmare. Well-connected international lawyers like Elliot Richardson would do well, but the average American would get it in the neck.

The Economics of Environmentalism

Once we reject utopianism, and realize that—for example—eight million people can't live in Los Angeles and have air like rural Colorado's—we can set about solving real environmental problems through the only possible mechanism: private property and the price system.

When the price system functions freely, it brings supply and demand into rough equality, ensuring that resources are put to their most-valued uses. To the extent that government meddles with prices, it ensures waste, hampers entrepreneurship, and makes people poorer.

If coffee—for whatever reason—becomes scarcer, its price goes up, which tells consumers to drink less. If more coffee comes on the market, its price goes down, telling consumers they can drink more. Prices thus constitute a system of resource conservation.

But environmentalists pretend—like Soviet central planners—to know economic values without prices. They claim we are "running out" of everything, and thus we need government controls on consumption. But if we really were running out of, say, oil, its price would skyrocket, telling consumers to use less and entrepreneurs to seek substitutes.

Neither do the voluntary eco-restrictions work as intended. The environmentalists are forever telling us to be poorer and use less water, less gasoline, less toilet paper, etc. But if they reduce their consumption, it lowers the price for the rest of us, and we can use more. (P.S.: don't pass this on to the environmentalists; it's the one favor they do the rest of us.)

When anything is commonly owned—like air and water—we see all the bad effects of socialism. People abuse the resource because they do not have to bear the price.

To solve this problem, anyone who is personally harmed, or his business damaged, by air pollution ought to be able to sue to stop it, and receive damages. But the federal government intervened in this common-law process in the 19th century to favor special interests, making it impossible, to take a real example, for a farmer to sue a railroad whose spark emissions burned down his orchard.

The federal government also nationalized the coasts and waterways specifically to smooth the way for industrial special interests.

If, as is the case with many waterways in England and other countries, people had property rights in the streams and rivers running through their land, they could prevent pollution just as they prevent trash dumping in their front yard. And if fishermen and homeowners held property rights in the coasts and adjacent waters, they could prevent pollution and properly allocate fishing rights.

The recent hysteria over African elephant tusks was another problem of property rights. If people were allowed to raise elephants and sell their tusks—as even the Zimbabwean government pointed out—there would be no more and no fewer elephant tusks than there should be. The same principle applies to all other resources. If left in common ownership, there will be misuse. If put in private hands, we will have the right amount: supply will meet demand.

An example of market conservation was the Cayman Turtle Farm in the British West Indies. The green sea turtle was considered endangered, thanks to over-harvesting due to common ownership. The Farm was able to hatch eggs and bring the hatchlings to maturity at a far higher rate than in nature. Its stock grew to 80,000 green turtles.

But the environmentalists hated the Cayman Turtle Farm, since in their view it is morally wrong to profit from wildlife. The Farm was driven out of business and the green turtle is again on the endangered species list.

GREENOMICS   Greens—like all liberals—justify government intervention because of what economists call "public goods" and "externalities."

A "public good" is supposed to be something we all want, but can't get, unless government provides it. Environmentalists claim everyone wants national parks, but the market won't provide them, so the government must. But how can we know, independent of the market, that everyone does want these expensive parks? Or how many parks of what sort?

We could take a survey, but that doesn't tell us the intensity of economic demand. More important, it is not enough to know that people want, for example, diamonds. That means something economically only if they are willing to give up other things to obtain them.

Amazingly, liberal economists have never developed a way to identify these so-called public goods, so—objective scientists that they are—they use intuition. Paul Samuelson's favorite example was the lighthouse, until Ronald Coase demonstrated that private entrepreneurs had provided lighthouses for centuries.

If we realize that only the market can give us *economic* information, the alleged problem of public goods disappears.

Absent government prohibitions and subsidies, or competition from "free" parks, the market will ensure that we have exactly the number and type of parks that the American people want, and are willing to pay for. Moreover, if we sell all the national parks, we can pay off the federal debt.

An "externality" is a side-effect. Your neighbors' attractive new landscaping is a positive externality; their barking dog is a negative one. One is a blessing, the other an irritant, but you voluntarily purchase neither.

Environmentalists say, for example, that trash is a negative externality of consumerism. So they advocate more regulation and bureaucracy to solve it. Yet the free market solves this much more justly and efficiently through property rights. Privatize everything and the externalities are "internalized," that is, those who ought to bear the costs do. But to environmentalists, human prosperity is itself a negative externality.

Chicken or chicory, elephant or endive, the natural order is valuable only in so far as it serves human needs and purposes. Our very existence is based on our dominion over nature; it was created for that end, and it is to that end that it must be used—through a private-property, free-market order, of course.

The environmental movement is openly anti-human and virulently statist. Is it any coincidence that the Nazis exalted animals, nature, and vegetarianism above humans, civilization, and civilized eating, or that our environmentalists have an air of green goose step about them?

The environmentalists must be opposed—if they will excuse the expression—root and branch.

6

THE COMMUNIST CRACKUP

Mises Vindicated

Llewellyn H. Rockwell

I f Ludwig von Mises were alive today, he could say: "I told you so." For in 1920, he wrote a long article on socialism, followed by a book two years later, that crafted socialism's tombstone.

In all the debates over socialism, he alone cut to the heart of the matter. Socialism doesn't qualify as an economic system because it seeks to abolish economics, he said. Without private property in the means of production, there can be no economic calculation and no price system. There can only be chaos.

"Whoever prefers life to death, happiness to suffering, well-being to misery," he said, must fight socialism and defend, without compromise, capitalism: "private owner-ship in the means of production."

As syndicated columnist Warren T. Brookes recently pointed out, "the real godfather of communism's European crackup" is Ludwig von Mises, whose "penetrating mind gave intellectual birth to Hayek, Friedman, and Buchanan, and rebirth to Adam Smith."

"Yet von Mises was completely shut out of the socialist/fascist-minded Austrian and German universities in the 1920s and 1930s," Brookes notes, "and was never offered any American post after exile by Nazism. Why? He wrote a book titled *Socialism*" and "showed with precise logic why socialism could never work." And "he coined the phrase 'statolatry' for the new Western irreligion."

The *Wall Street Journal*'s editorial page noted that "At the recent Comecon meeting, the strongest opposition to the communist status quo came from the Czechs—and in particular, their new finance minister Vaclav Klaus. 'The world is run by human action,' Klaus told Comecon, 'not by human design.' Some readers will note that Mr. Klaus was paraphrasing the famed Austrian economist Ludwig von Mises, whose 1949 book *Human Action*, is among his classic works on free-market economics. Mises, of course, was also a relentless critic of economic planning. We can't help but note the many Western intellectuals now proposing to teach the East Europeans how to live and work. It appears that the Czech finance minister has that well in hand."

And, as Yuri N. Maltsev, late of the U.S.S.R., points out, dissident Soviet economists look to Mises and his followers, not to Paul Samuelson, John Kenneth Galbraith, and other fellow travelers of socialism. And from similar testimonies, we know the same is true in Eastern Europe.

Austrian economics may undergo a second spring because of these emigre economists, who—like Mises—battle socialism and all other forms of statism without compromise.

In this country, we have never been subjected to full-blown socialism, but statolatry has still taken a dreadful toll: a spastic economy, a perverted culture, a swelling underclass, a declining standard of living, and a monstrous government.

As the freedom revolution leapt from country to country in Eastern Europe, some leftists claimed—as they whistled past their own graveyard—that the people were repudiating Stalinism, not Marxism. That's baloney, of course. People who have lived under Marxism make Joe McCarthy look like a pinko. Look for committees to investigate un-Bulgarian, un-Rumanian, and other activities.

Other leftists still cling to a mythical "third way" between communism and capitalism. But social democracy is inherently unstable. It pretends that some sectors of the economy—such as medicine—can be socialized, while others are left private, with no detriment to the economy. Such systems, as Mises pointed out, must ever trend towards freedom or totalitarianism, while wrecking economic havoc all the while.

Even Sweden—welfare-queen of the social democracies—is learning this lesson. Public opinion polls show that 78% of the people want much more privatization of state child care and socialized medicine. They're sick of having bureaucrats raise their kids and care for their sick.

In America, events seem to move at an Eastern-European pace, but in the opposite direction. While statism is being dismantled abroad, it is being constructed here at home.

EXHIBIT A: President Bush and the Democrats want to make the Environmental Protection Agency a cabinet department.

The EPA—a quintessential big business welfare agency—was founded by Richard Nixon in 1972 through an unconstitutional executive order. Ever since then, it has achieved bureaucratic success by handing out special-interest construction contracts while catering to the most anti-capitalist, indeed anti-human, forces in our society. The EPA should be dismantled, not exalted.

We have yet to learn that the environmental vision is just as impossible as the socialist one, and just as dangerous in the attempt.

EXHIBIT B: Sen. Joe Biden (D-Plagiarism) and unnamed "White House staff," not to speak of Drug Shah William Bennett, want to create a cabinet department of drugs, as if more government will win the unwinnable.

EXHIBIT C: The bipartisan S&L bailout will surpass $450 billion, which is a moral outrage. Why should this industry be funded on the backs of the American taxpayer?

If we are to have a bailout, along with picking the executives and directors clean, why not sell government assets for the rest? The feds own 40% of U.S. land. How about auctioning some of it? Taxpayers aren't responsible for the S&L fiasco, and they shouldn't pay for it.

EXHIBIT D: The Bush administration attacks Sen. Daniel Patrick Moynihan's (D-Phony British Accents) Social Security tax cut of $600 per American family as intended to raise other taxes.

Moynihan's motives may very well be bad (unlike the other senators, presumably), but so what? Any tax cut, any time, is a good idea. If anyone in D.C. had any guts, he's be calling for a reevaluation of the entire Ponzi scheme.

(Note: if tax cuts can be smokescreens for tax increases, what does one say about the 1981 Reagan cuts that were followed by five Reagan increases, including the monstrous SS increases?)

EXHIBIT E: The Bush administration has put an entire country—Panama—on welfare. The cost, we're told, is "only $1 billion," but don't believe it. We have only begun to pay the costs of Operation Noriega.

Given the way the Bush administration talks here at home, we might think it's encouraging a Panamanian capital-gains tax cut, privatization, less government, and more free enterprise. Instead, the administration is bilking us for Panamanian welfare checks and a gigantic public works program, plus subsidies to U.S. big business through the egregious Export-Import Bank, founded by FDR as part of the New Deal.

This all looks pretty discouraging, but it could be the final gasp of the securitate. I believe the global revulsion against government will finally reach the country where it all started 200 years ago: America.

Just as the Great Depression set us back decades—because the ideological scam-meisters succeeded in pinning the result of central bank inflation on capitalism—the freedom revolution will advance us decades.

With ideological history, a paradigm seems entrenched, until tossed out overnight through a thought revolution. Now the paradigm has shifted towards our side. Our job is to overthrow the idol of statolatry, and install in its place respect for the free market, for individual liberty, for private property, and for sound money. Ludwig von Mises told us so.

The Freedom Revolution

Murray N. Rothbard

I t is truly sobering these days to turn from a contemplation of American politics to world affairs. Among the hot issues in the United States has been the piteous complaint about the "martyrdom" of Jim Wright, Tony Coelho, and John Tower to the insidious advance of "excessive" ethics. If we tighten up ethics and crack down on graft and conflict of interest, the cry goes, how will we attract good people into government? The short answer, of course, is that we will indeed attract fewer crooks and grafters, but one wonders why this is something to complain about.

And then in the midst of this petty argle-bargle at home comes truly amazing, wrenching, and soul-stirring news from abroad. For we are privileged to be living in the midst of a "revolutionary moment" in world history. History usually proceeds at a glacial pace, so glacial that often no institutional or political changes seem to be occurring at all. And then, wham! A piling up of a large number of other minor grievances and tensions reaches a certain point, and there is an explosion of radical social change. Changes begin to occur at so rapid a pace that old markets quickly dissolve. Social and political life shifts with blinding speed from stagnation to escalation and volatility. This is what it must have been like living through the French Revolution.

I refer, of course, to the accelerating, revolutionary implosion of socialism-communism throughout the world. That is, to the freedom revolution. Political positions of leading actors change radically, almost from month to month. In Poland, General Jaruzelski, only a few years ago the hated symbol of repression, threatens to resign unless his colleagues in the communist government accede to free elections and to the pact with Solidarity. On the other hand, in China, Deng Hsiao-ping, the architect of market reform ten years ago, became the mass murderer of unarmed Chinese people because he refuses to add personal and political freedom to economic reform, to add *glasnost* to this *perestroika*.

Every day there is news that inspires and amazes. In Poland, the sweep by Solidarity of every contested race, and the defeat of unopposed Communist leaders by the simple, democratic device—unfortunately unavailable here—of crossing their names off the ballot. In Russia, they publish Solzhenitsyn, and a member of the elected Congress of Deputies gets on nationwide TV and denounces the KGB in the harshest possible terms—to a standing ovation. The KGB leader humbly promises to shape up. In the Baltic states, not only are *all* groups, from top Communists down—calling for independence from Soviet Russia, but also the Estonians come out for a free market, strictly limited government, and private property rights. In Hungary, numerous political parties spring up, most of them angrily rejecting the very concept of socialism.

In the "socialist bloc" covering virtually half the world, there are no socialists left. What all groups are trying to do is to dismantle socialism and government controls as rapidly as possible; even the ruling elites—certainly in Poland and Hungary—are trying to desocialize with as little pain to themselves as possible. In Hungary, for example, the ruling *nomenklatura* is trying to arrange desocialization so that *they* will emerge as among the leading capitalists on the old principle of "if you can't beat 'em, join 'em."

We are also seeing the complete vindication of the point that Hayek shook the world with in the *Road to Serfdom*. Writing during World War II when socialism seemed inevitable everywhere, Hayek warned that, in the long run, political and economic freedom go hand in hand. In particular, that "democratic socialism" is a contradiction in terms. A socialist economy will inevitably be dictatorial.

It is clear now to everyone that political and economic freedom are inseparable. The Chinese tragedy has come about because the ruling elite thought that they could enjoy the benefits of economic freedom while depriving its citizens of freedom of speech or press or political assembly. The terrible massacre of June 4th at Tiananmen Square stemmed from the desire by Deng and his associates to flout that contradiction, to have their cake and eat it too.

The unarmed Chinese masses in Beijing met their fate because they made the great mistake of trusting their government. They kept repeating again and again: "The People's Army cannot fire on the people." They ached for freedom, but they still remained seduced by the Communist con-game that the "government is the people." Every Chinese has now had the terrible lesson of the blood of thousands of brave young innocents engraved in his heart: "The government is *never* the people," even if it calls itself "the people's government."

It has been reported that when the tanks of the butchers of the notorious 27th Army entered Tiananmen Square and crushed the Statue of Liberty, that a hundred unarmed students locked arms, faced the tanks, and sang the "Internationale" as the tanks sprayed them with bullets, and, as they fell, they were succeeded by another hundred who did the same thing, and met the same fate.

Western leftists, however, cannot take any comfort from the contents of the song. For "The Internationale" is a stirring call for the oppressed masses to rise up against the tyrants of the ruling elite. The famous first stanza, which is all the students were undoubtedly able to sing, holds a crucial warning for the Chinese or for any other Communist elite that refuses to get out of the way of the freedom movement now shaking the socialist world:

Arise, ye prisoners of starvation!
Arise, ye wretched of the earth,
For justice thunders condemnation,
A better world's in birth.

No more tradition's chains shall bind us,
Arise, ye slaves; no more in thrall!
The earth shall rise on new foundations,
We have been naught, we shall be all.

Who can doubt, any more, that "justice thunders condemnation" of Deng and Mao and Pol Pot and Stalin and all the rest? And that the "new foundations" and "the better world in birth" is freedom?

[Editor's note: this article was published in June 1989, before the changes in Eastern European.]

The Old Right Was Right

Sheldon L. Richman

The pace of change in the Soviet Union and Eastern Europe is so brisk that it is risky to write anything about it. Nevertheless, the virtual dismantling of the Berlin Wall and the beginning of liberalization in East Germany are exhilarating news, the climax of months of historic developments.

One's natural reaction is: "Incredible! Unbelievable!" But are these things really unbelievable? Shouldn't we have expected this all along? According to the Cold War orthodoxy, this was not to be expected. We were told that no communist government would ever voluntarily give up power. It was a law.

So the spontaneous disintegration of the communist world should come as a shock to us all, right? It would not have come as a shock to a group of men who predicted exactly what has happened. This was a varied group of journalists, scholars, and politicians that has become known as the Old Right.

The Old Right, whose activities spanned the 1930s to the mid-1950s, was characterized by its immense distrust of concentrated political power. Its members objected to the domestic policies of the New Deal precisely because it concentrated power in the Washington

bureaucracy. Just as important, they objected to concentrated power motivated by foreign-policy considerations.
For that reason, the Old Right opposed U.S. participation
in the Cold War, though they were also bitter enemies of
communism.

Among the leading figures of the Old Right were
Robert Taft, John T. Flynn, Frank Chodorov, Garet Garrett, Albert Jay Nock, H. L. Mencken, and Felix Morley.
Many lesser-known thinkers filled its ranks, qualifying
it as a bona fide movement beginning in the interwar
period. Looking back at what they counselled for America
versus the Soviet Union is instructive and fascinating.

Before examining what the Old Right said about the
Cold War, we should be clear on what is happening in
the Soviet Union and the Eastern Bloc. In broadest
terms, the people there have awoken to what they've
been missing. Two-thirds of households in the Soviet
Union have no running water. *Pravda* has written that of
276 basic consumer goods, 243 cannot be found in stores.
According to Paul Craig Roberts, "Soviet economists speak
openly of 40 million people in poverty and on the brink of
famine." The situation is similar in the Soviet Union's
Warsaw Pact allies. These are stagnant economies, more
like Third World nations than industrialized countries.

How long could people be expected to live under these
conditions if they have an inkling of what people in the
West have? In East Germany the answer was plain:
200,000 of the brightest young people fled the country
in 1989. Mikhail Gorbachev and his counterparts in
Poland, Hungary, and East Germany realized that the
stability of their countries, and their own futures, were
at risk if things went on as they have been.

Gorbachev seems to understand that big-power status and prestige would be denied a country that cannot grow enough food for its own people. His solution is to begin to integrate the Soviet economy with the world economy. He wants trade and technology, and to get it he must commence, however modestly, market reforms. The people have demanded change, and the rulers could not ignore it.

The Old Right knew this would happen some day. They were skeptical of those who said that the only way to break communism's hold was a belligerent foreign policy. This, they said, would be expensive and damaging to the U.S. economy, would risk a cataclysmic war, and would fail. Rather than loosen the totalitarian grip, it would probably tighten it.

What could America do, then? The Old Right answered that the best chance the U.S. had to roll back communism and protect its own security was to live up to its ideals and set a good example. American prosperity would make it the envy of the world and cultivate friendships with all nations. Meanwhile, the economic and spiritual shortcomings of communism would create the conditions for internal change. The Old Right grasped intuitively, if not theoretically, Ludwig von Mises's fatal criticism of socialism as incapable of rational economic activity. A policy that risks war could never have the same results.

As Taft, then-Republican leader in the Senate, put it in 1951, "there are a good many Americans who talk about an American century in which America will dominate the world." If "we confine our activities to the field of moral leadership we shall be successful if our philosophy is sound and appeals to the people of the world. The trouble with those who advocate this policy," he said, "is that they really do not confine themselves to moral leadership. They are inspired with the same kind of New Deal planned-control ideas abroad as recent Administrations have desired to enforce at home."

John T. Flynn, the Old Right journalist and America First Committee organizer, said in 1950 that regarding the Cold War, "the course of wisdom for the American people would be to sit tight and put their faith in the immutable laws of human nature." To do this, he said, Americans would have to "make an end to the Cold War."

Frank Chodorov, another Old Right journalist, agreed. In 1954 he wrote "That our culture—the body of ideas, habit, and traditions indigenous to America—is under severe attack there is no doubt. But can we save it by killing off or subjugating the communist natives of other lands?"

"Communism is not a person," he wrote "it is an idea. But you cannot get rid of the idea that has possessed the communist by killing him, because the idea may have spread and you cannot destroy every carrier of it. It is better, therefore, to attack the idea than to attack the natives."

The Old Rightists were confident that Soviet domination, left to its own devices, would fade as time went on. This was expressed by the diplomat and historian George F. Kennan, himself not an Old Rightist, but one whose foreign-policy views were largely compatible. In his memoirs Kennan wrote of his years observing the Nazi occupation of Europe:

"I was brought to recognize the continued and undiminished relevance in the world of Gibbon's assertion that 'there is nothing more contrary to nature than the attempt to hold in obedience distant provinces.' Out of this grew my feeling that one must not be too frightened of those who aspire to world domination. No one people is great enough to establish world hegemony. There are built-in impediments to the permanent exertion by any power of dominant influence in areas which it is unable to garrison and police, or at least to overshadow from positions of close proximity, by its own troops."

How was this Old Right view to be turned into policy? Free trade, without government assistance, was the prescription. The United States and its allies over the years have followed two opposite courses, both of which have delayed the communist disintegration. Liberals tended to favor subsidies and aid, that is, forced trade; the conservatives tended to favor trade restrictions. Shortly after the Bolshevik revolution, the Western countries tried to topple the Soviet Union by refusing to allow trade (and by invasion). Later, in the 1920s and 1930s, Western governments subsidized trade and loans to the communist bloc. At other times they provided foreign aid.

Although embargoes and subsidies seem like contradictory policies, they had one thing in common: they strengthened the communist regimes. The subsidies and transfers helped them cover up the inevitable failures of communism and prolong its life. Since, as Mises first pointed out in 1920, rational economic calculation is impossible under socialism, countries trying to carry out socialism must fail.

The Bolsheviks admitted failure in 1921 when they switched from War Communism to the New Economic Policy, which was essentially a reestablishment of the market. Later, under Stalin, the Soviet Union ended the NEP, but it never returned to a moneyless, trade-less economy. Instead, it put in place a highly bureaucratized, interventionist state that had a veneer of central planning. It too was doomed to failure. But the infusion of Western wealth through government policy camouflaged the core incompetence of the system. The West, at taxpayer expense, bailed out the East.

Mises in 1952 wrote that "the United States is subsidizing all over the world the worst failure of history: socialism. But for these lavish subsidies the continuation of the socialist schemes would have become long since unfeasible."

The policy of trade restriction fared no better. The rationale was that if trade were forbidden, the East would sink lower into poverty, prompting the people to rise up and overthrow the communist regimes. For several reasons, it didn't work. First, the deprivation caused by the West made good propaganda for the regimes. They could tell their people that a hostile world wishes them ill and only support for the government could assure their security. The Soviet state would justify its existence, and deflect blame for the misery, by saying that just as it had protected them from the Nazis, now it was protecting them from the aggressive capitalist countries. It could plausibly ask its people for patience until the external threat subsided.

Another reason the strategy did not work is that, as Alexis de Tocqueville pointed out, revolutions do not occur when people are ground into despair. Radical change occurs, rather, when people glimpse what is possible to them from rising expectations. Merely depriving the people subjected to communism of consumer products could not be expected to impel them to overthrow their governments.

V. Orval Watts, an Old Right educator, debunked the embargo strategy. He wrote that government restrictions on private trade with communist countries strengthen the Iron Curtain because embargoing trade also embargoes ideas. In a 1955 article he wrote that "An American, for example, cannot walk down a Moscow street without conveying to passersby certain truths about the outside world—through the quality of his shoes, the cut of his clothes, his unafraid bearing and peaceable manner. Everywhere he goes, and in every contact, he does or says things which teach the meaning of freedom and expose the lies on which the Soviet rulers depend for inculcating fear and hatred of capitalism and of the peoples practicing it."

We should "work for a revolution behind the Iron Curtain. But for this, we need carriers of revolutionary ideas. In selecting the best means of accomplishing this revolution in Russia, let us not arbitrarily and emotionally reject the effective means of peaceful traders and travelers."

The meaning of these criticisms, in light of today's events, is staggering: U.S. policy has prolonged communist rule and delayed the crack-up.

Those who reply that what is happening now is the result of U.S. containment policy and military spending, which forced the communists to spend resources on arms rather than consumer products, miss the point of

Mises's calculation argument. Given the inherent incompetence of bureaucratic economies, it would not have mattered if the Soviets spent *no resources* on arms. The consumer economy would still have been starkly inferior to the West.

There is another point implicit in this analysis that is contrary to the Cold War orthodoxy. It is a fallacy to believe that public opinion plays no role in communist countries because the regimes rule by brute force. Totalitarian regimes always spend immense resources on propaganda and the promotion of an ideology, which is nothing less than a moral rationalization of the regime. They must do this, as Etienne le Boetie wrote in *The Politics of Obedience*, because the people always outnumber the rulers. Without the people's acquiescence and cooperation, the regime could not last.

The Old Right view is really the traditional U.S. foreign policy view. It was what Washington meant when he warned against "political connection" with foreign countries and what Jefferson meant in his warning against "entangling alliances." John Quincy Adams put it most eloquently: "America does not go abroad in search of monsters to destroy. She is the well-wisher to the freedom and independence of all. She is the champion and vindicator only of her own."

As to be expected, many American political leaders and commentators want the U.S. to pour taxpayer money into Eastern Europe and even the Soviet Union in the view that without our help, their attempts at reform will fail. This is mistaken. To the extent the U.S. government transfers the taxpayers' wealth there, those countries will have less incentive to really reform.

A government transfer is always a give-away of wealth that shields the recipient from its folly. In contrast, a private investor will expect something concrete in return or he will not invest. This is a surer way to encourage true liberalization. If they want Western capital, they will have to do what is necessary to make investment attractive.

As Mises wrote: "Prosperity is not simply a matter of capital investment. It is an ideological issue. What the underdeveloped countries need first is the ideology of economic freedom," which the United States should send them.

But that means that we ourselves should be clear about what is desirable politically. Until we are, we are not likely to be a good example to those who are groping for solutions in the communist world. If the reform economists there call for anti-trust laws and taxes on "excess profits," it doesn't take much imagination to see what they are using for a model.

Most of the talk about reform has been associated with democracy, but democracy in itself will not improve the condition of the subjects of communism. Democracy is a method for selecting rulers. But the problem in these countries is that economic decisions are made by politicians and bureaucrats—not how they got into office. Popular election of commissars would not make the Soviet economy better able to serve consumers. What would change the economy is individual rights, private property, sound money, and the rule of law—in other words, libertarian capitalism. That should be our banner, not democracy.

I do not wish to depreciate the Soviet or East German's attraction to "popular rule." When distant rulers have been telling you what to do with your life, it is natural to want a say in one's governance. I only want to point out that if the reform ends with democracy, it will not have been worth thc candle. There is but a small difference between having no say in one's own affairs and in having one vote out of millions. How the rulers are chosen is far less important than what the rules are. The civility of a democratic country should be measured in how much of life is beyond the reach of the democratic process.

Finally, a related point: Implicit in much discussion about recent events is the belief that East and West are converging toward a system that is neither communist nor capitalist. Advocates of convergence usually believe that this middle position is a good thing, avoiding the "extremes."

In fact, as Mises taught, the middle of the road is an unstable mixture that must eventually move toward more or less freedom. There is no need to seek a mixture of freedom and slavery because slavery adds nothing of value to the mix.

We will have missed the point of the East's revolution if we remain complacent about our own situation. Contrary to Francis Fukuyama (author of the acclaimed article "The End of History?"), now that Marxism is dead, we must get on with the main debate, the one between freedom and statism of any form. The objective in this debate is to bring to America a fully free market and voluntary social order.

The Vanishing Spectre of Communism

Doug Bandow

Nine years ago Ronald Reagan based his presidential campaign not only on a pledge to shrink government spending, but also on a promise to expand the Pentagon. For, in Reagan's view, only a massive military build-up could counter the threat posed by the "evil empire" of Soviet communism.

Evil it was, and remains, but in retrospect we can see that the threat was already fading, though few in the U.S., or probably even the Soviet Union, then realized it. For four decades the U.S.S.R. had been the foe used to justify the most draconian of measures to suppress American liberties—crushing taxation for unending subsidies for an increasingly inept military-industrial alliance, conscription, restrictions on free speech, and government secrecy laws. But now the spectre of totalitarianism on the march—the excuse for the most execrable of Washington's conduct—has largely disappeared.

The totalitarian structure imposed by the Red Army can no longer hold back people's freedom impulse in the Eastern bloc. And the repressive system built upon the rubble of the Czarist empire is itself imploding. There, too, when given a choice, people—with no democratic tradition, not one prior opportunity to freely express their opinions—joyously go to the polls to unseat thugs and assorted party hacks.

Almost as satisfying is the disarray spreading through the American Left. As long as the U.S.S.R. claimed it was building a better world, leftists could delude themselves that they had found "the future." If sometimes they had to shift utopias—going from the Soviet Union to China to Cuba to Vietnam to Nicaragua, etc.—there was always yet another nation where they could look for true socialism. What, however, can they say when virtually every member of the Communist Party leadership—other than in such depressing, cultish states as North Korea, Cuba, and Albania—admits that its system has failed?

Poor U.S. Communist Party Chairman Gus Hall now argues that "much of the Soviet mass media is not pro-socialist" since it spreads "falsehoods and slander about socialism" and paints a "false fairy-tale picture about capitalism." Former Institute for Policy Studies staffer Michael Parenti warns that decrepit Eastern Europe's move towards capitalism could result in, yes, a lower standard of living and "rationing of the kind that occurs in this country, by the market."

But it is not enough to luxuriate in the spread of freedom. We should encourage the spread of this good virus to hasten the collapse of what remains of the communist relic around the world. The most obvious means of doing so is to continue spreading the ideas of liberty. The collapse of communism reflects the ideological triumph of the Western conception of human rights as well as the practical triumph of Western market economies. In countries such as China, it is the idea of liberty, buttressed by the successful model of the U.S. and allied states, that has stolen the younger generation away from the embrace of Marxism.

The U.S. should also issue the sort of policy challenges that will spur change within Eastern Europe and the Soviet Union. President Bush could suggest, for example, that Moscow end conscription. In return, the U.S. would drop draft registration and all "national service" schemes. America's allies, such as Germany, would abandon their systems of forced military service.

The U.S. government should not, however, flood Poland and Hungary, or any other reforming state, with aid. If foreign aid worked, Tanzania, Bangladesh, Egypt, and a host of other poor states would be rich today; if access to vast amounts of foreign credit guaranteed economic success, Brazil, Mexico, and Argentina, rather than Japan, would be economic powerhouses. Only drastic policy reform can restore economic health to communist states, and American aid would only reduce the pressure for meaningful change. *Socialist economics*, as well as communist politics, must be allowed to collapse.

A century ago collectivism effectively supplanted classical liberalism as the dominant ideology of the West; statism naturally infused the scores of new nations formed around the globe since then. But the competition between capitalism and communism is now over, and no one, aside from Gus Hall and a dispirited remnant on the socialist left, has any doubt as to which is the winner. It's time for modern libertarians to celebrate—and then to work even harder to help shape a new, free, social order.

The Socialist Holocaust in Armenia
Llewellyn H. Rockwell

A roar, a shudder, and the end of the world. That was Soviet Armenia on December 7, 1988, when the great earthquake struck. In moments, whole cities disappeared, as nurseries and factories, homes and offices collapsed into rubble, killing 55,000 men, women, and children.

But no matter what seemed to be the case, those people weren't victims of geologic forces; they were casualties of socialism.

The Armenian earthquake measured 6.9 on the Richter scale. In 1985, Mexico City had two back-to-back earthquakes measuring 8.1 and 7.5, yet they did far less damage, with almost all of the deaths caused by collapsing public housing. In Armenia, all the buildings were public, and they all collapsed.

After the earthquake, Brian Tucker, a California geologist, said the destruction in Armenia was 100 times as great as it would have been in California from a similar-size quake. In fact, the ratio is probably 1,000 to one. The 1989 Northern California earthquake measured 7.1 and the few who died were killed by a collapsed government highway. In 1971, a major San Fernando Valley earthquake, measuring 6.5, did relatively little damage, except to a federal government hospital, which caved in and killed 49 people.

Nature is often blamed for the failure of socialism: bad weather, for example, for 70 years of Soviet crop failure. The Ethiopian famine is blamed on a drought, even though socialist dictator Mengistu has deliberately starved the peasants, Stalin-style, to collectivize them.

Unlike natural disasters, the destructive effects of socialism are not capricious. They are necessary consequences of government control.

In his important book *A Theory of Socialism and Capitalism* (Kluwer Academic Publishers and the Mises Institute, 1988), Professor Hans-Hermann Hoppe shows that socialism must result in: (1) much less capital formation; (2) a gargantuan waste of resources; and (3) destructive overuse of the means of production. Armenia is an all-too-accurate illustration.

Under socialism, all capital goods are publicly owned. Without individual ownership, as Hoppe explains, under socialism there is almost no incentive to produce new capital goods, let alone to keep up older ones. Control over those capital goods is exercised by bureaucrats, not savers, contractors, and investors.

There is no market for Soviet buildings or building materials. Everything is decided by central government planners, and citizens must live or work in whatever the bureaucrats erect. As a result, builders have no stake in the value of their work. And since the buildings cannot be sold, there is no reason for tenants or managers to try to preserve what little value the structures have.

Making the best use of scarce resources is impossible under socialism. That's because, as Ludwig von Mises showed in 1920, socialism precludes the possibility of rational economic calculation. There is, to take a simplified example, only a limited amount of steel, which must be allocated to both industry and building. Without market prices, there is no way to tell which is the more highly desired end.

In our relatively free market, we assume that concrete is less valuable than steel and that both are less valuable than marble. But we know this only because the market-generated prices tell us so. Without private property, free exchange, and market-prices, nobody can know what anything is worth.

The Soviets get a rough idea from Western pricing schedules, but that's not enough for rational economic calculation. To know how, when, and where to use capital and resources, there must be trade so that each good can have a market price.

Without this process, the Soviet economy is necessarily chaotic, with random surpluses and shortages. Even if a builder wanted to build a sturdy apartment house in the Soviet Union, he probably couldn't get the necessary resources.

Under socialism, government builders must fulfill the Plan no matter what, which results in the overutilization of available resources. Quality, which can't be bureaucratically quantified, is ignored. In fact, it is an impediment to turning out the ordered amount of production with the least amount of effort. The result is incredibly flimsy buildings.

The efficient production of buildings is an enormously complex process, too complex to be encompassed in a central plan. There is no way that bureaucrats in Moscow can handle it, let alone discover, like the entrepreneur, more effective ways of doing it.

In a free market, consumers ultimately determine the pattern of production. If buyers would rather have brick houses than wooden ones, the structure of production reflects this by bidding up the price of bricks, which pulls them away from alternative uses where they are less highly valued.

We can see the importance of consumer sovereignty in this process, as value is imputed backwards from consumer goods to production goods. Not only socialists misconstrue this. Mainstream economists claim that each stage of production mechanistically "adds value" to the final output, when it is actually the value of the consumed good that determines the value of the capital that goes into producing it.

Under socialism, this process is thwarted. The decisions of consumers have little, if any, connection to the central plan. When goods are produced with little or no consumption value, as is usually the case, resources are wasted and everyone is made poorer.

It is no wonder that in Moscow, buildings come crashing down five or ten years after they are built; even the ones still standing must have nets hung out over the sidewalks to catch falling masonry. In the U.S.S.R.'s internal colonies, standards are even lower—so low that an earthquake that would have minimal effect in the U.S. turns Soviet cities into cemeteries.

The inconceivable death and destruction in Armenia is a vivid illustration that economics is not arcane. Good economics results in prosperity and freedom. Bad economics results in a holocaust.

How To Desocialize?

Murray N. Rothbard

Everyone in Soviet Russia and Eastern Europe wants to desocialize. They are convinced that socialism doesn't work, and are anxious to get, as quickly as possible, to a society of private property and a market economy. As Mieczyslaw Wilczek, Poland's leading private entrepreneur, and Communist minister of industry before the recent elections, put it: "There haven't been

Communists in Poland for a long time. Nobody wants to hear about Marx and Lenin any more." In addition to coming out solidly for private ownership and denouncing unions, Wilczek attacked the concept of equality. He notes that some people are angry because he recently urged people to get rich. "And what was I to propose? That they get poorer perhaps?" And *he* was rejected by the Polish voters for being too attached to the Communist Party!

Eastern Europeans are eager for models and for the West to instruct them on how to speed up the process. How *do* they desocialize? Unfortunately, innumerable conservative institutions and scholars have studied East European Communism in the past 40 years, but precious few have pondered how to put desocialization into effect. Lots of discussion of game theory and throw weights, but little for East European desocializers to latch onto. As one Hungarian recently put it, "There are many books in the West about the difficulties of seizing power, but no one talks about how to *give up* power." The problem is that one of the axioms of conservatism has been that once a country goes Communist, the process is irreversible, and the country enters a black hole, never to be recovered. But what if, as has indeed happened, the citizens, even the ruling elite, are sick of communism and socialism because they clearly don't work?

So how can communist governments and their opposition desocialize? Some steps are obvious: legalize all black markets, including currency (and make each currency freely convertible at market rates), remove all price and production controls, drastically cut taxes, etc. But what to do about state enterprises and agencies, which are, after all, the bulk of activity in communist countries? The easy answer—sell them, either on contract or at auction—won't work here. For where will the money come from to buy virtually all enterprises from the government? And how can we ever say that the government deserves to collect virtually all the money in the realm by such a process. Telling individual managers to set their own prices is also not good enough; for the crucial step, acknowledged in Eastern Europe, is to transform state property into private property. So, some people and groups will have to be *given* that property? Who, and why?

As Professor Paul Craig Roberts stated in a fascinating recent speech in Moscow to the U.S.S.R. Academy of Sciences, there is only one way to convey government property into private hands. Ironically enough, by far the best path is to follow the old Marxist slogan: "All land to the peasants" (including agricultural workers) and "all factories to the workers!" "Returning" the state property to descendants of those expropriated in 1917 would be impracticable, since few of them exist or can be identified, and certainly the *industries* could be returned to no one, since they (in contrast to the land) were created by the Communist regime.

But there is one big political and economic problem: what to do with the existing ruling elite, the *nomenklatura*? As the Polish opposition journalist Kostek Gebert recently put the choice: "You either kill them off, or you buy them off." Admittedly, killing off the old despotic ruling elites would be emotionally satisfying, but it is clear that the people on the spot, in Poland and Hungary, and soon in Russia, prefer the more peaceful buying them off to pursuing justice at the price of a bloody civil war. And it is also clear that this is precisely what the *nomenklatura* want. They want free markets and private ownership, but they of course want to make sure that the transition period assures them of coming out very handsomely in at least the initial distribution of capital. They want to start capitalism as affluent private entrepreneurs.

Interestingly, Paul Craig Roberts, whom no one could ever accuse of being soft on communism or socialism, also recommends the more peaceful course: "Historically in these transformations ruling classes have had to be accommodated or overthrown. I would recommend that the Communist Party be accommodated." In practice what this means is that "ownership of the state factories should be divided between the ruling class and the factory workers, and stock certificates issued." His solution makes a great deal of sense.

Alternatively, Roberts says that a national lottery could determine the ownership of the means of production, since whoever initial owners may be, an economy of private property will be far more efficient, and "resources will eventually find their way into the most efficient and productive hands." But the trouble here is that Roberts ignores the hunger for justice among most people, and particularly among victims of communism. A lottery distribution would be so flagrantly unjust that the ensuing private property system might never recover from this initial blow. Furthermore, it does make a great deal of difference to everyone where they come out in such a lottery; most people in the real world cannot afford and do not wish to take such an Olympian view.

In any case, Roberts has performed an important service in helping launch the discussion. It is about time that Western economists start tackling the crucial question of desocialization. Perhaps they might thereby help to advance one of the most welcome and exciting developments of the 20th century.

A Radical Prescription for the Socialist Bloc
Murray N. Rothbard

It is generally agreed, both inside and outside Eastern Europe, that the only cure for their intensifying and grinding poverty is to abandon socialism and central planning, and to adopt private-property rights and a free-market economy. But a critical problem is that Western conventional wisdom counsels going slowly, "phasing-in" freedom, rather than taking the always-reviled path of radical and comprehensive social change.

Gradualism, and piecemeal change, is always held up as the sober, practical, responsible, and compassionate path of reform, avoiding the sudden shocks, painful dislocations, and unemployment brought on by radical change.

In this, as in so many areas, however, the conventional wisdom is wrong. It is becoming ever clearer to Eastern Europeans that the only practical and realistic path, the only path toward reform that truly works and works quickly, is the total abolition of socialism and statism across-the-board.

For one thing, as we have seen in the Soviet Union, gradual reform provides a convenient excuse to the vested interests, monopolists, and inefficient sluggards who are the beneficiaries of socialism, to change nothing at all. Combine this resistance with the standard bureaucratic inertia endemic under socialism, and meaningful change is reduced to mere rhetoric and lip service.

But more fundamentally, since the market economy is an intricate, interconnected latticework, a seamless web, keeping some controls and not others creates more dislocations, and perpetuates them indefinitely.

A striking case is the Soviet Union. The reformers wish to abolish all price controls, but they worry that this course, amidst an already inflationary environment, would greatly aggravate inflation. Unfortunately, the Eastern Europeans, in their eagerness to absorb pro-capitalist literature, have imbibed Western economic fallacies that focus on price increases as "inflation" rather than on the monetary expansion which causes the increased prices.

In Soviet Russia and in Poland, the government has been pouring an enormous number of rubles and zlotys into circulation, which has increased price levels. In both countries, severe price controls have disguised the price inflation, and have also created massive shortages of goods. As in most other examples of price control, the authorities then tried to assuage consumers by imposing especially severe price controls on consumer necessities, such as soap, meat, citrus fruit, or fuel. As an inevitable result, these valued items end up in particularly short supply.

If the governments went cold turkey and abolished all the controls, there would indeed be a large one-shot rise in most prices, particularly in consumer goods suffering most from the scarcity imposed by controls. But this would only be a one-shot increase, and not of the continuing and accelerating kind characteristic of monetary expansion. And, furthermore, what consolation is it for a consumer to have the price of an item be cheap if he or she can't find it? Better to have a bar of soap cost ten rubles and be available than to cost two rubles and never appear. And, of course, the market price—say of ten rubles—is not at all arbitrary, but is determined by the demands of the consumers themselves.

Total decontrol eliminates dislocations and restrictions at one fell swoop, and gives the free market the scope to release people's energies, increase production enormously, and direct resources away from misallocations and toward the satisfaction of consumers. It should never be forgotten that the "miracle" of West German recovery from the economic depths after World War II occurred because Ludwig Erhard and the West Germans dismantled the entire structure of price and wage controls at once and overnight, on the glorious day of July 7, 1949.

In addition, the Eastern European countries are starved for capital to develop their economy, and capital will only be supplied, whether by domestic savers or by foreign investors, when: (1) there is a genuine stock market, a market in shares of ownership titles to assets; and (2) the currency is genuinely convertible into hard currencies. Part of the immediate West German reform was to make the mark convertible into hard currencies.

If all price controls should be removed immediately, and currencies made convertible and a full-fledged stock market established, what then should be done about the massive state-owned sector in the socialist bloc? A vital question, since the overwhelming bulk of capital assets in the socialist countries are state-owned.

Many Eastern Europeans now realize that it is hopeless to try to induce state enterprises to be efficient, or to pay attention to prices, costs, or profits. It is becoming clearer to everyone that Ludwig von Mises was right: only genuinely private firms, private owners of the means of production, can be truly responsive to profit-and-loss incentives. And moreover, the only genuine price system, reflecting costs and profit opportunities, arises from actual markets—from buying and selling by private owners of property.

Obviously, then, all state firms and operations should be privatized immediately—the sooner the better. But, unfortunately, many Eastern Europeans committed to privatization are reluctant to push for this remedy because they complain that people don't have the money to purchase the mountain of capital assets, and that it seems almost impossible for the state to price such assets correctly.

Unfortunately, these free-marketeers are not thinking radically enough. Not only may private citizens under socialism not have the money to buy state assets, but there is a serious question about what the state is supposed to do with all the money, as well as the moral question of why the state deserves to amass this money from its long-suffering subjects.

The proper way to privatize is, once again, a radical one: allowing their present users to "homestead" these assets, for example, by granting pro-rata negotiable shares of ownership to workers in the various firms. After this one mighty stroke of universal privatization, prices of ownership shares on the market will fluctuate in accordance with the productivity and the success of the assets and the firms in question.

Critics of homesteading typically denounce such an idea as a "giveaway" of "windfall gains" to the recipients. But in fact, the homesteaders have already created or taken these resources and lifted them into production, and any ensuring gains (or losses) will be the result of their own productive and entrepreneurial actions.

Mises in Moscow!
An Interview with an Austrian
Economist From the U.S.S.R.

Jeffrey A. Tucker

Dr. Yuri Maltsev was a professor at the University of Marxism-Leninism in Moscow, a member of the Soviet Academy of Sciences, and an economic advisor to the Central Committee of the Communist Party of the U.S.S.R. He defected during an academic meeting in Finland in 1989 and now lives in Washington, D.C. He is a senior adjunct scholar of the Ludwig von Mises Institute, and this summer, he is a faculty member of our Mises University.

Q: *You were recently teaching economics in Moscow, yet you are an advocate of private property and the free market. Shouldn't we be surprised?*

A: No. After decades of enslavement, almost no one in the U.S.S.R. is interested, for example, in the views of

John Maynard Keynes. People, both in and out of academics, are looking for freedom, not an alternative method of government control. Even if they haven't read Mises, Hayek, and Rothbard, they are instinctive libertarians.

Q: *People see government as the problem?*

A: Everyone knows that the government is responsible for giving them a Third-World economy. We joke that inside the Kremlin walls there is communism (no money, just prosperity); inside the Moscow beltway, there is socialism (money and some goods and services); and outside the beltway, there is feudalism. Three of Marx's stages, of course.

A lot of intellectuals in the U.S. think there is some sort of plan behind the Soviet system. And there is, but not what they think: it is simple political power. Imagine the U.S. if the Democratic Party ran everything, and I mean *everything*, down to the tiniest detail, and everybody was a post office employee. That's the Soviet Union. As Mises demonstrated so many years ago, such a system cannot work because there are no market prices and no profit and loss signals.

Q: *What about the morality of central planning?*

A: It fails on that ground as well. If you impose a Single Will on the citizenry, everybody who deviates from this Will must be exterminated. Between the 1930s and the 1950s, 40 million people were slaughtered to carry out the Plan. Today, the government seldom shoots people, but it does deprive them of their jobs. And because it is a monopolistic economy, they cannot get another one.

Q: *How are prices set?*

A: This is the most absurd part of the Soviet economy. They pretend to use a cost-plus basis for pricing. But the profit is planned for you. Say you have a planned profit rate of 15%, and the cost of a good is 1 ruble. The price of the good will be 1.15 rubles. But if you include the costs of your own mismanagement in the base, then you can make a higher profit. So the system favors the maximization of inputs, not outputs, spending not production.

There are 22 million prices in the Soviet Union, most of them are computed on the local level. The State Committee on Prices issues the "methodological materials," which are rules on what must be included in the price, for example, the costs of material inputs and labor inputs. These costs are based on other costs. Then you have to submit the price to the Committee and they will check it and sometimes revise it. When the price is approved, it is never changed.

One of the strongest points of Austrian economics is the logical theory of the business cycle. You cannot think of a recession as a bad thing. It cleanses the economy of everything it does not need. Everything that is not wanted by consumers goes by the wayside. But imagine this: in 72 years, the Soviet Union has never closed a single enterprise.

Q: *But they know they should?*

A: Sure, they know they must. But how do you do it? There are too many vested interests. The only thing the Soviet government has left to brag about is that they have no unemployment. Last year, about 40% of all the enterprises could not meet the planned profit target. Theoretically, that means they operated with losses. Say they introduce so-called market socialism—a concept which really has no meaning—then these enterprises must be self-supporting. That means 40% of the enterprises would have to go belly-up. Some good economists say these enterprises are a burden and should be eliminated. But the point is you can't trust the profit and loss figures. They don't reflect consumer preferences and they can be miscalculated. There are plenty of enterprises that are essential, like farming, that always operate at losses. The overall agricultural productivity is minus six percent. This shows absolute ignorance of economics and social science.

Q: *Who benefits from phony figures?*

A: The managers of the Soviet enterprises. The only measure of your success is how you meet the planned target. The output target is the most important, and sometimes it is even nice to pretend you are making a profit.

It is hilarious to attend the annual meetings of the ministers. They rush to the podium to brag about how much they have produced and how they fulfilled the plan. All the while they are looking at the higher-level minister they answer to. But they are faking it. If you have been ordered to produce 10,000 widgets, but you only produce 9,000, you have a very strong incentive to lie about it. And moreover, to say you produced 11,000. It is very difficult to calculate these things, and nobody really cares. That's why they have to rely on foreign statistics so much.

Gorbachev has admitted that he expects agricultural losses to be about 40% in this year's harvest. And people there say, oh, how open and honest he is. But I don't believe these figures. Much of the harvest will never be seen. The numbers are imaginary. When the time comes, they will say the rats ate the harvest, or it was lost in a storm, or fell out on the railway, or whatever.

Q: *We've heard only recently that the Soviet GNP is much lower than we—and the Soviets—were told.*

A: Soviet GNP figures are ridiculous. I have a close friend, a very smart economist, who estimates that the Soviet economy is seventh or eighth in the world. But we can't say for sure. We do know that the standard of living is Third World.

A main problem is double counting. Say someone wants to produce an irrigation tractor. First they excavate the ore for steel and count that. Then they make pig iron and count that. On and on it goes, with steel, spare parts, etc., until the final tractor. At each stage they have counted the product in its entirety, not just the value that is added. I approximated the value-added cost of the tractor to be 870 roubles. But the enterprise was reporting the cost at 11,870 roubles. That is what goes into GNP calculations.

Q: *The CIA has used Soviet statistics on production for years.*

A: That's sheer irresponsibility. But it is not as if the CIA knew the truth. Nobody, including the Soviets, knows the truth. I know people in Washington think-tanks that think the Soviets are tampering with the figures just to fool Americans. They think the Soviets know the true figures. The truth is, they don't know themselves. Today the CIA and several think-tanks are recalculating Soviet statistics, but they are doing so on the basis of other phony Soviet statistics.

Q: *Much concern over the Soviet military threat was based on these figures.*

A: Sure. There are groups in the U.S. with a vested interest in showing the Soviet economy as larger than it really is. And some people think you can compare U.S. output with Soviet output on a dollar for dollar basis. You can certainly make up some quotient, but it is absurd.

Q: *Our government has long said the Soviet economy doesn't produce consumer goods because all resources are poured into the military, a sector which is pretty efficient. Socialism can't produce margarine and soap, but it can make planes and tanks. What do you think?*

A: Socialism cannot produce anything efficiently. The reason they can't produce margarine and soap is not because the resources aren't there, but because the socialist system doesn't work. Plenty of Soviet military officials fabricate figures themselves, as I know from my own army experience.

Gorbachev is trying to reduce military spending this year by 15%. When I was in the Soviet Union, I headed the project on the civil service. The final goal is conversion of 40% of the military to the civilian sector by 1993. Gorbachev thinks this will free resources, and prosperity will bloom in the consumer sector. But it will not, thanks to socialism.

Q: *What about the state of economics in the U.S.S.R.?*

A: Most economists there are trained in practical, not theoretical, economics. But Mises is far more respected in the Soviet Union than Paul Samuelson or J.K. Galbraith. The government's official propaganda treats libertarians as Enemy Number One because they openly condemn the socialist system. But the more the government

criticizes them, the more they appear interesting. Moreover, ideas condemning the Soviet authorities carry more
weight than the official pronouncements themselves.
That is why Boris Yeltsen is so popular. It is not his charm
and charisma. He was singled out as an enemy by the
official propaganda and it backfired.

Q: *Does the public believe what the Soviet authorities
say about America?*

A: If I went back to the Soviet Union today and said,
"I live in Washington, D.C., and there is widespread street
crime, corruption, crack wars, and people without
homes," everybody would assume I was a KGB agent.

No one believes the authorities. If a Soviet official
says, the economic plan has achieved and exceeded its
goals, people know it has failed as usual. There is a joke
that if the government forecasts warm weather, people
assume it will be cold.

Q: *What do you think about America?*

A: I love the American people and American society.
Americans are unbelievably good-hearted and generous.
This is the most wonderful country in the world. On the
other hand, I don't love government, any place, Moscow
or D.C. Thanks to democracy, your government is much
less extensive, and much less corrupt, but with a very
few exceptions, all politicians and bureaucrats are engaged in the same protection of vested interests through
economic and political manipulation. And they issue the
same sort of ridiculous orders.

One of the first things I encountered in the U.S. was
a Soviet system of newspaper pickup. Here is a newspaper which I have bought and paid for. Under the Constitution, I thought I had the right to eat it, burn it, or

dispose of it in any way. In the condominiums where I live, we received an order from the D.C. government. Each week you must surrender this newspaper in special bags, which you must get from the local supermarket. If you do not obey, you can be fined $400. In other words, I am told to surrender my property free of charge to the government according to their irrational standards. And I thought I was escaping socialism!

Q: *What do you predict for* perestroika?

A: It will be a failure. The overwhelming problem is the monopoly of the Communist Party. They are running the reforms. There are a myriad of vested interests. That is why I am more optimistic about Eastern Europe. They have all but eliminated their Communists. For years, the people living under socialism didn't know how bad they had it. Only with *glasnost* did people realize that socialism is built on lies.

Q: *Does Gorbachev deserve any credit?*

A: Yes, for *glasnost*. And he went all over Eastern Europe telling the people that the U.S.S.R. would not intervene militarily. That was the signal to throw the governments out. And they did. His foreign policy has been right on target.

In fact, many people in the Soviet Union believe Gorbachev is an anti-communist. If you are General Secretary of the Communist Party, you cannot just say, "This system is baloney." You must go about it slowly and covertly. If he is not an anti-communist, then he is a fool.

Q: *How can the U.S. help the capitalist revolution?*

A: Not through foreign aid! It will actually hurt by entrenching bureaucrats. The more money they get, the less eager they are to reform. And diplomatic missions to murderous regimes are disastrous too, both practically and morally. The best thing the U.S. can do is to export good economic thought, as the Ludwig von Mises Institute does, and set a good example by reducing the size of government here.

The Cambodian Catharsis

Lawrence W. Reed

I t is always better to kill by mistake than to not kill at all" was the slogan of Pol Pot's communist Khmer Rouge. From April 17, 1975, until January 7, 1979, the tiny southeast Asian nation of Cambodia endured a nightmare of mass murder, torture, and oppression at the hands of the fanatical Khmer Rouge. In an attempt to brutally reshape society, Pol Pot waged a campaign of genocide. Money was abolished. So was private property. The institution of the family was nearly erased. An all-out assault on religion led to the deaths of thousands of Buddhist monks and worshippers. Churches and pagodas were demolished. Schools were closed down and modern medicine forbidden in favor of quack remedies and sinister experimentation. Even eating in private or scavenging for food were considered crimes against the state.

Mass graves have been unearthed all over Cambodia, giving rise to the title of the movie, *The Killing Fields*. At one place I visited known as Choeung Ek, a memorial houses more than 8,000 human skulls—all found nearby. Rivers near places like this ran so red with blood that cattle would not drink from them.

Peace talks in Paris in the summer of 1989 convened to find a way to form a coalition government of reconciliation, but broke down over the U.S.-Red China demand that Pol Pot and the Khmer Rouge play a role in the new government. Should these monsters shoot their way back into Phnom Penh, the stage would surely be set for Act Two of the Cambodian Holocaust.

With that awful prospect dangling over this tragic nation, I went to Phnom Penh expecting the worst. A million land mines and other horrors of war have left behind many crippled and legless people. The city's drainage and sewer systems are in such disrepair that even a moderate rainfall produces flooded and often smelly streets. Peeling paint, crumbling stucco, and filthy walls and floors have taken over what once were glistening and majestic French colonial-style buildings. Routine power outages blacken whole sections of the city from 10 minutes to an hour every day. I visited a military hospital where young men blinded and maimed subsisted on the barest of medical care. Orphans were as prevalent as children with parents.

The Khmer Rouge had forced people to leave the capital. When the city was repopulated after 1979, housing was reclaimed—homesteaded is the word—in a free-for-all. So much had been damaged that the 750,000 people who now live in the capital are crowded into tiny apartments. One house I visited had been home to a family of five; now it is home to 63 people from no less than seven different families. All this was depressing. But it's not the whole story.

The big news in Cambodia is the revival of life, the reconstruction of markets, and incredible growth of economic activity. The city was humming with vitality and enterprise—with more optimism than any visitor could reasonably have hoped to witness.

Progress is palpable, even astonishing. A French relief worker told me that since the government began implementing "free-market reforms" a few years ago, the progress has come "almost hourly."

Indeed as the Vietnamese pull out and their influence in the Cambodian government wanes, Cambodians are putting markets in charge of the economy. Agriculture has been largely de-socialized; farms are now chiefly in private hands, by either lease or outright ownership.

There are no wage controls, no price restrictions, almost no controls over the movement of people and capital, no rationing, and no lines in front of stores. Having just visited the Soviet Union for the fourth time, days before arriving in Phnom Penh, I found myself thinking how envious my friends in Moscow would be if they could see the variety and abundance of goods in Phnom Penh's still officially communist markets.

In the city's Central Market, one of its many commercial hubs, hundreds of women hawk all sorts of produce from fish to fruit. Others push gold and silver jewelry, watches and calculators and televisions from Japan, bluejeans and T-shirts emblazoned with American logos and city names, a wide array of cosmetics, and all the Pepsi and Seven-Up one needs in the tropical sun-drenched land.

Along Phnom Penh's main thoroughfare, women are having their hair done in several privately owned beauty shops. Restaurants are humming with business and serve a variety of cuisines from "international" to native

Cambodian dishes of fried cricket, snake soup, duck feet, sweet and sour chicken, and, of course, white rice. Shops full of automobile and bicycle parts, carpets and mattresses, even tennis rackets and baseballs, dot the city.

The capital now boasts 20 theaters. For the equivalent of 50 cents or less, you can see a movie on the big screen, ride an elephant, play ping pong, or join a small audience of 20 or 30 crowded into a darkened shop to view an American film or a music video. Pleasure boaters ply the city's large lake, Voeung Kak, while families nearby enjoy a small zoo and amusement park.

Four months ago, there wasn't a photocopier to be found in Phnom Penh, except for a few in government or private offices. In recent weeks, a half dozen small shops have opened advertising photocopy services. Cambodians love to have their pictures taken, and entrepreneurs have responded by opening photographic studios all over the city. And the country's first one-hour film developing business has just been inaugurated by a man who committed more than 10 years of his family's savings to the venture.

People who aren't on foot get about town via bicycle, motorcycle, bicycle-rickshaws called "cyclos," or car—and there are now several thousand cars; whereas, six months ago there were barely 200. Gasoline can be purchased from a few government gas stations when they have it, but for about 20% more, you can get it anytime from the free-market vendors along the curbside.

Not even high inflation—which I estimate to be running at 75% plus—has put much of a damper on the business boom. Checkbooks and savings accounts are rarely used, but the cash economy is growing feverishly

without them. Though the government fixes the Cambodian currency—the riel—at 150 to the U.S. dollar, it
permits a thriving exchange business in the streets
where the buck fetches 210 riels.

Service with a smile seems to be the order of the day
all over town. I found that little more than eye meeting
eye quickly produces a broad, friendly grin from almost
every Cambodian. In the markets, even a prospective
patron who declines a purchase usually warrants a smile
and a polite thank you.

By the end of my stay, I was asking people to tell me
just what was "communist" about Cambodia anymore.
Aside from the one-party political monopoly, the country
is relying substantially on free enterprise to direct every-
day life. Even former beggars, I was advised, are getting
into business.

To be sure, Phnom Penh has a long way to go before
it achieves the level of prosperity it had before the
Vietnam War spilled over into Cambodia in the late
1960s. And in the countryside, where conditions are
generally harsher than in the capital, the reconstruction
of normal life has been painfully slow. A rising tide of
political corruption threatens to undermine the regime's
progress in currying favor with the public.

But the advances to date, coming on the heels of near
national annihilation, are a remarkable testament to the
curative powers of private enterprise and to the determination of the Cambodian people. Three years and nine
months of Pol Pot's horror could not erase the spirit of
enterprise in the Cambodian people, or their desire to
survive and rebuild.

Mises's Blueprint for the Free Society

Sheldon L. Richman

The bravery of the masses in China, Russia, and Eastern Europe are an inspiration to lovers of liberty everywhere. They are calling for freedom of speech and assembly and an end to official corruption. These are laudable objectives, but they cannot be guaranteed without more fundamental changes in the communist system. And the most consistent and integrated alternative is classical liberalism, a philosophy and tradition that built Western civilization.

The best place to explore the foundations of classical liberalism is in Ludwig von Mises's classic work *Liberalism*. This is Mises's succinct statement of the meaning of the political philosophy that liberated mankind from the old order of feudalism and mercantilism and raised man's standard of living such that the noblemen of old would envy the position of today's poor.

Early in the book, Mises acknowledges that "Liberalism...has nothing else in view than the advancement of [men's] material welfare and does not concern itself directly with their inner, spiritual and metaphysical needs." He realizes that classical liberalism has been attacked through the ages for not being concerned with man's nonmaterial needs, and he answers the charge forthrightly: "It is not from a disdain of spiritual goods that liberalism concerns itself exclusively with man's material well-being, but from a conviction that what is highest and deepest in man cannot be touched by any outward regulation." Liberalism seeks "outer well-being because it knows that inner, spiritual riches cannot come to man from without, but only from within his own heart."

Mises identifies seven tenets that form the foundation of classical liberalism:

1. *Private Property*. This is the most misunderstood part of liberalism. It is the key that separates advocates of capitalism from its opponents, even those who are otherwise concerned with individual liberty. To the Marxist or Maoist, property is exploitation; to the real liberal it is liberation. Mises says, "the program of liberalism, therefore, if condensed into a single word, would have to read *property*, that is, private ownership of the means of production." "All the other demands of liberalism result from this fundamental demand," he writes.

2. *Freedom*. Mises is concerned to tie the case for individual liberty to the progress of society and the material advancement of the human race. He writes: "What we maintain is only that a system based on freedom for all workers warrants the greatest productivity of human labor and is therefore in the interest of all inhabitants of the earth." Freedom for Mises means the right to enter contracts, to move as one pleases, to immigrate, and to emigrate. When we get to Mises's discussion of limits on government power, we'll see what else he attaches to this concept.

3. *Peace*. Classical liberalism from the beginning was associated with peace. When the martial virtues were extolled, it was the liberals who vouched for the superiority of production and commerce. As Mises puts it, "The liberal critique of the argument in favor of war...starts from the premise that not war, but peace, is the father of all things. What alone enables mankind to advance and

distinguishes man from the animals is social cooperation. It is labor alone that is productive.... War only
destroys; it cannot create." Mises differentiates the liberal case against war from the "humanitarian" case by
pointing out that the liberal "is convinced that victorious
war is an evil even for the victor...."

4. *Equality*. No concept that began with liberalism has
been more subject to abuse than "equality." The various
doctrines of egalitarianism ride on the achievements and
goodwill created by liberalism, but would destroy them
if practiced consistently. For Mises, equality means no
more and no less than equal treatment under the law.
"Nothing, however, is as ill-founded as the assertion of
the alleged equality of all members of the human race,"
writes Mises. "Even between brothers there exist the
most marked differences in physical and mental attri-
butes."

5. *Limited Government*. Under liberalism, government
power is to be limited to protecting people and their
property from aggression. Anything beyond that makes
the individual a slave. "We see that as soon as we
surrender the principle that the state should not interfere in any questions touching on the individual's mode
of life, we end by regulating and restricting the latter
down to the smallest detail," he writes. The danger of
government's moving beyond its narrow function is the
suppression of the innovators. "All mankind's progress
has been achieved as a result of the initiative of a small
minority that began to deviate from the ideas and
customs of the majority until their example finally moved
the others to accept the innovation themselves," writes
Mises. "To give the majority the right to dictate to the

minority what it is to think, to read, and to do is to put a stop to progress once and for all."

6. *Tolerance*. Mises makes a poignant plea for tolerance: "Liberalism," he says, "must be intolerant of every kind of intolerance." It "proclaims tolerance for every religious faith and every metaphysical belief, not out of indifference for these 'higher' things, but from the conviction that the assurance of peace within society must take precedence over everything and everyone." "Only tolerance," he says, "can create and preserve the condition of social peace without which humanity must relapse into the barbarism and penury of centuries long past."

7. *Democracy*. Mises's democracy is to be sharply distinguished from other theories of democracy. For Mises, democracy is the method of choosing the "rulers," not the rules. The difference is critical. Under the latter conception, no one is safe from the whims of the majority or the well-organized minority, as under the absolute democracy of Athens or of Rousseau's fantasies.

For Mises, democracy is the method of making violent internal political upheaval unnecessary. "There can be no lasting economic improvement if the peaceful course of affairs is continually interrupted by internal struggles," Mises writes. "Democracy is that form of political constitution which makes possible the adaptation of the government to the wishes of the governed without violent struggles."

The passionate people of Russia, Eastern Europe, and China, and those who struggle for freedom all over the world, can learn from Mises and his integrated philosophy of a free society.

APPENDIX

A Foreign Policy for a Free-Market America: Two Views

A New Nationalism

Patrick J. Buchanan

Ben Franklin told the lady in Philadelphia, "A republic if you can keep it." Surely, preservation of the Republic, defense of its Constitution, living up to its ideals—that is our national purpose.

"America does not go abroad in search of monsters to destroy," John Quincy Adams said. "She is the well-wisher of the freedom and independence of all. She is the champion and vindicator only of her own."

Yet, when the question is posed, "What is America's national purpose?" answers vary widely. To Randall Robinson of TransAfrica, it is overthrow of South Africa; to Jesse Jackson, it is to advance "justice" by restoring the wealth the white race has robbed from the colored peoples of the earth; to AIPAC, it is to keep Israel secure and inviolate; to Ben Wattenberg, it is to "wage democracy" around the world.

Each substitutes an extra-national ideal for the national interest; each sees our national purpose in another continent or country; each treats our republic as a means to some larger end.

In Charles Krauthammer's "vision," the "wish and work" of our nation should be to "integrate" with Europe and Japan inside a "super-sovereign" entity that is "economically, culturally and politically hegemonic in the world." This "new universalism," he writes, "would require the conscious deprecation not only of American sovereignty but of the notion of sovereignty in general."

While Krauthammer's super-state may set off onanistic rejoicing inside the Trilateral Commission, it should set off alarm bells in more precincts than Belmont, Mass.

When Adams spoke, he was echoing Washington's farewell address that warned his fickle countrymen against "inveterate antipathies against particular nations, and passionate attachments for others.... The nation which indulges toward an habitual hatred, or an habitual fondness, is in some degree a slave. It is a slave to its animosities or to its affections, either of which is sufficient to lead it astray from its duty and its interest."

For a century after Washington's death, we resisted the siren's call of empire. Then, Kipling's call to "take up the white man's burden" fell upon the receptive ears of Bill McKinley, who came down from a sleepless night of consulting the Almighty to tell the press: "God told me to take the Philippines." We were launched.

Two decades later, 100,000 Americans lay dead in France in a European war begun, as Bismarck predicted it would begin, "because of some damn fool thing in the Balkans."

"To make the world safe for democracy," we joined an alliance of empires, British, French and Russian, that held most of mankind in colonial captivity. Washington's warning proved prophetic. Doughboys fell in places like the Argonne and Belleau Wood, in no small measure to

vindicate the Germanphobia and Anglophilia of a reg-
nant Yankee elite. When the great "war to end all war"
had fertilized the seed bed that produced Mussolini,
Hitler, and Stalin, Americans by 1941 had concluded a
blunder had been made in ignoring the wise counsel of
their Founding Fathers.

The isolationism of our fathers is today condemned,
and FDR is adjudged a great visionary, because he
sought early involvement in Britain's war with Hitler. Yet
even the interventionists' arguments were, and are,
couched in terms of American national interest.

America wanted to stay out. Americans saw, in the
world's bloody conflict, no cause why our soldiers should
be sent overseas to spill a single drop of American blood.
Pearl Harbor, not FDR, convinced America to go to war.

After V-E Day and V-J Day, all America wanted to
"bring the boys home," and we did. Then, they were sent
back, back to Europe, back to Asia, because we Americans were persuaded—by Joseph Stalin—that the Cold
War must be waged. As the old saw goes, you can refuse
almost any invitation, but when the man wants to fight,
you've got to oblige him.

If the Cold War is ending, what are the terms of
honorable peace that will permit us to go home? Are they
not withdrawal of the Red Army back within its own
frontiers, liberation of Central Europe and the Baltic
republics, re-unification of Germany, and de-Leniniza-
tion of Moscow, i.e., overthrow of the imperialist party
that has prosecuted the 70 Years War against the West?

The compensating concession we should offer: total
withdrawal of U.S. troops from Europe. If Moscow will
get out, we will get out.

There is another argument for disengagement. When the cheering stops, there is going to be a calling to account for the crimes of Tehran, Yalta, and Potsdam, where the Great Men acceded to Stalin's demand that he be made cartographer of Europe. In the coming conflicts, over Poland's frontiers east and west, over Transylvania, Karelia, Moldavia, the breakup of Yugoslavia, our role is diplomatic and moral, not military.

As the United States moves off the mainland of Europe, we should move our troops off the mainland of Asia as well. South Korea has twice the population, five times the economic might of North Korea. She can be sold the planes, guns, missiles and ships to give her decisive superiority.

We are not going to fight another land war in Asia; no vital interest justifies it; our people will not permit it. Why, then, keep 30,000 ground troops on the DMZ? If Kim Il Sung attacks, why should Americans be first to die?

It is time we began uprooting the global network of "trip wires," planted on foreign soil, to ensnare the United States in the wars of other nations, to back commitments made and treaties signed before this generation of American soldiers was even born.

The United States has been drained of wealth and power by wars, cold and hot. We cannot forever defend wealthy nations that refuse to defend themselves; we cannot permit endless transfusions of the lifeblood of American capitalism into the mendicant countries and economic corpses of socialism, without bleeding ourselves to death. Foreign aid is an idea whose time has passed. The Communist and socialist world now owe the

West a thousand billion dollars and more, exclusive of hundreds of billions we simply gave away.

Our going-away gift to the globalist ideologues should be to tell the Third World we are not sending the gunboats to collect our debts, neither are we sending more money. The children are on their own.

Americans are the most generous people in history. But our altruism has been exploited by the guilty-and-pity crowd. At home, a monstrous welfare state of hundreds of thousands of drones and millions of dependents consumes huge slices of the national income. Abroad, regiments of global bureaucrats siphon off billions for themselves and their client regimes.

With the Cold War ending, we should look, too, with a cold eye on the internationalist set, never at a loss for new ideas to divert U.S. wealth and power into crusades and causes having little or nothing to do with the true national interest of the United States.

High among these is the democratist temptation, the worship of democracy as a form of government and the concomitant ambition to see all mankind embrace it, or explain why not. Like all idolatries, democratism substitutes a false god for the real, a love of process for a love of country.

How other people rule themselves is their own business. To call it a vital interest of the United States is to contradict history and common sense. And for the republic to seek to dictate to 160 nations, what kind of regime each should have, is a formula for interminable meddling and endless conflict; it is a textbook example of that "messianic globaloney" against which Dean Acheson warned.

"We must consider first and last," Walter Lippman wrote in 1943, "the American national interest. If we do not, if we construct our foreign policy on some kind of abstract theory of rights and duties, we shall build castles in the air."

"Enlightened nationalism," was Mr. Lippman's idea of a foreign policy to protect America's true national interest. What we need is a new nationalism, a new patriotism, a new foreign policy that puts America first, and not only first, but second and third as well.

America First, Once More

Bill Kauffman

As the Cold War approaches the midnight hour, and the Soviet threat turns into a pumpkin, typewriter hawks in Washington and Manhattan are scrambling to find a new foreign bogeyman: Hispanic drug lords? Russian nationalists? German neutralists?

Their quest is urgent, even a little pathetic. The swiftness of revolution in Eastern Europe has caught everyone off guard. As the Soviets chip off the old bloc, the rationale for keeping 300,000 U.S. troops in Europe—the "field of slaughter," Jefferson called it—vanishes. Poof! At the same time, the strategic importance of foreign aid clients like Israel, El Salvador, and Pakistan diminishes.

Put yourself in the place of a Cold War intellectual. For years you've lived comfortably on the foundation and government dole, Truman and Churchill quote books at your side, composing paeans to the majesty of $325 billion defense budgets. And the grant money flows like blood.

In little more than a revolutionary fortnight, your world crumbles. The Soviet Union admits the failure of communism and starts withdrawing troops from its satellites. Poland is governed by union democrats. Czechoslovakia elects as president a playwright with libertarian tendencies. Romanians send their dictator to hell with a chorus of shotgun blasts. It is glorious and beautiful and inspiring and it's gonna put you out of a job.

Maybe.

For the more astute Cold Warriors had a backup plan, fusing the messianism of Woodrow Wilson with the saber-rattling of John F. Kennedy. Using the talismanic language of "democracy," they propose to spend tax dollars sticking Uncle Sam's nose into the political affairs of Chile, Nicaragua, Angola, and a host of obscure African and Asian countries that the overwhelming majority of Americans don't give a damn about. No emirate is too small or too remote to escape the meddling of these crusading PhDs, who are more fervent than World Federalists and twice as dangerous.

These new Wilsonians are the fulfillment of Senator Richard Russell's dire prophecy: "If it is easy for us to go anywhere and do anything, we will always be going someplace and doing something."

Opposed to these globaloney mountebanks is the common sense of the American people, who still cherish the isolationist wisdom of the Founders. The problem is, the people are unorganized. They have no voice in the chambers of state; their spokesmen do not parry with

Secretary of State Baker or Lord Kissinger on the *David Brinkley Show*.

The rock band The Who once sang, "Let's get together before we get much older," and boy, were they ever right. It's high time to get together and revive—in spirit if not in name—America First.

America First was a broad-based coalition of men and women who opposed the drift toward war in 1940 and 1941. Its celebrity leaders were a diverse lot: Oswald Garrison Villard of *The Nation*, liberal John T. Flynn, General Robert E. Wood of Sears Roebuck, actress Lillian Gish, and populist Burton K. Wheeler. The great aviator Charles Lindbergh expressed the still-relevant creed of America First: "What happens in Europe is of little importance compared with what happens in our own land. It is far more important to have farms without mortgages, workmen with their homes, and young people who can afford families, than it is for us to crusade abroad for freedoms that are tottering in our own country."

America First was a casualty of Pearl Harbor, and the American republic was a casualty of the war and its aftermath. But the long dark night of the Cold War is about over. In the sunshiny morrow of Eastern European liberation, modern-day Washingtonians, Jeffersonians, and even Hamiltonians (for all his sins, Alexander did ghost-write sections of Washington's Farewell Address) can recoalesce under a new America First banner.

The signs are auspicious. Young Americans—farmboys in North Dakota, ghetto kids in Watts, heretofore mere fodder for Harvard militarists in their endowed chairs—are no longer willing to die for foreign politicians.

A 1988 poll for *Rolling Stone* magazine found that three-quarters of American youth would *not* willingly shed blood in a European war. The *Rolling Stone* reporter saw "skepticism that resembles the public's isolationism in the days before Pearl Harbor."

Meanwhile, the Cold War's expiry has renewed the promise of a broad-based coalition on foreign policy. The lineaments of this alliance were sketched in the mid-60s by economist Murray Rothbard and historian William Appleman Williams.

Behold: a quarter-century later, the American Right is at war with itself. "Paleoconservatives," defenders of small towns and limited government, have broken with neoconservative Cold Warriors. In books like Robert Nisbet's *The Present Age* and magazines like *Chronicles*, edited by Southern agrarian Thomas Fleming, the pale-ocons indict the military-industrial complex and eloquently reject the world policeman heresy. Patrick Buchanan, a forceful champion of putting America first, thunders: "It is not the business of the United States to dictate to 150 countries in the world what kind of government they ought to have."

To distinguish a neocon from a paleocon, ask him what he thinks about the 1940s. Neoconservatives view this decade as the apex of American achievement: Hiroshima, Nagasaki, total warfare, the draft and rationing and public employment and Archibald MacLeish's propaganda poetry and the two greatest presidents of all time, FDR and Harry Truman. Now that was paradise!

Paleocons, like libertarians, consider the '40s to be the single worst decade in American history. War and regimentation filled "so many blood-lakes," in poet

Robinson Jeffers's words, and entrenched the New Deal and delivered us unto Leviathan.

Significantly, decentralists of the left share the paleocon-libertarian assessment. Dorothy Day, Dwight Macdonald, and Paul Goodman, giants of the last generation, were appalled by this senselessly destructive decade. So are their heirs. We are, all of us—decentralists, libertarians, Main Street conservatives—basically on the same side in the America First vs. World Policeman debate. If only we realized it!

Finally, there is a large and articulate reservoir of anti-empire sentiment that is usually overlooked: American writers. From the republic's birth, the majority of home-grown novelists and poets have been children of 1776. The three titans of the mid-nineteenth century, Walt Whitman, Nathaniel Hawthorne, and Herman Melville, were all "Loco Focos," or libertarian Democrats. In FDR's heyday, an impressive roster of Middle American men and women of letters were isolationist, some of them card-carrying America Firsters: Sinclair Lewis, Sherwood Anderson, Robinson Jeffers, Edmund Wilson, Kathleen Norris, John P. Marquand, e.e. cummings, and Robert Lowell, among others.

The rebel American spirit endures, despite the many neutering successes of the NEA. Consider our three best-selling "serious" novelists: Gore Vidal is a patrician republican and die-hard isolationist; Kurt Vonnegut is an iconoclast who wrote America First editorials for the Cornell student newspaper; and Norman Mailer is a self-described "left conservative" whose 1969 New York City mayoralty campaign was based on the principle of secession. Not a liberal internationalist among 'em.

So we've got true conservatives, decentralists, libertarians, writers, Main Street Americans...the one missing piece is politicians.

Have no fear. The most comic aspect of the Revolution of 1989 was the breathtaking speed with which communist appartchiks and "legislators" changed their plumage. Overnight, ugly Brezhnevite ducklings sprouted brilliant Jeffersonian feathers. The same will happen here, once the hacks hear vox populi screaming in their ears.

The largely peaceful overthrow of communism in Europe is a godsend—to the formerly subjugated people, yes, but also to us. We have a once-in-a-lifetime chance to restore sanity to U.S. foreign policy. We can stand on the sidelines and watch the empire-lovers—the liberals who gave us Vietnam and the phony conservatives who gave us Iranamok—determine our future. Or we can speak up, with others of like mind, and bring the boys home, dismantle the garrison state, and shrink the federal budget. We can put America First, again, as it should be. If not now, when?

Index

Compiled by Richard Hite

Abbey, Edward, 292
Acheson, Dean, 367
Acid rain, 299-300
Acton, Lord, 120-21
Adams, John Quincy, 329, 364
Advertising, 244-46
Affirmative action, 160, 184-85
Agency for International Development, 44
Agnos, Arthur, 142
Agriculture, 191-96, 349, 350
AIDS, 179, 216, 220, 249-53, 292, 305
Airline industry, 190
Airline Pilots Association, 26
Alar, 297-98
Albania, 191, 333
Alcohol; *See* Prohibition
American Broadcasting Corporation (ABC), 244
American Federation of Labor-Congress of Industrial Organizations (AFL-CIO), 20, 23
American Future Systems, 245
American Medical Association (AMA), 252
Amnesty International, 72
Anderson, Sherwood, 372
Andreas, Dwayne, 116
Angell, Wayne, 101-03
Angola, 369
Animal Liberation Front, 303
Animal rights, 272-76, 284, 301-05
Antoinette, Marie, 248
Appalachian Regional Development Act, 179
Aquinas, Saint Thomas, 75

Argentina, 115, 334
Aristotle, 165
Armey, Richard, 201, 206-07
Asian Law Caucus, 248
Astrology, 66, 68
Auburn University, 225
Audubon Society, 302
Austrian economics, 48, 70, 95
Austrian Institute for Business Cycle Research, 105
Azpilcueta, Martin de, 75

Bailouts
farm 195; *See also* Savings & Loan Industry
Baker, James, 33, 35, 87, 117, 370
Bank for International Settlements, 254, 260
Bank of Japan, 254
Bank Secrecy Act, 257
Banking
central, 32-35, 105, 107, 175, 254, 261-62, 282, 317
deposit insurance, 80-83, 89-91
fractional reserve, 79-82, 83, 84, 89-90, 92, 93, 108
in West Germany, 34
international, 33-34, 257-259, 261-62
offshore, 259
private, 110-12
reserve requirements, 80, 83
world, 32, 34-35
See also Federal Reserve
Barnes, Fred, 280, 281, 284, 304
Bastiat, Frederic, 167
Baumol, William J., 39

Bell, Terell, 240
Bennett, Pauline, 137, 139
Bennett, William, 135, 153, 162, 204, 223, 226, 231, 233, 234, 316
Berg, Jerome, 194
Berlin Wall, 322
Bernardino of Siena, Saint, 76
Bernstein, Edward M., 33
Biddle, Livingston, 206
Biden, Joseph, 316
Bill of Rights, 155, 157, 176
Bimetalism, 110
Bipartisanship, definition of, 281
Bismarck, Otto von, 364
Black markets, 222, 225, 339
Blinder, Alan S., 39
Blood supply, 216
Boetie, Etienne le, 329
Böhm-Bawerk, Eugen von, 106
Boland Amendment, 145
Bolshevik Revolution, 326-27
Bonds, 96
Bonin, Jose Miguez, 277, 279
Borman, Frank, 21
Boxer, Barbara, 302
Bradford, M.E., 204
Bradley, Ed, 297-98
Brady, Nicholas, 47, 51, 85-88
Breeden, Richard, 72
Bretton Woods, 32-33, 103, 116, 261
Brookes, Warren, 297, 314
Brooklyn Academy of Music, 206
Brower, David, 148-49, 292, 293
Browne, Tom, 140
Buchanan, James, 189, 314
Buchanan, Patrick J., 88, 371
Bureaucracy
    failure of, 74, 119-23, 124-27, 128, 130, 164, 170, 173, 180, 193, 242, 253, 283, 297, 300, 308, 343, 353, 367
    paternalism of, 121, 176, 316
    of the World Bank, 117

Bureau of Indian Affairs, 126
Bureau of Land Managment, 152
Burnham, James, 223
Burroughs, John, 291
Bush administration, 31
    bureaucracy of, 126, 133, 137, 177, 189, 190, 204, 207
    on deficits, 30
    on drugs, 234
    education, 238-41
    on environmentalism, 300, 304, 306, 307
    on globalism, 254-57
    on gun control, 153
    on Savings & Loans, 89, 283
    on taxes, 53, 144, 317
    on the Third World, 85, 235
    See also Drug War
Bush, Barbara, 304
Bush, George Herbert Walker, 18, 64, 90, 132, 161, 235, 238, 239, 263, 268, 280, 285-88
Business cycles, 29, 95, 96, 104-08, 255, 348

Calculation, economic, 14-15, 265-66
Cambodia, 354-58
Canadian Animal Rights Network, 273
Capital markets, 159-60
Capitalism
    and competition, 87, 334
    enemies of, 13, 277, 291
    See also Free Market
Carcinogens, 298
Carroll, John, 72
Carter administration, 206, 282
Carter, James E., 133, 177, 228, 240, 285
Cass, Ronald, 61
Castro, Fidel, 277
Catholics, 243
Cavazos, Lauro F., 136

Cayman Turtle Farm, 310-11
Census, U.S., 63
Central Intelligence Agency, 350
Chafuen, Alejandro A., 73, 75
Charity, private, 173
Chase, Alton, 299
Chase Manhattan Bank, 71
Cheney, Richard, 212, 215
Chesterton, G.K., 233
Chicago Board of Trade, 48
Chicago School of economics, 95
Chile, 369
China, People's Republic of, 114, 319-22, 333
Chodorov, Frank, 175, 323, 325
Chocung Ek, 354
Chomsky, Noam, 282
Christianity, 276-79, 289
Chrysler Corporation, 57, 86
Church World Services, 141
Churchill, Winston, 282, 368
Civic duty, 264
Civil Aeronautics Board, 188
Civil rights, 16, 182-87
    Act of 1964, 179, 250
    Rehabilitation Act of 1973, 250
Civil service, 171
Clarke, Robert L., 83
Clean Air Bill, 307
Clean Water Act, 296, 306
Coase, Ronald, 311
Coast Guard, 248
Cocaine, 225
Cockburn, Alexander, 289
Coelho, Tony, 318
Cold War, 211, 213, 216, 322-25, 329, 365, 367, 368, 371
Collectivism, 163, 191, 334; See also Communism; Socialism
Columbia University, 63
Comecon, 314
Committee on Government Operations, 260

Commodity Futures Trading Commission, 48
Communism, 247, 327, 332, 347; See also Socialism
Communist Party, 235, 236, 333, 346, 353
Community Development Block Grants, 133
Compassion, 171
Competition, 71, 243, 271
Comptroller of the Currency, 258
Conable, Barber, 114, 115
Congress, U.S., 116, 124, 171
    and arts, 204
    and pay raise, 124, 125
    in defense of, 144-48
Conscription, 332, 333-34
Conservatives, 159-64, 169, 204, 207, 240
Constitution, U.S., 109-12, 120, 123, 145-46, 155, 175, 244-46, 288, 352
Consumers, 49-51, 59, 269-70, 344
Continental Illinois Bank, 84
Contras, 169
Coolidge, Calvin, 24
Corcoran Gallery of Art, 202
Corporate Average Fuel Efficiency (CAFE) standards, 307
Corporate control, 71
Cost-benefit analysis, 123, 130, 208, 348
Council of Economic Advisers, 188
Counterfeiting, 175
Coxe, Tench, 155
Cranston, Alan, 230
Credit
    expansion, 83, 105, 107
    markets, 80-81
    See also Inflation Crisis, 172
Crockett, Davy, 143
Cuba, 235, 333

Cuddihy, John Murray, 184
Currency Transaction Report, 258

Darman, Michael, 88
Day, Dorothy, 373
Dean, Deborah, 119
Debt
  foreign, 58, 86
  government, 85-86
  of Third World, 83, 85-88
Declaration of Independence,
  176, 177, 179
Deficits, 29-30, 104, 267, 282-83
Democracy, 166, 167, 330-31,
  352, 362, 367
Democratic Party, 17, 120, 125,
  133, 160, 169, 186, 207, 280,
  283, 305, 308, 347
Demsetz, Harold, 40
Department of Agriculture, 126,
  192-94
Department of Commerce, 120, 283
Department of Defense, 293
Department of Education, 120,
  126, 136, 283, 285
Department of Energy, 136
Department of Health and
  Human Services, 120, 124, 145
Department of Housing and
  Urban Development, 119-20,
  122, 124-25, 127, 132-36, 163,
  186, 283, 286, 287
Department of the Interior, 120
Department of Justice, 261, 273,
  295
Department of Labor, 120, 283
Department of State, 230, 261
Department of Transportation,
  120, 286, 287
Department of Treasury, 170,
  258, 259, 261
Department of Veteran's Affairs,
  126, 188
Deregulation, 187, 201

Deukmejan, George, 144
Dewey, Thomas, 66
Diapers, 198
Dingell, John, 157
Direct Relief International, 141
Disaster relief, 136-40, 141-45
Discrimination, 184-85, 250-51
Dodd, Thomas, 154
Dolphins, 301-02
Dornan, Robert, 304, 305
Dornbusch, Rudiger, 39
Dresser Industries, 116
Drexel-Burnham-Lambert, 72
Dreyep, Robert, A., 194
Drugs
  addiction, 224, 229
  crime and, 224
  war on, 154, 221-34, 258
  war compared with War on Infi-
    delity, 228
Dukakis, Michael, 64, 268
Dumping, 60, 62

Earth Island Institute, 292
EarthFirst! movement, 292
Earthquake
  Armenian, 144, 334-38
  California, 141-45
  Mexican, 335
  San Fernando Valley, 335
Eastern Airlines, 21-22, 26
Eastern Europe, 14, 15, 101,
  107, 113, 138, 156, 201, 211,
  215, 288, 314-15, 322, 329,
  333, 338, 342-45, 368
Econometric Society, 67
Economic calculation, 122, 126,
  128, 129-30, 132, 201, 212,
  313, 326, 329, 336-37, 347-48,
  See also Price; Mises; Socialism
Economic Opportunity Act, 179
Economists
  liberal and mainstream, 28-29,
    31, 36-38, 44-45, 48, 200, 311, 337

Education, 238-43, 286
Edwards, Donald, 144
Efron, Bradley, 65
Egalitarianism, 219, 361
Egypt, 334
Ehrlich, Paul, 149
Eisenhower, Dwight D., 67
Ellul, Jacques, 278, 279
England, 34, 310, 365
    common law in, 151-52
    education in, 242-43
Enterprise Zones, 134
Entrepreneurs
    and labor, 48, 266
    and trash disposal, 199, 200
    calculation by, 48-50, 265, 337
    discovery by, 129-130, 242-43,
    361
    investment by, 49, 107
Environmental Protection Agency
    (EPA), 286, 298, 308, 316
Environmentalists
    activities of, 139-40, 150-53,
    190, 198, 248-49, 281, 284,
    287, 289-312
    anti-human, 138-39, 153, 312
    economics and, 308-12
    ethics, 149-50, 284
    on oil spill, 148-50
Episcopal Church, Bishop's
    Fund, 141
Equitable Life Assurance Soci-
    ety, 202
Erhard, Ludwig, 344
Estonia, 319
Ethiopia, 235-37, 335
    and forecasting, 69
    World Bank funding of, 112-
    13, 114, 115
European Central Bank, 34, 172
European Community, 34, 301, 308
European Currency Unit (ECU),
    34, 262

Evangelicals, 276, 278
Exchange, mutually beneficial,
    59, 278
Exchange rates, 33, 261-62
Export-Import Bank, 317
Exports, 55-56
Externalities, 36, 38-41, 200, 311-12
Exxon, 116, 148-153, 294-95

Fabians, 13
Farmer's Home Administration, 194
Fascism, 13, 173
Faust, 98-101
Federal Bureau of Investigation
    (FBI), 214
Federal Deposit Insurance Cor-
    poration (FDIC), 81, 82, 91, 93
Federal Emergency Manage-
    ment Agency (FEMA), 136-37,
    141-45
Federal Home Loan Board, 91
Federal Register, 188
Federal Reserve System, 47, 50,
    79, 80, 83, 91, 93, 96-98, 101,
    104, 108, 111, 172, 175, 231,
    254, 255, 258, 282
    Act of 1913, 82
Federal Savings and Loan Insur-
    ance Corporation, 92-93
Federalist, The, 155
Feed the Children, 141
Fees, user, 88
Feudalism, 295, 347, 359
Financial markets, 47-50, 190,
    254, 259-61, 344
Financial Times of London, 72,
    260
Firearms Owners' Protection Act
    of 1986, 157
Fischer, Stanley, 39
Fishing industry, 247-49, 301, 302
Fleming, Thomas, 371
Fluorocarbons, 151
Flynn, John T., 323, 325, 370

Foley, Thomas, 285
Ford, Henry, 294
Forecasting, 66-70
Foreign aid, 112-17, 325, 329, 334, 353
Foreman, David, 292
Forest Service, 152
Founding Fathers, 109-10, 127, 145, 147, 175, 286, 369
Franklin, Benjamin, 363
Free markets, 73, 86, 174, 187, 208, 262, 310, 327, 331, 345
Free riders, 35-41
Free speech, 244-46, 332
French Revolution, 319
Friedman, Jerome, 65
Friedman, Milton, 314
Friends of the Earth, 148, 292
Fukuyama, Francis, 331
Fur industry, 275-76, 301, 303

Gaia, 197, 290-91, 292
Galbraith, J.K., 38, 314, 351
Garbage; See Trash
Garbage Project, 197, 199
Garden of Eden, 290
Garn, Jake, 131
Garrett, Garet, 323
Gartner, Michael, 244
Gebert, Kostek, 340
General Accounting Office, 194, 215
Georgetown, 143
Ghana, 113
Gilder, George, 257
Gingrich, Newt, 125, 144
Ginsberg, Allan, 293
Gish, Lillian, 370
Glasnost, 319
Global warming, 151, 298-99, 307
Globalization, 257-62
Goethe, J.W. von, 98-101
Gold standard, 32, 94, 101-04, 261
Goodman, Paul, 373

Gorbachev, Mikhail, 38, 152, 182, 212, 289, 323-324, 349, 351, 353
Gosbank, 101-03
Government
  the growth of, 169-74, 268, 288
  the meaning of, 109, 111
Gramm-Rudman-Hollings Balanced Budget Amendment, 283
Great Depression, 24, 107, 317
Great Society, 120, 133, 159, 177, 178-82, 287, 305
Greed vs. need, 169
Greenhouse effect; See Global Warming
Greenmail, 71
Greens, 16, 311; See also Environmentalists
Greenspan, Alan, 83, 96
Gregory, Paul R., 39-40
Gross National Product, 189
Gun control, 153-58, 281
  Act of 1968, 154
Gwartney, James, 41

Hall, Edwin Arthur, 157
Hall, Gus, 333, 334
Hamilton, Alexander, 370
Hammer, Armand, 147
Harding, Warren G., 24
Harley Davidson, 41
Harrington, Michael, 222
Hawthorne, Nathaniel, 372
Hayashi, Dennis W., 248
Hayek, F.A., 37-50, 105-08, 141, 167, 314, 320, 347
Haywood, Frances, 240
Hazlitt, Henry, 66, 175-76, 279
Heilbroner, Robert, 38
Heritage USA, 86
Heyne, Paul, 41
Higgs, Robert, 172
Higher Education Act, 179
Hillside Strangler, 124
Hiroshima, 371

Hitler, Adolph 365; *See also* Nazism
Hodsoll, Frank, 204, 206
Hollings, Ernest F., 142
Home Ownership for People
    Everywhere (HOPE), 286
Homesteading, 345-46
Hoover, Herbert 24
Hoppe, Hans-Hermann, 335-36
Hotelling, Harold, 63
Housing, 133-36
Humane Society, 274, 302
Humphrey, Hubert, 184
Hungary, 319, 320, 340
Hurricane
    Hazel of 1954, 139
    Hugo of 1989, 136-41
Hutt, William H., 269, 272
Huxley, Aldous, 294

IBM, 116
Iacocca, Lee, 56, 57
Icahn, Carl C., 72
Immigration, 216-20
    German, 218
    Haitian, 216, 217
    Iran, 219
    Vietnamese, 247-49
Imports, 55-57, 59-61
Incumbency, 186
Individualism, 121
Industrial Revolution, 149, 245
Inflation, 28-29, 35, 74-75, 95-97,
    98-101, 102-03, 104-105, 109,
    175-76, 253, 262, 343, 357
    expectation of, 96
    hyper-, 98, 100, 103
Ingersoll Rand, 116
Insider trading, 260
Insurance
    government, 268-70, 277
    private, 136-137, 250-51, 271
Interest rates, 92, 95-96
International Criminal Police Or-
    ganization (Interpol), 258

International Finance Corpora-
    tion, 113
International Monetary Fund
    (IMF), 33, 44, 85, 86, 114, 254
International Organization of Secu-
    rities Commissions (IOSC), 260
International Trade Commis-
    sion, 59-62
"Internationale," 321
Interventionism, 28-29, 48-53,
    73, 170, 173, 176, 190, 100,
    365
Investment, 53-54, 270
    foreign, 58
    level of, 51-52
Iran-Contra Scandal, 180, 373
Iraq, subsidies to, 195
Iron Curtain, 328
Isolationism, 324, 363-68, 370-73
Israel, 363
Ivory, 310

Jackson, Jesse, 363
James, Ron, 293-94
Japan, 34, 51, 55, 58, 334, 364
Jaruzelski, General, 319
Jeffers, Robinson, 373
Jefferson, Thomas, 165, 171,
    237, 286, 329, 368
Johns, Michael, 235
Johnson administration, 120,
    125, 133, 160, 164, 178-82,
    203, 280, 285-88
Johnson, Lyndon B., 125, 133,
    160, 164, 178-81, 280, 287-88,
    305
Johnson, Skip, 141
Jones Act, 247-49

Katuna, Michael, 139
Keating Five, 125
Kemp, Jack, 123, 132-36, 163,
    164
Kennan, George F., 325
Kennedy, Edward, 18, 268, 283

Kennedy, John F., 369
Keynesianism, 27-35, 105-06, 120, 254, 282, 347
Kipling, Rudyard, 364
Kirk, Andrew, 276-77, 279
Kissinger, Henry, 370
Klaus, Vaclav, 314
Koch, Ilse, 275
Koop, C. Everett, 252
Korea, 115, 333
Krauthammer, Charles, 363-64
Kwanda, 116

Labor markets, 18-19, 265-72
Labrador Indians, 40
Ladd, Everett, 282
Lampe, Keith, 293
Landfills, 198, 200-01, 296
Latin America, 103
Law
  antitrust, 330
  concept of, 166-68
  enforcement, 223
  ex post facto, 185
  legal tender, 108
  moral, 52
  natural, 166
Lee, Henry, 231, 232
Leland, Mickey, 235-37
Lenin, V.I., 277, 289, 290, 339
Lennon, Gered, 139
Lewis, C.S., 166
Lewis, Sinclair, 372
Liberalism
  left-, 20, 42, 53, 159-64, 169, 184-86, 189, 198, 207, 332
  classical, 187, 359-62
Libertarianism, 162, 166, 187, 217, 347, 351, 371, 372
Lichtenstein, Harvey, 206
Lindbergh, Charles, 370
Lippman, Walter, 281, 368
Lockheed Corp., 86
Logging, 149, 152

London Institute for Contemporary Christianity, 276-77
London School of Economics, 105
Lorenzo, Frank, 22
Los Angeles Times, 149
Lovelock, James, 290
Lowell, Robert, 372
Loyal Legion of Loggers and Lumbermen 24

McCabe, Katie, 303
McCarthy, Joseph, 315
McDonald's, 274
McKibben, William, 291, 292
McKinley, Bill, 364
McNeil-Lehrer News Hour, 263
MacAuliff, Christa, 131
MacDonald, Dwight, 372
MacLeish, Archibald, 371
Madison, James, 155, 157
Mailer, Norman, 372
Malthus, Thomas, 114
Maltsev, Yuri, 314, 346-54
Mandated benefits, 267-72
Mao Tse-Tung, 277, 321
Mapplethorpe, Robert, 202-03, 288
Mariana, Juan de, 73, 74
Marine Mammal Protection Act, 302
Market failure, 36, 120
Marquand, John P., 372
Martino, Giulio, 97
Marx, Karl, 14, 46, 290, 339, 360
Marxists, 13, 101, 115, 167, 277, 289, 315, 331, 333, 340, 347; See also Socialism
Matthews, Christopher, 141, 144, 236
Mead, Walter Russell, 255
Media, 172, 174, 186, 202, 282, 303
Medicaid, 170, 179

Medicare, 179, 219
Melcher, John, 304
Melville, Herman, 373
Mencken, H.L., 323
Mendelsohn, Robert, 65
Menger, Carl, 106
Mengistu, Haile Mariam, 113, 235, 236, 335
Mephistopheles, 98-99
Mercado, Tomas de, 75
Mercantilism, 359
Meyer, Frank, 145, 146, 177, 178
Mexico, 334
Military economy, 211-16, 328, 332-34, 351, 368-69
Military-Industrial-Congressional-Complex (MICC), 213-16
Milken, Michael, 70-72
Miller, Sanford, 298
Miller, Vicki, 273
Minorities, 183-95
Mises, Ludwig von
    as humanitarian, 237
    Institute, 15, 135, 335, 346, 354
    on bureaucracy, 120-21, 122, 126-27, 132
    on business cycles, 105, 106-08
    on capitalism, 15, 297
    on freedom, 330, 359-62
    on interventionism, 37, 173, 182, 200, 331
    on law, 167
    on markets, 58, 279, 347
    on peace, 360-61
    on socialism and planning, 13-14, 69, 122, 174, 212, 313-15, 318, 324, 326, 336, 345
    on statistics, 68
    on world government, 256
Mitterand, François, 46
Molina, Luis de, 75, 76
Monetarists, 31, 35, 95
Money market mutual funds, 92

Money
    fiat, 108-10
    honest, 102
    supply of, 93-94, 95-97, 343
    See also Gold Standard
Monsanto Corporation, 116
Montagnois Indians, 41
Morality
    and markets, 73, 77
Morgan, J.P., 306
Moyers, Bill, 181
Moynihan, Daniel P., 317
Muir, John, 291
Multilateral Investment Guarantee Agency (MIGA), 115
Murphy, Eddie, 124
Murray, Charles, 179, 181
Mussolini, Benito, 365

Nader, Ralph, 125, 149
Nagasaki, 371
Nash, Ronald, 73, 278, 279
National Aeronautics and Space Administration (NASA), 22, 127-32
National Education Association (NEA), 25, 136, 240, 285
National Endowment for the Arts (NEA), 201-07, 286
National Endowment for the Humanities (NEH), 203, 204, 205, 207
National Foundation for the Arts and Humanities, 179
National Review, 144, 146, 177, 255
National Security, 267
National Service, 263-67
National Taxpayers Union, 135
Nationalism, 128
Natural Resources Defense Council, 294, 297
Natural rights, 176

Navarrete, Fernandez, 74
Nazis, 13, 312, 314, 325-26, 327
  and gun control, 155-57
Neoconservatism, 371
Ness, Eliot, 232
New Deal, 13, 24-25, 91, 159, 163,
  178, 188, 305, 317, 322, 325, 372
New Economic Policy, 327
New Republic, The, 255, 280, 304
New York City Clearing House
  Association, 82
New York Stock Exchange, 47
New York Times, 72, 85, 112,
  135, 189, 308
Newkirk, Ingrid, 272, 305
Nicaragua, 333, 369
Nisbet, Robert, 371
Niskanen, William, 188
Nixon, Richard, 133, 177, 306,
  316
Nock, Albert Jay, 176, 177, 294,
  323
Nomocracy, 167
Nomenklatura, American, 215
Norris, Kathleen, 372
Norris-LaGuardia Act 24
Novak, Michael, 73
Nunn, Sam, 263, 264

Oakeshott, Michael, 166-67
Old Right, 322-331, 370
O'Neill, Thomas P., 236
Operation California, 141
"Opinion Cartel," 280-84
Opium, 225, 231
Oppenheimer, Franz, 121-22
Opportunity costs, 129
Orem, John, 303
Organization of Petroleum Ex-
  porting Countries (OPEC), 95
Ozone layer, 151, 299

Pacheco, Alex, 272, 273, 274, 305
Packard Commission, 215

Paganism, 273
Pakistan, 113
Paleoconservative, 371-72
Paleolibertarian, 227
Panama, 317
Pantheism, 273, 289, 290, 291,
  292, 293
Parenti, Michael, 33
Parklands, national, 150, 151,
  311-12
Patterson, Isabel, 237, 290
Paul, Ron, 135
Pearl Harbor, 365, 370, 371
Peel, Gary E., 246
Penn Fishing Tackle, 60-61
Pentagon, 126, 212, 215
People for the Ethical Treatment
  of Animals (PETA), 272-75,
  302, 304-05
Perestroika, 319, 353
Permanent Subcommittee on
  Investigations (PSI), 259
Pesticides, 297-98
Philadelphia Institute of Con-
  temporary Art, 202
Phnom Penh, 355-58
Pickens, T. Boone, 72
Pierce, Samuel, 119
Pilgrims, 294
Pilkey, Orrin H., 139
Planning, central, 69, 178, 180,
  210-11, 309, 327, 336-38, 347;
  See also Socialism
Plant-closing legislation, 268,
  271
Poison pills, 71
Poland, 319, 320, 340
Pol Pot, 235, 321, 354, 358
Police, 223
Politics
  definition of, 187
Politicians
  and scandals, 119, 284

Pollution, 310
Ponderosa Pine, 292-93
Population growth, 114
Postdam, 366
Potter, Ted, 206
Poverty
  programs, 179-82
  war on, 179-82, 222
Pozsgai, John, 296
Pravda, 323
Presidential powers, 145, 288
Prices
  agricultural, 192-96
  and supply of goods, 68
  by gouging, 138
  consumer, 96, 208
  controls on, 138, 190, 192-93,
  343-45
  for roads, 207-11
  for trash, 199
  "just," 75
  of drugs, 225
  role of, 14, 49-50, 106, 107,
  152, 267, 270, 309, 313, 336-
  37, 346, 347-48, 350
Prisons, 234
Privatization, *See* Property
Production, 49, 270, 337
Profits, 48, 122, 265-66, 270,
  348-49
Progressive Era, 177
Prohibition, alcohol, 231-34;
  See also Drug War
Propaganda, 275, 281-82
Property rights, 35-41, 45-46,
  141, 152, 168, 175, 176, 183,
  220
  common property, 35, 41, 76
  private, 15, 35-41, 44, 182-83,
  220, 224, 276, 300, 309, 313,
  330, 341, 345
Proposition 13, 144
Protectionism, 56-57, 61-62

Proudon, Pierre Joseph, 182
Proxmire, William, 135
Public choice, 284
Public goods, 36, 39, 41, 213, 309-
  12
Puerto Rico, 245
Purdy, Patrick, 153, 157

Quayle, Dan, 141, 230

"Racial Justice," 184
Ratajczak, Donald, 96
Rathje, William L. 197, 198, 296-
  97
Reagan administration, 31, 190,
  200, 235, 267, 280, 285, 302
  and deficits, 30
  bureaucracies, 126, 133, 177,
  204
  conservatism of, 159-69
  credit risk during, 80
  internationalism of, 258, 261
  on agricultural subsidies, 196
  on arts subsidies, 203
  on education, 239-40
  on minimum wage 17, 20
  and World Bank, 116
Reagan revolution, 159-63, 167-
  68, 187-89, 317, 332
Reagan, Ronald W., 132, 159-63,
  168, 177, 196, 239, 258, 280,
  285, 302, 332
Recession, 28-29
  inevitability of, 97
  of 1982, 66, 95
Recycling, 297
Red Cross, American, 141
Redistributionism, 182, 183,
  222, 254, 270, 330
Regan, Donald, 31
Regulation, 45, 47-48, 50-51,
  176, 187-88, 245, 253, 255, 259-
  61, 343, 359
Reign of Terror, 290
Religion, 242; *See also* Christianity

Republican party, 17-18, 119, 120, 125, 133, 145, 169, 207, 238, 280, 285, 286, 306, 308
Reynolds, Morgan, 23, 26-27
Richardson, Elliott, 308
RICO, 176, 273
Rifkind, Jeremy, 149
Rights, human, 177
Robbins, Lord Lionel, 105
Roberts, Paul Craig, 323, 340, 341-42
Robinson, Randall, 363
Rockefeller, David, 71, 116, 255
Rockwell, Llewellyn, H., 224
Rogers, Will, 128
Rohrabacher, Dana, 201, 206-07
Roosevelt administration, 82, 305, 371, 372
Roosevelt, Franklin D. 24, 31, 317, 365
Roosevelt, Theodore, 306
Rothbard, Murray N., 17, 24, 69, 83, 347, 371
    on bank runs, 80, 82, 84
    on environmentalism, 149, 295
Rousseau, Jean Jacques, 290, 362
Ruder, David, 48, 260
Ruffin, Roy J., 39, 40
Rule of Law, 165-68, 330, 341
Russell, Richard, 369
Russia; See Soviet Union

Salvation Army, 141
Samuelson, Paul, 38, 43, 311, 314, 351
San Francisco Examiner, 140, 292
Saturday Night Live, 137
Savings
    level of, 51
    private, 52-54, 92-93
Savings & Loan Industry, 88-94, 186, 188, 281, 283, 316
    bankruptcy of, 92, 94, 126
    creation of, 91

deregulation of, 91
Scholastics, 73-77
Schroeder, Pat, 135
Securities and Exchange Commission, 47-48, 72, 172, 260-261
Serrano, Andres, 201-02, 206, 288
Seybolt, Robert, 243
Shortages, 138
Shriver, Sargent, 180
Sider, Ronald, 276, 279
Siegal, Steve, 275
Sierra Club, 148-49, 292, 294
Simpson, Richard, 120-21
Singapore, 114-15
Singer, Fred S., 299
Slavery, 183, 265, 361
Smith, Adam, 76
Smith, Al, 181
Snow, Tony, 306
Sobran, Joseph, 305
Social democracy, 315
Social engineering, 178
Social justice, 167
Social sciences
    compared with natural, 67-68
    theory of obsolescence, 65
Social security, 190, 205, 219, 269, 286
Socialism, 46, 47, 113-14, 289-90
    Christianity and, 77, 276-79
    decline of, 13, 15, 152, 160, 318-21, 322, 326, 332-34, 347, 368, 369, 373
    defense of, 14
    dismantling of, 338-42, 342-46
    failure of, 38, 122, 178, 200, 236, 314, 335-38
    inevitability of, 173, 174
    market, 37, 241, 349
    response to Mises, 15
Society for the Prevention of Cruelty to Animals (SPCA), 302

Solidarity, 319
Solzhenitsyn, Alexander, 319
Soto, Domingo de, 76
Southern Carolina Coastal Council, 139
Soviet Academy of Sciences, 340
Soviet Union, 37-38, 195, 211, 215, 275, 322, 323-24, 327, 329, 332-33, 337, 340, 342-43, 346-54, 356
    and monetary reform, 101, 104
    IFC funding of, 113
    and wheat purchases, 195
Space
    exploration, 128-32
    shuttle, 127, 131
Speakeasies, 232
Special interests, 86, 125, 127, 167, 170-71, 172, 173, 185-86, 213, 254, 255, 265, 283, 306, 310, 316
Speciesism, 274
Spending
    federal, 53-54, 160, 190, 268, 283
Sputnik, 127
Stagflation, 104
Stalin, Joseph, 236, 289, 315, 321, 327, 365, 366
Statecraft, 282
Statistics
    destruction of method, 63-65
    economic, 55, 56
    fallacies of, 56, 64-65, 349-50
    monetary, 97
Statolatry, 314, 315, 318
Stern, William J., 215
Stiff, David, 134
Stillman, James, 81
Stock market, 48-50
    and crash of 1987, 47, 66, 259
    and crimes, 70, 259-61
    drop of 1955, 67
    See also Financial markets

Stone, Merlin, 290
Strategic Defense Initiative (SDI), 162-63, 169
Stroup, Richard, 41
Structure of production, 337-38
Subsidies
    agriculture, 192-96
    art, 201-07
    education, 239
    maritime, 247-49
    to AIDS carriers, 251
Sudden Infant Death Syndrome, 303
Sugar, 194
Sunday, Billy, 231
Supply-side economics, 31, 41-45, 163
Supreme Court, U.S., 146, 244-46
Sweden, 315-16

Taft, Robert, 323, 324
Taft-Hawley Act, 25
Taiwan, 114
Tang, 129
Tanzania, 334
Tariffs, 57, 59-62
Taxes, 45, 54, 166, 167, 168-69, 172, 175, 187, 189, 191, 282, 327
    and national service, 264-65
    and Reform Act of 1986, 53
    and World Bank, 112-13
    and world government, 256
    as bailouts for debt, 85-88, 93, 188, 316
    business, 191
    collectors of, 74, 166
    for garbage collection, 197
    global treaty on, 259
    havens, 259
    income, 41-43, 46, 282
    international, 230
    on money, 111
Tehran, 366
Teleocracy, 167, 168

Teodorico, King, 74
Thatcher, Margaret, 135
Theft, 174
Theresa, Mother, 43, 237
Third World, 14, 103, 198, 276, 367
    and the World Bank, 114, 15
3M Corporation, 61, 62
Tiananmen Square, 320-21
Thornburgh, Richard, 295
Thornton, Mark, 225
Tocqueville, Alexis de, 327
Toronto Globe and Mail, 274
Torrington Company, 60, 61
Tower, John, 318
Trade, international, 55-59, 257, 326
Traditionalists, 162
Traffic congestion, 207-11
TransAfrica, 363
Transportation, *See* Traffic
Trans-Species Unlimited, 275
Trash, 197-201, 296-97, 312, 352-53
Tree huggers, 200
Triffin, Robert, 33
Trilateralism, 255, 308, 364
Trucking industry, 190
Truman, Harry, 25, 368, 371
Tucker, Brian, 335
Tucker, Robert, 150
Tuition tax credits, 238-41
Tupperware, 245-46
Turkey, 115

Underclass, 179
Underground economy, 165, 67
Unemployment, 348
    compensation, 269
    insurance, 277
Unions, 20-23, 25-27, 219, 268, 283
Uniroyal, 298
Unitarians, 290
United Nations, 230, 254, 258, 308

Urban Development Action
    Grant Programs (UDAGs), 133, 134
U.S.S.R.; *See* Soviet Union
USX Corporation, 57

V-E Day, 365
V-J Day, 365
Valdez, Alaska, 148-49
Value, subjective, 49, 73, 75, 76, 338

Victimhood, 168, 169, 184-86
Vidal, Gore, 372
Vietnam War, 280, 288, 333, 373
Vieira, Edwin, 25
Villard, Oswald Garrison, 370
Vincent de Paul Society, St., 141
Voluntarism, 141-42
Vonnegut, Kurt, 372
Voting Rights Act, 179
Vouchers, 238-41, 263-64

Wages
    control of, 17-21, 24-25, 27, 190, 267, 277, 281, 283
    determination of, 26, 75-76, 265-66, 269-72
Wagner Act, 24
Wall Street Journal, 101, 135, 144, 189, 314
Walters, Sir Alan, 35
War Powers Act, 145
War
    of Independence, 110
    on poverty, 164, 178-182, 221-22
    on terrorism, 222
    U.S. Civil, 23, 110, 183
    See also Drug War; Vietnam War
Warburton, Clark, 233
Warsaw Pact, 288, 323
Washington, George, 364
Washington Post, 72, 135, 236, 296

Washington Project for the Arts, 202-03
Washington Times, The, 306
Washingtonian, 303
Watt, James, 119
Wattenberg, Ben, 363
Watts, V. Orval, 328
Weaver, Paul, 188
Wedtech, 215
Weimar Republic, 98
Welfare state, 138, 168, 170-71, 173, 179-82, 192, 218, 227, 231, 253, 283, 285
Wetlands, 295-96
Wheeler, Burton K., 370
When God Was a Woman, 290
White, Harry Dexter, 32
White, Lynn Jr., 291
Whitman, Walt, 372
Wilczek, Mieczyslaw, 338-39
Wilde, Oscar, 19
Wilderness Society, 292
Will, George, 141, 144, 231, 232, 233
William Park Group, 47-48
Williams Act, 71
Williams, Harrison, 71
Williams, Walter, 171

Williams, William Appleman, 371
Wilson, Edmund, 372
Wilson, William R., 60
Wilson, Woodrow, 177, 308, 369
Wood, Robert E., 370
World Bank, 44, 85, 112-17, 254, 256
World Central Bank, 33, 34, 172
World government, 253-56, 257-62, 307-08
World Policy Institute, 255
World Relief Incorporated, 141
World War I, 23, 25
World War II, 25, 33-34, 44, 320
Wright, Jim, 318
Wright, Robert, 304-05

Xenophobia, 58

Yalta, 366
Yates, Sidney, 206
Yellowstone National Park, 151, 294
Yeltsin, Boris, 352
Yippie Party, 293

Zambia, 113, 116
Zero-sum game, 278
Zimbabwe, 113, 310

About the Contributors

Doug Bandow is a syndicated columnist and author of *The Politics of Plunder.*

Tom Bethell is a media fellow at the Mises Institute and the Hoover Institution and Washington editor of the *American Spectator*.

Walter Block is chief economist at the Fraser Institute and senior fellow at the Mises Institute.

James Bovard is an author and public policy analyst in Washington, D.C.

Patrick J. Buchanan is a nationally syndicated columist.

Carl C. Curtis, III, is a writer and novelist living in Tyler, Texas.

John V. Denson is an attorney in Opelika, Alabama, and vice chairman of the Mises Institute.

James Grant is editor and publisher of *Grant's Interest Rate Observer* in New York City.

Stephen P. Halbrook is an attorney in Fairfax, Virginia, and the author of *That Every Man Be Armed*.

Robert Higgs is Thomas F. Gleed Professor in the Albers Business School at Seattle University and is an adjunct scholar of the Mises Institute.

Richard Hite is a graduate student and Mises Institute fellow at George Mason University.

Matthew Hoffman is an economics major at George Mason University.

Greg Kaza is vice president for public policy at the Mackinac Center for Public Policy in Midland, Michigan.

R. Cort Kirkwood is an editorial writer for the *Washington Times*.

Graeme B. Littler is editor of *Central Bank Watch* and a Mises Institute research fellow.

Bradley Miller is director of publications for the Heritage Foundation, a Mises Institute media fellow, and author of *Beyond Left and Right*.

William Murchison is editorial-page editor of the *Dallas Morning News* and a Mises Institute media fellow.

Lawrence W. Reed is president of the Mackinac Center for Public Policy in Midland, Michigan.

Sheldon L. Richman is senior editor at the Institute for Humane Studies at George Mason University and an adjunct scholar of the Mises Institute.

Llewellyn H. Rockwell is founder and president of the Ludwig von Mises Institute.

Murray N. Rothbard is S. J. Hall distinguished professor of economics at the University of Nevada, Las Vegas, and vice president for academic affairs at the Ludwig von Mises Institute.

Joseph Sobran is a senior editor of *The National Review* and a Mises Institute media fellow.

Alex Tabarrok is a graduate student and Mises Institute fellow at George Mason University.

Jeffrey A. Tucker is managing editor of the *Free Market* and a graduate student and Mises Institute fellow at George Mason University.

Edwin Vieira, Jr., is an attorney at the National Right to Work Foundation and author of *Pieces of Eight*.